INTRODUCTION TO TRADE, INDUSTRIAL, AND TECHNICAL EDUCATION

INTRODUCTION TO TRADE, INDUSTRIAL, AND TECHNICAL EDUCATION

MERLE E. STRONG
University of Wisconsin

CARL J. SCHAEFER
Rutgers University—The State University of New Jersey

CHARLES E. MERRILL PUBLISHING COMPANY
A Bell & Howell Company
Columbus, Ohio

THE MERRILL SERIES
IN CAREER PROGRAMS

Published by
Charles E. Merrill Publishing Company
A Bell & Howell Company
Columbus, Ohio 43216

International Standard Book Number: 0-675-08787-2

Library of Congress Catalog Card Number: 74-81198

1 2 3 4 5 6—79 78 77 76 75
Printed in the United States of America.

THE
MERRILL SERIES
IN CAREER
PROGRAMS

In recent years our nation has literally redis-
covered education. Concurrently, many nations are considering educational
programs in revolutionary terms. They now realize that education is the
responsible link between social needs and social improvement. While traditionally Americans have been committed to the ideal of the optimal development of each individual, there is increased public appreciation and
support of the values and benefits of education in general, and vocational
and technical education in particular. With occupational education's demonstrated capacity to contribute to economic growth and national well
being, it is only natural that it has been given increased prominence and
importance in this educational climate.

With the increased recognition that the true resources of a nation are its
human resources, occupational education programs are considered a form
of investment in human capital—an investment which provides compara-
tively high returns to both the individual and society.

The Merrill Series in Career Programs is designed to provide a broad
range of educational materials to assist members of the profession in providing effective and efficient programs of occupational education which contribute to an individual's becoming both a contributing economic producer
and a responsible member of society.

The series and its sub-series do not have a singular position or philosophy concerning the problems and alternatives in providing the broad range of offerings needed to prepare the nation's work force. Rather, authors are encouraged to develop and support independent positions and alternative strategies. A wide range of educational and occupational experiences and perspectives have been brought to bear through the Merrill Series in Career Programs National Editorial Board. These experiences, coupled with those of the authors, assure useful publications. I believe that this title, along with others in the series, will provide major assistance in further developing and extending viable educational programs to assist youth and adults in preparing for and furthering their careers.

Robert E. Taylor
Editorial Director
Series in Career Programs

ADDITIONAL PUBLICATIONS IN THE CAREER PROGRAMS SERIES

Career Development in the Elementary School
Robert L. Gibson

Principles of Post-Secondary Vocational Education
Angelo Gillie

Career Education: Perspective and Promise
Goldhammer/Taylor

Developing Careers in the Elementary School
Gysbers/Miller/Moore

Teaching Related Subjects in Trade and Industrial and
Technical Education
Milton E. Larson

Principles and Techniques of Vocational Guidance
H. H. London

Curriculum Development for Trade and Industrial and
Technical Education
Gordon G. McMahon

Planning Facilities for Occupational Education Programs
Richard F. Meckley

Coordination of Cooperative Vocational Education
Meyer/Klaurens/Crawford

Women's Careers: How They Develop
Samuel H. Osipow

Teaching Shop and Laboratory Methods
Albert J. Pautler

Individualizing Vocational and Technical Instruction
Pucel/Knaak

Vocational Education and Guidance—A System for the Seventies
James A. Rhodes

Career Guidance: An Individual Developmental Approach
K. Norman Severinsen

Leadership in Administration of Vocational and Technical Education
Wenrich/Wenrich

FOREWORD

Probably one of the more difficult vocational areas to understand is that of trade, industrial, and technical education. This is due to not only the similarities, but also the differences among its discrete parts. The intent of this text is to clarify the various educational roles of each. In doing so, it is hoped that those engaged in these aspects of vocational education will be able to perform more effectively as to their challenge as well as bring more dedication to the tasks for which each is held accountable.

It is helpful to have some feel for "from whence one came." In a sense trade, industrial, and technical education serves as the backbone of all vocational education. In our highly developed technological society it has been the heritage of trade, industrial, and technical education to develop man, his skill, and his creative mind. The trades having been passed down from father to son; apprentices have learned from the master and the craftsman; and the notion of an artisan* has not been void in our American way of life. Such is the heritage of those engaged in trade, industrial, and technical education.

---

*Artisan has been more closely associated with the arts and crafts of recent years in contrast to the colonial day definition.

The student of this subject will quickly grasp the full meaning of the need for setting clear-cut objectives of what is to be taught, the differentiating of functions of each segment of trade, industrial, and technical education, and the practicality of the present-day term "accountability." The authors have tried to blend the philosophical bases of this important aspect of education with an ample portion of operational technique which assures functional and successful programs. Student-centered needs are not overlooked; neither is the reality of assuring the worth of the end product.

What has been said in this text should be of value to not only the practitioner of trade, industrial, and technical education but the implementator as well. To have done less would have been to ignore the total potential of these discrete yet related educational areas.

Merle Strong and Carl Schaefer are not dreamers of what they have written. Each has had considerable experience as a teacher, local director, teacher-educator, and administrator. Their careers have been tempered by employment in several states, state departments of education, the U.S. Office of Education, and at a number of universities. Their writing has been collaborative throughout, and the serious reader will find their thoughts and ideas both inspiring and challenging.

Robert M. Reese
Professor & Chairman
Academic Faculty of
    Vocational—Technical Education
The Ohio State University

PREFACE

The thrust of this book is to provide the reader with an understanding of trade, industrial, and technical education. But even more than this, it hopefully will enable those engaged in trade, industrial, and technical education to identify more precisely their mission on the educational continuum. This book, therefore, is intended for those present and future teachers, administrators, and leaders who make up the ranks of educators who are willing to devote their careers to the preparation of skilled manpower and the occupational needs of our society.

We, the authors, do not intend our work to be popularized treatment of the field; we do intend it to be of aid to the practitioner. We did not write the book as a historical piece; we did write it as a contemporary philosophical position. And finally, we did not write it from theory without supporting evidence; the examples cited are real and existing. There is a reflection of practicality and concreteness of practice throughout which hopefully can serve as an interface to other, more in-depth subject treatments of the field of trade, industrial, and technical education.

Each chapter is written to stand on its own. Such an approach enables the book to be read chapter by chapter, contrary to the sequential reading required by most texts. In this respect, the organization of the book somewhat reflects that of a handbook. For example, if the reader wants to acquire an understanding of the Vocational Industrial Clubs of America, it becomes but necessary to refer directly to chapter 11. Administrative, staff recruitment, guidance, professional organizations, and other pertinent aspects of trade, industrial, and technical education are treated in the same manner. The Appendices contain additional examples and information for use that should not be overlooked.

To the keen reader, obviously much more could have been said about each of the topics. Further readings are of course essential and to those who aspire to greater understanding, we would refer you to other texts in the Merrill Series in Career Programs.

To those who have contributed to our thinking and to those we have cited, we the authors, are appreciative.

C.J.S.
M.E.S.

CONTENTS

INTRODUCTION TO TRADE, INDUSTRIAL, AND TECHNICAL EDUCATION

Chapter 1 HISTORICAL BACKGROUND

The early foundations of trade, industrial, and technical education in America are reflected in the growth of America itself. Any detailed study of forces which led to the beginnings of trade, industrial, and technical education and to its development into the significant role it plays in our present system of training would require a complete analysis of the growth of our technological society. Such a study is beyond the capability of this volume. However, it seems appropriate to discuss some of the highlights.

Social and Economic Forces

While it would be fair to say that man has always been engaged in the pursuit of skills in order to provide food and shelter, the foundations of trade and industrial education in America are found in the conditions brought about by the industrial revolution. Some historians have suggested that the term industrial revolution is too strong a term since revolution implies sudden and catastrophic change. In the case of the United States there can be little doubt that the social and economic change was quite dramatic.

1

A few centuries ago when the early settlers arrived on the eastern shores they found native Indians with their agrarian culture. Open conflict arose with the white man because the Indians had, until that time, held undisputed use of the land. Although the conflicts were fierce, the Indian was forced to retreat further and occupy new areas of wilderness.

In the broadest sense this retreat provided Indian youth with a type of vocational training similar to that given to the Indian youth in preceding decades and centuries. The training was concerned with securing food mainly by hunting, providing shelter, building crafts for transportation on the rivers and lakes, and protecting themselves against enemies. Their system was a static system of training as compared with that developed by the settlers.

In an undeveloped society there is no wealth of usable knowledge on which to build. Discoveries of new ways of doing things are slow and the struggle toward a better existence is slow indeed. Under these conditions work skills must be shared with the succeeding generation.

In this sense the phenomena of vocational training existing in our present society had their roots in the past. In a way then, we are not dealing with something new but with the development of a system of training with a flexibility which permits it to adjust to new conditions.

Vocational education for early youth of our nation was accomplished as an outcome of family living or through observing the practices of adults. It was primarily the development of work tasks. Periodically, someone would discover a better way of doing something which would be passed on mainly by observation. Observation as a form of training will always be with us; however, the success of our nation from its early beginnings has been due to a great extent to successful efforts to develop and implement more efficient methods for passing on new skills and knowledge to future generations.

Antecedent Movements

APPRENTICESHIP

In this country the earliest system of training to qualify for jobs that would be considered as trade and industrial jobs was apprenticeship. The system was brought to America from Europe and though it served a purpose for that day, it had many deficiencies. However, it was the only system of that period, for no program of public education existed in the colonies or in any of the states prior to 1789.

At that time parents of means usually sent their children to private schools which were operated as a part of some religious denomination.

However, apprenticeship served many of the other youth. Two patterns existed: (1) The voluntary system which followed closely the pattern transported from England in which a youth "bound himself" by his free will to an employer in order to learn a trade; (2) Involuntary apprenticeship which provided a means under the Poor Law to take care of poor children and orphans. In the case of the volunteer apprentices the town governments provided laws relating to apprentices with the result that authorities provided some supervision to see that agreements were honored. In the case of the involuntary apprentice he was bound over to a master who was responsible for his personal and occupational needs. In general, the agreement provided that the youth would be given food, clothing, and shelter, as well as general education as needed in the trade, and trade skills.

Early writers disagree somewhat on whether the system allowed the exploitation of youth or provided a sound education for that period. Regardless, it was the most used educational scheme until about 1830. It is important to realize that apprenticeship of that period served both boys and girls at the young age of fourteen.

The industrial revolution in the colonies came a little later than in England where it was well established by the beginning of the nineteenth century. The restrictive legislation imposed upon the colonies during the eighteenth century very definitely retarded industrial growth. England sought in various ways to keep the colonies dependent. It is said that it was not until after 1812 that manufacturing got well started in the United States and not until after the Civil War that manufacturing was of considerable consequence.

The early factory years created new demands for labor. In some of the factories this demand was met to a great degree by the employment of youth. The factory system caused new kinds of demands which were not readily met through the apprenticeship system. It became evident that apprenticeship with its extended training period was inadequate to meet the needs for skill development in a developing country. Child labor laws varied among the colonies if indeed they did exist, and in too many cases apprenticeship may have been abused to the point that it became a term for indentured servitude. Although child labor laws improved somewhat relating to factory work, it was really not until the beginning of the twentieth century that federal and state laws relating to child labor became somewhat effective in eliminating "sweatshop" working conditions.

In spite of the weaknesses, early apprenticeship did provide both social and economic solutions for several groups of that day. First, it provided a means without public tax support to give youth job skills that would make them economically self-supporting. It also provided a means for literacy training of all youth since this was a requirement placed on the master. The system also provided a means of support for the poor since an apprentice received food, shelter, and clothing from the employer. Even though life was often hard for an apprentice, the system provided to some degree the dimensions with which we still struggle as we attempt to serve the poor. These attempts include the placing of a youth in a training situation where his support will be assured, followed by placing him in a wage-earning job, and finally providing him with the opportunity to become a master craftsman.

Population growth, the rise of the factory system, increased mechanization, and shortcomings of the apprenticeship system highlighted the need for occupational education in the United States. Private trade schools developed, and although they served small numbers very well, they were not the answer to meeting industrial labor requirements.

During the last part of the nineteenth century, manual training spread rapidly into the schools of the nation. Manual training was based on the concepts of faculty psychology with its idea of transfer of training. While this greatly influenced the nature of efforts that were to follow, it failed as a movement to meet the needs of industry or of individuals who needed preparation for work. In fact, the vocational values of manual training were not stressed in its early years.

During the early 1900s, a number of states were concerned about the development of a more relevant educational program. In any discussion of the foundations of trade and industrial education, it is necessary to highlight the work of the Douglas Commission which was appointed in 1905 by Governor William A. Douglas of Massachusetts. This seemed to mark the beginning of the acceptance of the idea of supporting training for employment through public funds. The report of the commission was directed to both the social and economic problems of that period. Concern was shown for both the welfare of the rapidly growing industry and the social welfare of adult and young prospective wage earners.

> Describing the youth situation of that time, it was stated that 25,000 Massachusetts children between 14 and 16 years of age were either at work or idle. It was estimated that one out of six completed the grammar grades. The years from 14 to 16 were wasted since these children were neither learning a trade nor preparing for any kind of life occupation (Fitzpatrick 1944).

Through the recommendations of the Douglas Commission, Massachusetts established the first state system of public vocational education. Central to the program was training related to the trade and industrial needs of the industries of that period. At the same time, training in agriculture and homemaking was also provided.

Of particular historical note was the activity in Wisconsin, stimulated, to a great extent, by Charles McCarthy. "Democratic education" was the philosophy of education he purported as basic to his efforts. His concern was that education should reach all of the people, not merely those who could survive the hurdles of the high school or the "semester-hour credits" of the college. His chief concern was for the dropout—or those who were dropped from the system. He thought in terms of the chain image, that the social structure was only as strong as its weakest links. McCarthy did not want to give these weak links merely skills or abilities for a higher rate of productivity, he wanted to make them better workers, better citizens, and better individuals.

McCarthy was instrumental in starting the continuation-school movement in Wisconsin, as well as being an influence on future federal legislation. This continuation-school movement formed the foundation for the growth of the unique system of dominantly trade training vocational schools in Wisconsin.

Nationally, the growing movement was spearheaded from 1906–1917 by the National Society for Promotion of Industrial Education. This society was composed of outstanding men from the field of business and industry. A Statement of Aim in their Constitution was "To bring to public attention the importance of industrial education as a factor in the industrial development of the United States." Evidence indicates that the Society was successful in its aim as shown by Congress creating the Commission on National Aid to Vocational Education through an act approved January 20, 1914. The Commission was appointed by the president of the United States with the task of considering the subject of national aid for vocational education. The commission whose membership included representatives from Congress, industry, and education addressed themselves to the following questions:

1. To what extent is there a need for vocational education in the United States?

2. Is there a need for national grants stimulating the states to give vocational education?

3. What kinds or forms of vocational education should be stimulated by national grants?

4. How far can the Federal Government aid through [providing] expert knowledge [for] vocational education in the various states?

5. To what extent should the Federal Government aid the states through national grants for vocational education?

6. Under what conditions should grants to the states for vocational education be made (U.S. Office of Education 1963)?

There appeared to be recognition for the need for support of many kinds of education; however, priority was centered on the kind of education that would prepare workers for the common occupations which employed the greatest number of workers. The following is a quote from their report:

> There is a great and crying need of providing vocational education of this character for every part of the United States—to conserve and develop our resources; to promote a more productive and prosperous agriculture; to prevent the waste of human labor; to supplement apprenticeship; to increase the wage-earning power of our productive workers; to meet the increasing demand for trained workmen; to offset the increased cost of living. Vocational education is therefore needed as a wise business investment for this Nation, because our national prosperity and happiness are at stake and our position in the markets of the world cannot otherwise be maintained (U.S. Office of Education .1963).

The commission made its report to Congress June 1, 1914. It was more than two years later, however, before final action was taken on a bill which resulted from the study.

Federal Legislation*

History indicates that the federal government has always provided encouragement for education of all types. However, one of the first areas of education to receive federal funds has been education designed to stimulate the growth and development of occupational competencies. Although it is not the purpose of this chapter to provide an in-depth historical treatment of trade and industrial education, a brief description of the most significant federal legislation will be provided.

SMITH-HUGHES ACT

February 23, 1917, is the historic date on which P.L. 64–347, commonly called the Smith-Hughes Act, became law. The act provided the first categorical financial support for vocational education. The act is important not only for the funds that it provided but for the fact that it established a pattern for federal-state cooperation in vocational education that continues to exist even under the most recent federal legislation. In fact, while additional acts and amendments supporting vocational education have been passed throughout the years, the Smith-Hughes Act remained in effect as originally passed with only minor amendments until the passage of the

---

*The authors have used materials extensively in this section from *Education for a Changing World of Work*, U.S. Department of Health, Education and Welfare, Office of Education, Report of the Panel of Consultants on Vocational Education, O.E.–80021 (Washington: U.S. Government Printing Office, 1963), pp. 20–26.

Vocational Education Amendments of 1968; even with these amendments the act was not erased. Funds are still appropriated under the title; however, these funds are administered under the provisions of the 1968 Act. The act has served well as a foundation on which to build the federal-state cooperative program, and it remains a symbol of the early leaders responsible for its passage and for those who worked in the early years in the development of vocational education.

The act included provisions for several types of programs in trade and industrial education including: (1) evening classes for employed persons with instruction designed to supplement employment skills and knowledge, (2) preemployment day-trade classes, and (3) part-time classes. In the earlier years of the program, part-time continuation classes that were designed to increase the civic intelligence of young workers under 18 years of age made a very great contribution to the education of youth.

Additional monies were subsequently authorized by Congress to provide for futher development of vocational education beyond the amounts appropriated by the Smith-Hughes Act. In general, the provisions of the Smith-Hughes Act applied to the George-Reed and the George-Ellzey Acts. These statutes differed from the Smith-Hughes Act primarily in that they contained terminal dates and that they only authorized funds to be appropriated.

GEORGE-REED ACT

The George-Reed Act (Public Law 702, 70th Congress, approved February 5, 1929) authorized an appropriation of $500,000 for the year ending June 30, 1930, and an additional $500,000 each year thereafter for 4 years. The act expired on June 30, 1934.

The appropriation was divided equally between agriculture and home economics. Each state received for agriculture an amount equal to the ratio of its farm population to the total farm population of the United States; for home economics, the ratio used was the state's rural population to the total rural population of the United States. The act also provided $100,000 for the Federal Board for Vocational Education for administration and other purposes.

GEORGE-ELLZEY ACT

The George-Ellzey Act (Public Law 245, 73rd Congress, approved May 21, 1934) authorized an appropriation of $3 million each year for 3 years. The money was divided equally among agricultural education, home economics education, and trade and industrial education. The ratios for distribution of money to the states were determined for agriculture by using the farm population; for home economics, the rural population; and for trade and industrial education, the nonfarm population. An amount of $100,000 was authorized for the Department of the Interior, Office of Education, for administrative and other purposes in connection with the act.

GEORGE-DEEN ACT

The short-term enactments demonstrated the necessity of additional funds for the promotion and further development of vocational education. Accordingly, the Congress approved the George-Deen Act (Public Law 673, 74th Congress, approved June 8, 1936) to replace the George-Ellzey Act which was to expire in 1937. This new act was a continuing statute with no expiration date. The George-Deen Act became effective on July 1, 1937; the annual authorization for agriculture, home economics, and trade and industrial education was $12 million. The money was divided equally among the three services; allotments to the states were made on the basis of farm population for agriculture, rural population for home economics, and nonfarm population for trade and industrial education.

An annual allotment of $1.2 million was authorized for vocational programs in the distributive occupations. This money was allocated to the states on the basis of total population. For teacher training, the act authorized $1 million annually, distributed on the basis of total population. An allotment of $350,000 was made to the Office of Education for administrative and other purposes. The total annual authorization of the George-Deen Act was approximately $14,550,000.

GEORGE-BARDEN ACT

On August 1, 1946, the Congress approved the Vocational Education Act of 1946, which authorized an appropriation of $28,850,000 annually for the further development of vocational education. This act, technically an amendment of the George-Deen Act, is known as the George-Barden Act (Public Law 586, 79th Congress). The funds were to be expended "for the same purpose and in the same manner" as had been provided in the Smith-Hughes Act, with several specified differences.

Ten million dollars was authorized for agricultural education, to be allocated among the states on the basis of farm population. Authority was given in the act for the expenditure of funds in support of two youth organizations in agriculture: the Future Farmers of America and the New Farmers of America. For home economics, $8 million was authorized, the basis of allotment being the rural population of the state. For trade and industrial education, $8 million was authorized, to be allocated among the states on the basis of nonfarm population. An authorization for distributive occupations was made in the amount of $2.5 million allocated to the states on the basis of total population. Funds for distributive occupations were limited to support for part-time and evening courses for employed workers. An appropriation of $350,000 was authorized to enable the Office of Education to carry out the provisions of the act. The act also included an open-end authorization to guarantee states minimum amounts for each occupational category of vocational education.

Practical Nursing. The trades and industry appropriation authorized by the George-Barden Act was utilized to some extent for practical nurse training. The Health Amendments Act of 1956 (Public Law 911, 84th Congress, approved August 2, 1956), specifically authorized practical nurse training under the George-Barden Act. The act authorized $5 million for practical nurse training annually for a period of 5 years. In 1961 the authorization was extended to June 30, 1965 (Public Law 87–22, 87th Congress, approved April 24, 1961), and then made permanent by the Vocational Education Act of 1963. The practical nurse training provision of the Health Amendments Act became title II of the George-Barden Act and the previous authorization became title I.

Fishery Amendment. An act of Congress approved August 8, 1956 (Public Law 1027, 84th Congress, approved August 8, 1956), authorized an appropriation of $375,000 for vocational education in the fishery trades and industries and in the distributive occupation. Distribution of the funds was to be determined by the U.S. Commissioner of Education in consultation with the Secretary of the Interior. The purpose of the act was to promote the fishing industry by providing for the training of personnel. The act was an amendment to title I of the George-Barden Act.

NATIONAL DEFENSE EDUCATION ACT

Title VIII of the National Defense Education Act (Public Law 85–864, 85th Congress, approved September 2, 1968), "Area Vocational Education Programs," authorized an appropriation of $15 million annually for 4 years to support programs limited exclusively to the training of highly skilled technicians in recognized occupations necessary to the national defense.

These provisions of the National Defense Education Act became Title III of the George-Barden Act. In October 1961, Congress extended the National Defense Education Act for 2 years to June 30, 1964 (Public Law 87–344, 87th Congress, approved October 3, 1961). It was further extended by the Vocational Education Act of 1963, remaining in force until superseded by the Vocational Education Amendments of 1968. Allotments were made to the states according to a state's proportion of the total amount allocated under the George-Barden Act for agriculture, home economics, trades and industries, distributive occupations, and fisheries.

AREA REDEVELOPMENT ACT

The Area Redevelopment Act (Public Law 87–27, 87th Congress, approved May 1, 1961) authorized $4.5 million annually until 1965 for vocational education. The legislation recognized the critical need for training which arose from unemployment and underemployment in economically distressed areas. The act authorized vocational education for unemployed and underemployed residents of certain geographic areas which were designated as redevelopment areas by the Secretary of Commerce. The act further provided that the Secretary of Labor would select and refer persons for training. The Secretary of Health, Education and Welfare was given the authority to contract with other public and private educational institutions if the required services were not available through state and local vocational education agencies.

Funds appropriated under this act were given to the states for use only in designated redevelopment areas; there were no state allotments and no requirements for matching of funds for training programs.

MANPOWER DEVELOPMENT AND TRAINING ACT

The Manpower Development and Training Act (Public Law 87–415, 87th Congress, approved March 15, 1962) provided for the federal government to appraise the nation's manpower needs and resources and to work toward a solution to the unmet skill requirements and persistent unemployment. The act with its several amendments provides for research in problems affecting employment and unemployment and for the training and retraining of unemployed and underemployed workers. The act is jointly administered by the United States Department of Labor and the Department of Health, Education and Welfare. Under the law the Employment Security Division of the U.S. Department of Labor through its State Employment Service Offices is responsible for determining the need for training, for the referring of persons for training, and for job placement.

The act has been important to trade and industrial educators since training is conducted by local school systems, community colleges, and technical institutes. A good portion of the training continues to be in trade, industrial, and technical type jobs. The cost of the training is borne to a great extent by federal funds. The act provides for reimbursement to employers for on-the-job training given to trainees. In such cases vocational educators are often asked to provide related instruction.

THE VOCATIONAL EDUCATION ACT OF 1963

Legislation usually does not just happen but rather comes about after a series of events prompted by social, economic, or other concerns. The Vocational Education Act of 1963 (Public Law 88–210, 88th Congress, approved December 18, 1973), one of the milestones in vocational education, marks a new era in the program. Although those involved in programs of trade, industrial, and technical education may wish to review the events leading up to the passage of this act in more detail, this volume will provide a brief summary of the background and events leading to the passage of the act.

A beginning point of significance was the fact that the budget proposed to Congress for the fiscal year 1961 called for a $2 million dollar cut in appropriations for vocational education. In the course of the yearly budget hearings of a congressional committee the proposed cut came into full view of the congressional committee as well as other concerned persons. The United States Commissioner of Education, Lawrence G. Derthick, and the Secretary of the Department of Health, Education and Welfare, Arthur S. Flemming, were not in favor of the cuts. However, there was some feeling that the program needed some redirection because of the many changes in society. The trade, industrial, and technical education programs received less criticism than other parts of the vocational education programs because it was generally agreed that the trade, industrial, and technical programs had made a greater effort to relate to the needs of the labor market. However, it would be less than accurate to say that there was complete satisfaction with the programs and the need for expansion was very evident.

Evidence was provided to the congressional committee that vocational education had indeed made adjustments related to social, economic, and manpower requirements. New courses were being added, the area school concept was gaining momentum stimulated by the Area Redevelopment Act, and special programs were being provided for the unemployed. On the basis of this testimony the committee decided that cuts at that time were inappropriate with the needs of the nation and the funds were restored to the budget.

The American Vocational Association, as is customary, made inquiry of the presidential candidates, Senator John F. Kennedy and Vice President Richard M. Nixon, for the 1960 election year. In a letter the candidates were asked specifically about their reactions to the proposed cut in vocational education appropriations. Both candidates responded in favor of increasing the funds for vocational education. Senator Kennedy's response was as follows:

The continuation of federal funds for vocational education at the full amounts authorized by existing law is vital to the security and economic health of our nation. This is why I co-authored the area vocational education measure that became a law in 1958.

Vocational education plays an important part in the program of the Democratic Party for acceleration of our nation's growth. Growing needs mean expansion of vocational education. As the skill of our workers increase, their contribution to the economy increases.

I wholly subscribe to the pledge contained in the 1960 Democratic Platform to "further federal support for all phases of vocational education."

I am aware of the efforts of the present administration to make drastic cuts in appropriations for such education or to repeal existing laws dealing with the subject. I am proud of the record of the Democratic Congress in continuing this effort (*American Vocational Journal* October, 1960).

Vice President Nixon's response was equally supportive as evidenced by excerpts from his letter:

The nation's growing economy demands that we use the talents of every worker to the fullest degree. Vocational education plays a vital role in ensuring that each individual may make the greatest contribution to our economy.

I concur that today millions of Americans who have received vocational training are making a great contribution to the nation's welfare and economy. They must continue to make that contribution (*American Vocational Journal* November, 1960).

It was evident to vocational educators that there was support for programs of vocational education but that the program must develop and undergo changes if it was to play a continuing and significant role in the educational scheme of the nation. Vocational educators through the American Vocational Association made known their desire for an extensive study of vocational and technical education. These feelings were communicated through the new Secretary of Health, Education and Welfare to the President.

President Kennedy demonstrated his faith and concern for vocational and technical education in his message to Congress on American Education on February 20, 1961, when he said:

The National Vocational Education Acts, first enacted by the Congress in 1917 and subsequently amended, have provided a program of training for industry, agriculture, and other occupational areas. The basic purpose of our vocational education effort is sound and sufficiently broad to provide a basis for meeting future needs. However, the technological changes which have occurred in all occupations call for a review and re-evaluation of these acts, with a view toward their modernization.

To that end, I am requesting the Secretary of Health, Education and Welfare to convene an advisory body drawn from the education profession, labor, industry, and agriculture, as well as the lay public, together with representatives from the Departments of Agriculture and Labor, to be charged with the responsibility of reviewing and evaluating the current National Vocational Education Acts, and making recommendations for improving and redirecting the program.

Vocational educators were pleased with the President's message which assured a study would be made. There was concern, however, that members selected to carry out the study would have an understanding of the program and its potential for meeting national needs.

On October 5, 1961, the President announced the names of a panel of consultants to the Secretary of Health, Education and Welfare to review and evaluate the vocational education legislation and to make recommendations for improving and redirecting the program. (See Barlow 1967 for additional information.)

The panel worked more than a year and reported its findings and recommendations in a document entitled *Education for a Changing World of Work* (U.S. Office of Education 1963). Its recommendations proved to be highly significant in that they formed the basis for the development of the legislation that ultimately was passed by Congress. The panel's general recommendations were that vocational education in a changing world of work must

Offer training opportunities to the 21 million noncollege graduates who will enter the labor market in the 1960's.

Provide training or retraining for the millions of workers whose skills and technical knowledge must be updated, as well as those whose jobs will disappear due to increasing efficiency, automation, or economic change.

Meet the critical need for highly skilled craftsmen and technicians through education during and after the high school years.

Expand vocational and technical training programs consistent with employment possibilities and national economic needs.

Make educational opportunities equally available to all, regardless of race, sex, scholastic aptitude, or place of residence.

The panel was strong in their belief that the federal government must continue to work with the states and local communities to develop and improve the skills of its citizens. They departed from tradition, however, in that they spoke to groups of people in contrast to occupation categories when they recommended: "that the local-state-federal partnership increase support of vocational and technical education for":

High school students preparing to enter the labor market or become homemakers.

Youth with special needs who have academic, socio-economic, or other handicaps that prevent them from succeeding in the usual high school vocational education program.

Youth and adults who have completed or left high school and are full time students preparing to enter the labor market.

Youth and adults unemployed or at work who need training or retraining to achieve employment stability.

Adequate services and facilities to assure quality in all vocational and technical education programs.

For services required to assure quality in all vocational and technical education, they recommended that

Teacher and leadership training programs be improved and enlarged. Institutions of higher education, especially land-grant colleges and state universities, should provide for the professional growth of vocational and technical teachers.

Basic education material oriented to specific occupations be available for all programs. For this purpose, instructional materials laboratories should be established in appropriate institutions and financed and coordinated through the Division of Vocational and Technical Education, U.S. Office of Education.

Occupational information and guidance services be available for all students. State and national leadership for these programs should be supported and coordinated by the Division of Vocational and Technical Education, U.S. Office of Education.

Research and development in vocational and technical education be encouraged, supported, and coordinated at the national level. The results of this research and development should be made available on a nationwide basis.

The panel recognized that if the the training needs of the youth and adults were to be met that financial resources at all levels would need to be increased substantially. At that time over $400 million was being spent by local and state governments. Their recommendation for the federal government's effort was as follows:

For youth in high school who are preparing to enter the labor market or to become homemakers ($200 million)

For high school youth with academic, socio-economic, or other handicaps that prevent them from succeeding in the usual high school vocational education program ($10 million)

For youth and adults who have completed or left high school and are full-time students preparing to enter the labor market ($50 million)

For youth and adults unemployed or at work who need training or retraining to achieve employment stability ($100 million)

For services required to assure quality in all vocational and technical education programs ($40 million)

Details on the passage of the 1963 Act should be of interest to all trade and industrial educators because they relate the concerns and philosophy for the program and the tremendous support by many Congressmen. There is no doubt that the act commonly referred to as the Morse-Perkins Act which recognized the leadership of Carl D. Perkins in the House and Senator Wayne Morse in the Senate, ushered in a new day for trade, industrial, and technical education for the country. (For further details on the passage of the legislation see Barlow 1967; Kliever 1965.)

Carl Perkins' remarks before the House in the final days before the passage of the act when he gained acceptance of the bill as changed by the conference committee showed not only his great support for the bill but also his faith in the program of vocational and technical education.

Mr. Speaker, the conference compromise on H.R. 4955, in my judgment, will enable federal, state and local education authorities to cooperate in providing an expanded vocational education program so urgently needed to fit our young people for remunerative and productive careers in vocational occupations. It has been 17 years since the Congress last enacted any major legislation in the field of vocational education. Since that time the nature of employment opportunities and the training required has undergone drastic changes. Employment is demanding more and more education and higher degree of skills. Yet under our present trends some 30 to 40 percent of our children now in grade school will not be graduated from high school. About half of those who graduate from high school will end their educational careers at that time and attempt to secure employment. In spite of these trends, only about 13 percent of our 15 to 19 year olds are enrolled in vocational education programs embraced by the Smith-Hughes and George-Barden Acts. The conference agreement maintains the important provisions of the original House passed bill with respect to:

First. Permitting states to transfer funds between categories under the Smith-Hughes and George-Barden Acts.

Second. Broadening the definition of vocational agriculture to include agriculture related occupations.

Third. Authorizing assistance to business and office and other occupational training not now covered by Smith-Hughes and George-Barden.

Fourth. Periodic analysis of job market conditions so as to assure that the vocational education program will be actually geared to meet employment opportunities.

Fifth. Emphasis on the construction and operation of area vocational schools and that type of program which assures an
opportunity in all areas for persons to attend a full-time
course of occupational training in the vocational field of his
preference.

Main Provisions   The Vocational Act of 1963 authorized the appropriations in the amount of $60 million for fiscal year 1964 with amounts
increased to $225 million for each year thereafter. Ninety percent of the
funds was to be allocated to the states on a formula basis for extending and
improving present programs and for developing new programs, while ten
percent was reserved by the U.S. Commissioner of Education to pay a part
of the cost of research and training programs, designed to meet the special
vocational education needs of youth.

The sum allocated to the states were to be used for (1) occupational
training programs not requiring a baccalaureate degree for all persons,
youth or adults, (2) for ancillary services to assure quality programs which
included but were not limited to teacher education, administration, supervision, research, program evaluation, and instructional materials, (3) construction of area vocational school facilities.

Funds received for fiscal year 1965 and thereafter were to be matched on
a dollar-for-dollar basis. One-third of each state's annual allotment prior to
July 1, 1968, and 25 percent thereafter was required to be spent for youth
who have left school and/or construction of area schools. At least 3 percent
was required to be spent for ancillary services.

A separate authorization of $30 million for fiscal year 1965, $50 million
for 1966, and $35 million for fiscal years 1967 and 1968 was made for
residential schools and the work study program. The U.S. Commissioner
of Education had the responsibility of determining the division of funds
appropriated between work-study and residential schools.

The administration of the act was through a state board for vocational
education. A state plan was a requirement which must include provision for
cooperating with the state employment service.

Several significant amendments were made to the Smith-Hughes and
George-Barden Acts including the following provisions:

1. Funds allotted to the states from the Smith-Hughes and George-
   Barden Acts could be used for the purposes and subject to the
   conditions set forth in the Vocational Act of 1963.

2. Training in agriculture was broadened to include any occupation
   involving knowledge and skills in agricultural subjects. Formerly
   instruction was for occupations involving work on the farm only.

3. Funds allotted for home economics could be used for vocational
   education to fit individuals for gainful employment in occupations

involving knowledge and skills in home economics subjects and a requirement that at least 10 percent of funds be spent for that purpose.

4. Restrictions for distributive education programs requiring that preemployment programs must be of the cooperative type were removed.

5. Minimum time requirements for trade and industrial programs designed to train for single or semiskilled occupations were removed.

6. Titles II and III of the George-Barden Act relating respectively to practical nurse and area vocational education programs were removed.

VOCATIONAL EDUCATION AMENDMENTS OF 1968

Among the provisions of the Vocational Education Act of 1963 was one requiring a periodic review of the national program. In compliance with this requirement an Advisory Council on Vocational Education was appointed by the President of the United States on November 22, 1966, under the Chairmanship of Martin W. Essex, Superintendent of Public Instruction in Ohio. The Council's review of the program was submitted to the President on December 1, 1967, in a report entitled *Vocational Education: The Bridge Between Man and His Work* (U. S. Government Printing Office 1968). This evaluation in addition to identifying program weaknesses and highlighting unmet needs, contained recommendations which formed the basis for development of legislation which culminated in the Vocational Education Amendments of 1968 (Public Law 90-576, 90th Congress, October 16, 1968). The provisions of the Vocational Education Act of 1968 does not reflect all recommendations. For example, recommendation number two calls for a Cabinet level Department of Education and Manpower Development. However, at the date of this writing, discussions at high levels in government are taking place on this issue.

The following were the recommendations of the Advisory Council:

1. All federal vocational education acts administered by the Office of Education should be combined into one act.

2. A Department of Education and Manpower Development should be established at cabinet level.

3. Funds and permanent authority should be provided for the Commissioner of Education to make grants or contracts to state boards and with the approval of the state board to local educational

agencies, organizations, or institutions for planning, development, and operation of exemplary and innovative programs of occupational preparation.

4. Funds and permanent authority should be provided to develop and operate new and expanded vocational education programs and services specifically designed for persons who have academic, social, economic, or other handicaps.

5. The act should provide permanent authority for work study and include work study and work experience programs in the secondary schools and those at the postsecondary levels related to vocational and technical education.

6. Funds and permanent authority should be provided for the Commissioner to make grants to state boards of vocational education and, with the approval of the state board, to colleges and universities, and/or to public educational agencies to construct facilities and operate residential vocational schools.

7. The act should provide for at least 25 percent of the funds appropriated for allocation to the states to be used for purposes set forth in postsecondary schools and adult programs of the Vocational Education Act of 1963.

8. The act should include vocational homemaking education in a separate section of the act with specific funding authorization.

9. The act should provide for the distribution of funds to the states on bases which will encourage increased enrollment, attendance, and improved performance.

10. The act should permit matching of the federal allotment on a statewide basis.

11. Provision should be made for states to receive allotments earlier in the calendar year and expenditure of funds be authorized through the succeeding year.

12. The act should provide that salaries and expenses needed for the administration of vocational and technical education be included in the annual appropriation for this act.

13. Provisions for developing a state plan in the act should provide that a state shall, through its designated state board for vocational education:
    a. Submit for approval a properly executed legal contract to the Commissioner of Education on such forms and in such detail as the Commissioner deems necessary to assure compliance with the provisions of the act and regulations;

b. Submit a five-year projected plan for administering and operating programs of vocational and technical education. An annual updating of the plan to reflect changes and modifications contemplated would be submitted on or before the beginning of each fiscal year.

14. The act should recognize the need and provide support for professional and paraprofessional staff recruitment, preparation, and upgrading at all levels, including leadership, administration, teacher education, and counseling and guidance on a state, regional, and national basis.

15. Twenty-five percent of the funds appropriated for Title IV of the Higher Education Act of 1965 should be set aside for opportunity grants for students interested in entering postsecondary technical and vocational programs.

16. Funds should be authorized for pilot projects to study the feasibility of reimbursement to employers for unusual costs of supervision, training, and instruction of part-time cooperative students in publicly supported education.

17. Ten percent of the sums appropriated for the purposes listed in Section 4(a) of VEA 1963 shall be used by the Commissioner of Education for the following purposes:
    a. For grants or contracts to colleges and universities and other public or nonprofit private agencies and institutions to pay part of the cost of research and dissemination of research results in vocational and technical education;
    b. For grants or contracts approved by the operating bureau for evaluation, demonstration, and experimental programs in vocational and technical education and for dissemination of results;
    c. For grants to states for paying part of the cost of state research coordinating units, state research, evaluation, demonstration, and experimental programs in vocational and technical education and dissemination of results.

18. The act should provide funds and require the Office of Education to be responsible for collecting data and preparing an annual descriptive and analytical report on vocational education to be submitted to the President and Congress.

19. The act should provide that each state conduct a periodic statewide review and evaluation of its vocational education program.

20. The act should include within the definition of vocational education "prevocational" education and "employability skills."

21. Section 4(a) of the Vocational Education Act of 1963 should be changed to delete the word "area" and that section 8.2 be changed to read: "The term vocational education facilities refers to. . . ."

22. The definition of vocational education in the act should be expanded to include the responsibility of education for initial job placement and follow-up for persons who:
    a. Have completed or are about to complete a program of education;
    b. Require part-time employment to remain in school;
    c. Need work experience which is an integral part of an education program.

23. That in order to meet current needs, authorization levels for administering and operating programs of vocational and technical education under the act should be established as follows:
    I. Grants of $500 million to states and grants authorized by the Commissioner of Education. (Students served—8 million.)
        A. Grants to states for: (1) Maintenance and expansion of operating programs; (2) construction; (3) ancillary services; (4) teacher education and professional development—($437,500,000) (50–50).
        B. Grants to be authorized by the Commissioner for: (1) Research, development, evaluation, and experimentation (10 percent)—$50 million (100); (2) Special programs for teacher education and professional development (25 percent)—($12,500,000) (100).
    II. Work-Study Program—$350 million (90–10). (Students served—575,000.)
    III. Innovative Programs—$200 million (100). (Students served—175,000.)
    IV. Residential Vocational Schools (50)—$200 million (90–10). (Students served—25,000.)
    V. Program for socially, economically, and culturally disadvantaged—$300 million (90–10). (Students served—175,000.)
    VI. Vocational Homemaking—$15 million (50–50). (Students served—2 million.)
    Total authorization—$2,565 million.
    (Total students served—10,950,000 including 2 million in home economics.)

The following recommendations were directed to the attention of the Commissioner of Education. They were recommendations which the council felt would make decided improvement in the status and quality of vocational education.

24. There be established two to four centers for curriculum development in vocational education.

25. The Office of Education provides staff for the National Advisory Committee on Vocational Education and establishes guidelines for helping the states make more effective use of state advisory boards.

26. A learning corps be established on a pilot basis to provide improved learning experiences for economically disadvantaged youths, particularly, inner-city youths. Such corps would arrange for young people to have the opportunity of living in selected homes in rural, small city, and suburban communities and to enroll in the local schools where skill development for employment would be a part of their educational program.

The Vocational Education Amendments of 1968, P.L. 90–576, were passed by the Congress without a dissenting vote in either the House or Senate and became law on October 16, 1968. See table 1–1 for appropriations authorized. It should not be concluded that its development and passage was without a great effort on the part of those concerned. Its consideration came at a time when the executive branch of the government was committed to curbing expenditures and thus was not in a position to give full support to the legislation. Its passage is a tribute, however, to vocational educators and others across the nation who had demonstrated the benefits of vocational education and to members of Congress who were convinced of the worth and potential of the program.

PROVISIONS OF P.L. 90–576

TITLE I, Part A:

Declaration of Purpose: To assist the states to maintain, extend, and improve existing programs of vocational education, to develop new programs, and to provide part-time employment for youths who need the earnings to continue their vocational training, so that persons of all ages in all communities of the state—those in high school, those who have completed or discontinued their formal education and are preparing to enter the labor market, those who have already entered the labor market but need to upgrade their skills or learn new ones, those with special educational handicaps, and those in postsecondary schools—will have ready access to vocational training or retraining which is of high quality, realistic in light of

TABLE 1-1
PUBLIC LAW 90–576

Program	APPROPRIATIONS AUTHORIZED		Eligibility
	Funds Authorized	Matching Requirements	
I. Grants to the states for vocational education, including research and training		50–50 federal/state for state grants; 75–25 for research coordinating units; 90–10 for other research activities undertaken by states	Grants are made to State Boards; research contracts and grants (50 percent of research fund made by Commissioner with public and private agencies and institutions.[2]
FY 1969	$355,000,000[1]		
FY 1970	565,000,000		
FY 1971	675,000,000		
FY 1972	675,000,000		
Each year thereafter	565,000,000		
II. Programs for the Disadvantaged		Commissioner has discretionary authority to waive matching requirements	State Boards
FY 1969	$ 40,000,000		
FY 1970	40,000,000		
III. Administration of all new programs	Such sums as may be necessary		
IV. Administration by O.E. and states for comprehensive programs	Such sums as may be necessary	No matching requirements	
V. Work Study		80–20 federal/state	State Boards
FY 1969	$ 35,000,000		
FY 1970	35,000,000		
VI. Exemplary Programs		No matching requirements	State Boards receive 50 percent of funds; 50 percent used by Commissioner for grants to public and private agencies.
FY 1969	$ 15,000,000		
FY 1970	57,500,000		
FY 1971	75,000,000		
FY 1972	75,000,000		
VII. Cooperative Work Study		No matching requirements	State Boards
FY 1969	$ 20,000,000		
FY 1970	35,000,000		
FY 1971	50,000,000		
FY 1972	75,000,000		

22

		Matching requirements	Administering agencies
VIII. Demonstration Residential Schools		No matching requirements	State Boards, colleges and universities or other public agencies
FY 1969	$ 25,000,000		
FY 1970	30,000,000		
FY 1971	35,000,000		
FY 1972	35,000,000		
IX. Grants to States for Residential Schools		90–10 federal/state	State Boards
FY 1969	$ 15,000,000		
FY 1970	15,000,000		
X. Dormitories (interest subsidy)		None	State Boards, colleges, and universities, and/or local educational agencies
FY 1969	$ 5,000,000		
FY 1970	10,000,000		
XI. Consumer and Home-making Education		50–50 federal/state except the 1/3 set aside (at 90–10) for programs for disadvantaged	State Boards
FY 1970	$ 25,000,000		
FY 1971	35,000,000		
FY 1972	50,000,000		
XII. Curriculum Development			State Boards, colleges, and universities, other public and private agencies
FY 1969	$ 7,000,000		
FY 1970	10,000,000		
XIII. National Advisory Council			
FY 1969	$ 100,000		
FY 1970–73	150,000 for each fiscal year		
XIV. Vocational Education Professions Development			Colleges and universities; State Boards
FY 1969	$ 25,000,000		
FY 1970	35,000,000		

Notes: [1] 10 percent set aside for research and training activities.
[2] State Boards may also contract with private agencies for service.

opportunities for gainful employment, and suited to their needs, interests, and ability to benefit from such training.

National Advisory Council: The President will appoint the National Council consisting of twenty-one members, one-third of whom shall be representatives of the general public. Others on the council will come from fields representing agriculture, home economics, distribution and marketing, health, trades, manufacturing, office and service industries, and persons representative of new and emerging occupational fields; persons who are familiar with manpower problems and the administration of manpower programs; persons knowledgeable about the administration of state and local vocational education programs, including members of local school boards; persons experienced in the education and training of handicapped persons; persons familiar with the special problems of the disadvantaged; persons who have special knowledge of post secondary and adult vocational education programs.

This Council will advise the Commissioner concerning preparation of general regulations for, and the operation of, vocational programs supported with assistance under the Act (except in the case of the training of vocational education personnel); review programs and report findings and recommendations to the Secretary for transmittal to the Congress; conduct independent evaluations of programs, and review duplication of post secondary programs within geographic areas. The Council is authorized to employ staff and make studies to carry out its duties.

State Advisory Councils: Before any state can receive funds under the new Act, a State Advisory Council must be appointed and its membership certified to the Commissioner. The members must be representative of the various interests in vocational education, and though no specific number of members is indicated, it would appear that the State Councils will have a minimum membership of 13 persons. The Councils will be appointed by the governor of the state, or in the case of the states in which the members of the State Board are elected, the Council shall be appointed by the State Board. The State Councils are to be funded with federal funds at a minimum of $50,000 or a maximum of $150,000. The Council will employ staff and obtain such services as needed to carry out its functions. Duties shall include advising the State Board on the development of policy in administration of the state plan; evaluation of vocational education programs; and preparation of an annual report to the Commissioner of Education and to the National Advisory Council. The Council shall elect its own chairman, and must provide for not less than one public meeting each year at which the public is given an opportunity to express views concerning vocational education.

TITLE I, Part B:

State Vocational Education Programs: Funds are to be used to maintain, extend, and promote vocational education programs to meet the needs of the following categories of people:

1.   high school students (including programs to prepare them for advanced or highly skilled post secondary vocational-technical education)

2.   persons who have completed or left high school and who are available for study in preparation for entering the labor market

3. persons who have already entered the labor market and who need training or retraining to achieve stability or advance in employment

4. persons who have academic, socioeconomic, or other handicaps that prevent them from succeeding in the regular vocational education programs

5. persons who have handicaps (physical) and who need special educational assistance or require a modified vocational education program.

In addition, funds may be used for construction of area vocational education school facilities; for vocational guidance and counseling designed to aid students in the selection of, and preparation for employment in all vocational areas; provide vocational training through arrangements with private vocational training institutions; and to provide for ancillary service and activities to assure quality in all vocational education programs, such as teacher training, supervision, program evaluation, demonstration and experimental programs, development of instructional materials, and improved state administration and leadership.

One-fourth of the funds must be used for vocational education for the disadvantaged, and one-fourth for post secondary program; an additional 10 percent of the funds must be used to provide vocational education for the physically handicapped.

State Plans: Several new items are included in the state plan provisions to assure that more adequate funding will go to large metropolitan areas where there are concentrations of high youth unemployment; state plans must also provide that a public hearing shall be held in connection with development of the plan; it must set forth criteria for submission of projects by local education agencies. The state plan must also assure that funds authorized will not be used for any program of vocational education (except homemaking) which cannot be demonstrated to (a) prepare students for employment, (b) be necessary to prepare individuals for successful completion of such a program, or (c) be of significant assistance to individuals enrolled in making an informed and meaningful occupational choice.

The Commissioner is instructed, by law, not to approve a state plan until he has made specific findings as to the compliance of such plan with the requirements of the law, and until he is satisfied that adequate procedures are set forth to insure that the assurances and provisions of the state plan will be carried out.

TITLE I, Part C:

Research and Training in Vocational Education: Ten percent of the sums authorized for grants to the states shall be used for research and training in vocational education. One-half of the amount shall be allotted to the states to pay up to 75 percent of the costs of state research coordinating units, and 90 percent of the costs of projects for research and training, experimental and developmental, or pilot programs, and dissemination of information. The other half shall be used by the Commissioner to make grants and contracts for research in vocational education; training programs, experimental and demonstration projects; demonstration and dissemination projects; development of new vocational curricula; projects in the development of new careers and occupations, and evaluation of vocational-technical education programs.

TITLE I, Part D:

Exemplary Programs and Projects: One-half of the funds will be expended for projects approved by the Commissioner of Education, and the remaining one-half shall be allotted to the states. No matching of federal funds is required. The program is authorized for a period of four years. Each state shall receive a minimum allotment of $200,000, with the remainder allotted to the states on the basis of population aged 15 to 19. The funds shall be used for programs that will broaden the occupational aspirations and opportunities for youths, with special emphasis given to youths who have academic, socioeconomic, or other handicaps. Effective procedures must be adopted by grantees to coordinate with the appropriate state plan the development and operation of programs and projects carried out under this section.

TITLE I, Part E:

Residential Vocational Education: Funds are authorized to construct, equip, and operate residential schools to provide vocational education for youths at least 15 years of age and less than 21 years of age at the time of enrollment. Schools may be on a demonstration or pilot basis, or funded through special set-asides for state programs. Federal funds may be used by the states for planning residential facilities.

TITLE I, Part F:

Consumer and Homemaking Education: The state plan shall set forth a program under which federal funds will be used to support educational programs to encourage home economics to give greater consideration to social and cultural conditions and needs, especially in economically depressed areas; encourage preparation for professional leadership; prepare youths and adults for the role of homemaker, or to contribute to the employability of such youths and adults in the dual role of homemaker and wage earner; include consumer education programs, and must be designed for persons who have entered, or are preparing to enter, the work of the home. Funds may also be used for teacher training and supervision, curriculum development research, program evaluation, instructional materials, and provision of equipment, and for state administration and leadership. States will match federal funds on a fifty-fifty basis except that one-third of the federal allotment shall be used for programs in economically depressed areas or areas with high rates of unemployment to assist consumers and to help improve home environments and the quality of family life (in which case the Federal funds are available on a 90–10 matching basis).

TITLE I, Part G:

Cooperative Vocational Education Programs: The purpose of this section of the Act is to assist the states to expand cooperative work-study programs by providing assistance for personnel to coordinate such programs and to provide instruction related to the work experience; to reimburse employers when necessary for certain added costs incurred in providing on-the-job training, and to pay other costs of cooperative work-study programs. Such programs must be a part of the state plan. Each state shall receive a minimum allocation of $200,000. Funds may be used to prepare students for work in any occupational field.

TITLE I, Part H:

Work-Study Programs for Vocational Education Students: The amendments extend for two years the provisions of the Vocational Education Act of 1963 that fund work-study programs for vocational students who need financial assistance in order to remain in school.

TITLE I, Part I:

Curriculum Development in Vocational-Technical Education: Authorizes funds to enable the U.S. Office of Education to promote the development and dissemination of vocational-technical education curriculum materials for use in teaching occupational subjects, including curricula for new and changing occupational fields; to develop standards for curriculum development in all occupational fields; to coordinate efforts of the states in the preparation of curriculum materials and prepare current lists of curriculum materials available in all occupational fields; survey curriculum materials developed by other agencies of government, including the Department of Defense; and to evaluate vocational-technical education curriculum materials and their uses; and to train personnel in curriculum development.

TITLE II, Part F:

Training and Development Programs for Vocational Education Personnel: It is the purpose of this Title to provide opportunities for experienced vocational educators to spend full-time in advanced study of vocational education for a period not to exceed three years in length, and to provide opportunities to up-date the occupational competencies of vocational education teachers through exchanges of personnel between commercial, industrial, or other public or private employment related to the subject matter of vocational education, and to provide programs of in-service teacher education and short-term institutes for vocational education personnel.

Leadership development awards (graduate study) will be available through institutions of higher education and will be designed for students who are eligible for admission as graduate students. Awards will be apportioned among the states.

The Commissioner is also authorized to make grants to State Boards to enable them to make grants or contracts with public and private agencies for the purpose of providing in-service and exchange programs for vocational education personnel.

TITLE III

Miscellaneous Provisions: The George-Barden Act and the Vocational Education Act of 1963 are, in effect, repealed, with new and additional language added by the 1968 amendments. The Smith-Hughes Act is not repealed, though the only feature remaining is the appropriate language. Funds appropriated under the Smith-Hughes Act are to be spent under the provisions of the 1968 Amendments. Advance funding for vocational education programs is provided; the Commissioner of Education is instructed to make a special study of the means by which the Job Corps might most effectively and expeditiously be transferred by state or joint federal-state operation in conjunction with the program of residential vocational schools authorized under the amendments; use of private schools is authorized; the National Advisory Council is instructed to review the possible local duplication of vocational education programs at post secondary and adult levels and to report its findings; a reserve of $5 million is to be transferred to the Secretary of Labor to finance national, regional, state and local studies and to project manpower needs; the Commissioner of Education is instructed to prepare and disseminate information concerning federal assistance for educational programs, and shall make available, upon request, advice, counsel, demonstrations, and technical assistance to state educational agencies and local educational agencies or to institutions of higher education.

Although the act authorized the appropriation of funds for the fiscal year ending July 1, 1969, appropriations were not passed until almost midway in the 1970 fiscal year. The provisions of the act, however, became effective as of July 1, 1969.

EDUCATION AMENDMENTS OF 1972

The Education Amendments of 1972 (P.L. 92–318) was signed into law by President Nixon on June 23, 1972. This law represents one of the most comprehensive pieces of federal education legislation passed to date and it has special significance for community colleges and technical (postsecondary) education. For purposes of this chapter, however, only those parts will be discussed which are of most significance to vocational and technical education.

By far the most important title of the act for trade, industrial, and technical education is Title X. The main provisions of this title are summarized as follows:

PART A. ESTABLISHMENT AND EXPANSION OF COMMUNITY COLLEGES

Subpart 1   State Plans

Purpose: Each state shall establish a Postsecondary Education (1202) Commission which shall develop a statewide plan for the expansion or improvement of postsecondary education programs in community colleges which shall:

- Designate areas where access to two years of low tuition or free tuition postsecondary education is not available within reasonable distance.
- Set forth a comprehensive plan for establishing, expanding, improving community colleges which would achieve goal of making available to all residents of the state an opportunity to attend a community college.
- Establish priorities for use of federal and non-federal financial and other resources.

- Make recommendations with respect to adequate state and local financial support.
- Analyze duplications of postsecondary programs and recommend coordination.
- Set forth a plan for use of new and existing resources, including recommendation for modification of plans for federally assisted vocational education, community services and academic facilities as they affect community colleges.

Administration
and Revenues: Fifteen million seven hundred thousand dollars is authorized nationally for fiscal years 1973 and 1974. These monies would be administered by the Postsecondary Education (1202) Commission to accomplish the purpose of Part A, subpart 1, statewide plans. Wisconsin's share of the national appropriation is roughly two percent. Therefore, if the total authorization is appropriated, Wisconsin would receive approximately $314,000 for planning for fiscal years 1973 and 1974. However, as noted earlier, the actual amount will probably be less.

The Postsecondary Education (1202) Commission shall establish an Advisory Council on Community Colleges which shall:

1. be composed of—
   a. A substantial number of persons in the state (including representatives of state and local agencies) having responsibility for the operation of community colleges;
   b. representatives of state agencies having responsibility for or an interest in postsecondary education; and
   c. the general public.
2. have responsibility for assisting and making recommendations to the State Commission in developing the statewide plan required under this section;
3. conduct such hearings as the State Commission may deem advisable; and
4. pursuant to requirements establish by the State Commission, provide each state and local agency with the state responsible for postsecondary education an opportunity to review and make recommendations with respect to such plan.

Subpart 2   Establishment and Expansion of Community Colleges

Purpose: Encourage and assist those states and localities which so desire in establishing and/or expanding community colleges.

Establishment grants will be provided for planning, developing, establishing and conducting initial operations of new community colleges in areas of the state in which there are no existing community colleges or in which existing community colleges cannot adequately provide postsecondary educational opportunities for all the residents.

Expansion grants will be provided to existing community colleges to assist them—

1. in expanding enrollment capacities

2. in establishing new campuses

3. in altering or modifying their educational programs to:
   • more adequately meet the needs of the community they serve
   • provide educational programs especially suited to the needs of the educationally disadvantaged.

Administration
and Revenues: Congress authorized the following appropriations for Part A, subpart 2, Establishment and Expansion of Community Colleges: The Act authorizes a national appropriation of:

$50,000,000 fiscal year 1973
$75,000,000 fiscal year 1974
$150,000,000 fiscal year 1975

These monies would be distributed from the U.S. Commissioner directly to individual institutions. All applications submitted by institutions to the Commissioner for establishment and expansion grant monies under Part A, subpart 2 must be consistent with the plan approved by the Commissioner which is developed by the Postsecondary Education (1202) Commission under Part A, subpart 1. Monies available under Part A, subpart 2 may be used to remodel or renovate existing facilities, lease facilities or to equip new and existing facilities. They may not be used for construction of new facilities or the acquisition of existing facilities.

PART B. OCCUPATIONAL EDUCATION PROGRAMS

Purpose: The Postsecondary Education (1202) Commission shall develop plans for occupational education programs which shall:
   • assess existing capabilities and facilities for providing postsecondary occupational education and the need for such education.
   • consider the most effective utilization of all existing institutions capable of providing occupational education.

- develop administrative procedures for resolving differences between various educational groups with respect to administration of the occupational program.
- develop long range strategy for infusing occupational education into elementary-secondary schools on an equal footing with traditional academic education.
- develop procedures to insure continuous planning and evaluation. A state Administrative Agency (1055) will have sole responsibility for fiscal management and administration of the occupational program in accordance with the Part B plan prepared by the 1202 Commission. The Administrative (1055) Agency shall be responsible for:
  — designing, establishing and conducting programs of post-secondary occupational education.
  — designing, establishing and conducting programs to infuse occupational preparation into elementary-secondary schools.
  — development of an order of priorities of high quality post-secondary occupational education.
  — special training to prepare persons to teach occupational education.
  — leasing, renting or remodeling of facilities in the delivery of occupational education.

Administration
and Revenues: Congress has authorized the following national appropriations for Part B Occupational Education.

The law provides that the State Advisory Council for Vocational Education shall perform the same role with respect to Part B, Occupational Education, as it does under the 1968 Vocational Education Amendments.

PART C. ESTABLISHMENT OF AGENCIES

Purpose: Establishment of Bureau of Occupational and Adult Education
The law established this bureau in the U.S. Office of Education to administer Title X, the Vocational Education Act of 1963, the Adult Education Act, functions of the U.S. Office relating to vocational, technical and occupational training in community and junior colleges and any other Act vesting authority in the Commissioner for vocational, occupational, adult and continuing education and for certain relevant portions of career education.

NATIONAL INSTITUTE OF EDUCATION

The Education Amendments of 1972 also established the National Institute of Education (NIE). This institute was labeled after the National Institute of Health (NIH) for the purpose of expanding the quantity and quality of research in education.

In reality a new structure for administering educational research was established which removes the primary research responsibility from the U.S. Office of Education.

Legislative Dilemma

The future nature of federal legislation funding is being debated at this point in time. The administration is pressing hard for some form of educational revenue sharing which could affect drastically the role played by the federal government. The funding picture in many of the states is also somewhat clouded by the fact that there continues to be pressure for property tax relief, a taxing method upon which education has been highly dependent in most states.

The fact remains, however, that the need for trade, industrial, and technical education programs has never been greater. The support for such programs is found at all levels. The challenge to vocational educators is to find ways to work aggressively within new organizational structures and through possible new funding structures and patterns.

Program Developments

It would be inaccurate to infer that trade and industrial education or programs of a trade and industrial nature began with the Smith-Hughes Act. However, it is accurate to say that prior to this act there was no national plan for development of trade and industrial programs. Also, it could be said that there was no recognizable pattern of programs across the nation. Programs did exist, however, usually established in response to locally identified interests and need. Several of the states were engaged in a statewide effort; however, there was little uniformity in effort and program.

It should be recognized that we were speaking of a period prior to 1917 when there was not the total commitment to education that exists today. It was also a period in which the administrative structure for providing education at the state, intermediate, and local levels was not as well developed as at present. In the case of trade and industrial type training programs there were not recognized standards for program development, content, or achievement. An organized group of leaders did not exist to encourage or give program direction. It was the success of these early programs, however, which gave rise to recognition that the benefits of such programs should be made available to more youth. There was a recognition of the needs of the work force for better trained people, coupled with the idea that millions of individuals just were not prepared to meet industrial employment standards.

Private schools had developed primarily in the population centers where industrial development had taken place. Many of these schools did an outstanding job but served only limited numbers compared to the need of an expanding industrial nation. Factory schools existed, also, particularly in the larger establishments. These were designed to serve their own organizational needs. It is clear that throughout the nation many commendable training activities existed. However, it seems quite clear that there was need for a system of training for industrial type jobs that would make such training more generally available to young people who could profit from such education and training.

The Smith-Hughes Act was passed in 1917 with the specific purpose of promotion of vocational education in agriculture, home economics, and trades and industries in cooperation with the states. Some of the early leaders spoke of it as an attempt to "democratize" the program of the public school system of the nation by providing practical instruction leading to useful employment.

World War I

Some historians have pointed out the fact that the congressional leaders were influenced to pass the Smith-Hughes Act because of the possibility of war. The provisions of the act, particularly the trade and industrial education provisions, were well suited to training for not only national defense but also for the economic improvement of the nation. It is really an academic question that could stir much debate as to the influence of the impending war on the passage of the Smith-Hughes Act. The fact remains, however, that vocational education, particularly those phases related to trade and industrial education, received an immediate challenge as a result of the efforts to prepare for war, particularly World War I in which we soon became engaged.

Discussions and plans took place almost immediately between the state board and other departments of the federal government, particularly the War Department and the United States Shipping Board. The importance of the role that the state board and in turn vocational educators across the nation were to play was expressed by an order signed on November 3, 1917, to all commanding generals and chiefs of bureaus which follows:

1. The Secretary of War directs that you be informed as follows:
   a. The Federal Board of Vocational Education, authorized by act of Congress, February 23, 1917, of which Dr. C. A. Proser is Director, is now organized and is in close cooperation with vocational schools of the country. This board is prepared to initiate a comprehensive system of preliminary training of the men of the second and subsequent drafts prior to their reporting to cantonments.
   b. It is the desire of the Secretary of War that the Chiefs of Bureaus maintain close cooperation with this board, furnishing such information as to the number of men desired to be trained, necessary courses, etc. For this purpose the chiefs of the bureaus will deal directly with Dr. Proser (U.S. Government Printing Office 1917).

World War II

Without a doubt the victory of World War II was assisted by the know-how of vocational educators. Operating under the War Production Training Act of 1940, sometimes called Vocational Education for National Defense (VEND), the shops and laboratories of vocational schools and programs readily lent themselves to the training of skilled manpower to produce the materials needed by the servicemen. During this period the lights burned late in the vocational wings of local high schools and postsecondary institutes. Just as the war industries ran three shifts a day so did vocational educators train around the clock. The outpour of over seven million production workers to meet the needs of industry was no small achievement of this historical period.

In all, the War Production Training Act provided $100 million to do the job. As a result, Congress expressed considerable confidence in vocational education as a delivery system. This was substantiated by the passage of the George-Barden Act in 1946.

Program Growth

Vocational and technical education has sustained continuous growth throughout its history, both in terms of its mission, its enrollments, and its financial support. Table 1–2 provides a brief summary of enrollments, federal legislation, and dollar support.

Figure 1–1 and table 1–3 provide a more detailed picture of total expenditures for vocational and technical education including state, local, and federal funds for the years 1965 through 1971. The increase in expenditures as illustrated has been consistent. It should be noted that for every federal dollar spent approximately six state and local dollars were expended.

Trade and industrial education has been and continues to make up a significant part of the enrollment in vocational and technical education. For historical purposes figure 1–2 is included which shows trade and industrial enrollments by types of programs through 1972.

The changes in reporting and program classification of the Office of Education make it difficult to report growth of program on a single graph. However, the enrollments for trades and industry and technical programs for the years 1966 through 1970 are shown in table 1–2.

The story of trade, industrial, and technical programs and their growth is incomplete without some understanding of the breadth of the program. The U.S. Office of Education and the states have struggled throughout the existence of the programs for a meaningful and accurate way to classify and report instructional programs in such a way that they would relate to actual job titles and classifications. Figure 1–3 provides a summary of enrollments by O. E. Instructional Code with projections to 1976. It should be noted that under each broad instructional category training may be provided for a number of job titles.

TABLE 1–2

ENROLLMENTS FOR TECHNICAL, TRADE, AND INDUSTRIAL PROGRAMS. (FISCAL YEARS 1966–1970)

	1966	1967	1968	1969	1970
Technical	253,838	368,981	270,400	318,612	277,658
Secondary	28,865	27,614	36,286	31,833	34,386
Postsecondary	100,151	97,156	104,746	130,564	151,621
Adult	124,730	140,431	127,418	151,714	85,723
Special Needs	92	853	1,382	2,000	13,373
(in regular programs)		2,927	568	3,301	2,555
Trade and Industrial	1,269,051	1,506,194	1,646,069	1,743,087	2,118,930
Secondary	318,961	367,789	421,719	458,554	692,396
Postsecondary	115,539	123,374	137,732	174,201	261,182
Adult	803,901	966,301	1,030,723	1,042,362	952,555
Special Needs	30,650	33,343	38,368	45,742	182,642
(in regular programs)		15,387	17,527	22,148	30,155

SOURCE: *Trends in Vocational Education,* U.S. Department of Health, Education and Welfare, June 1971.

TABLE 1-3

EXPENDITURES FOR VOCATIONAL EDUCATION FISCAL YEARS
1965–1976 BY SOURCE OF FUNDS

	1965	1970	1971	1976 (Projected)
Amount				
Grand Total	$604,645,727	$1,841,846,345	$2,347,353,175	$4,000,000,000
Federal	156,936,015	300,045,568	396,378,405	667,000,000
State/Local	447,709,712	1,541,800,777	1,950,974,770	3,333,000,000
Ratio: State/Local to Federal	$2.90	$5.14	$4.92	$5.00
Percentage Distribution				
Grand Total	100.0	100.0	100.0	100.0
Federal	26.0	16.3	16.9	16.7
State/Local	74.0	83.7	83.1	83.3
Percentage Change from Previous Year				
Grand Total	81.7	34.6	27.4	- - -
Federal	185.2	17.8	32.1	- - -
State/Local	61.2	38.4	26.5	- - -
Federal Allotments				
Total Allotments	$168,607,278	$365,347,467	$412,812,093	
Smith-Hughes Act	7,266,455	- - -	- - -	
George-Barden Act	49,690,823	- - -	- - -	
VE Act of 1963	111,650,000	- - -	- - -	
1968 Amendments		365,347,467	412,812,093	

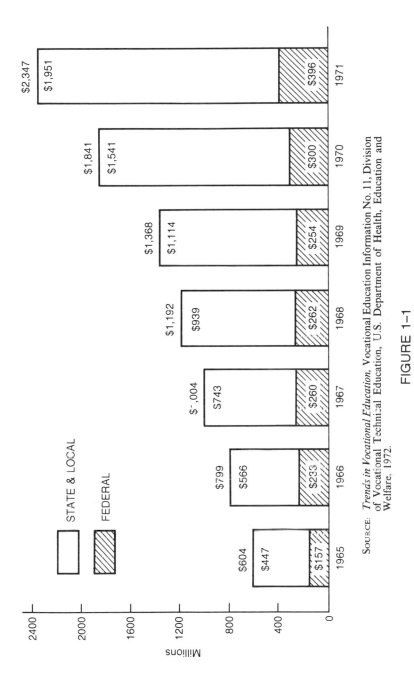

FIGURE 1-1

EXPENDITURES BY SOURCE OF FUNDS, 1965–1971 (IN MILLIONS)

SOURCE: *Trends in Vocational Education,* Vocational Education Information No. 11, Division of Vocational Technical Education, U.S. Department of Health, Education and Welfare, 1972.

37

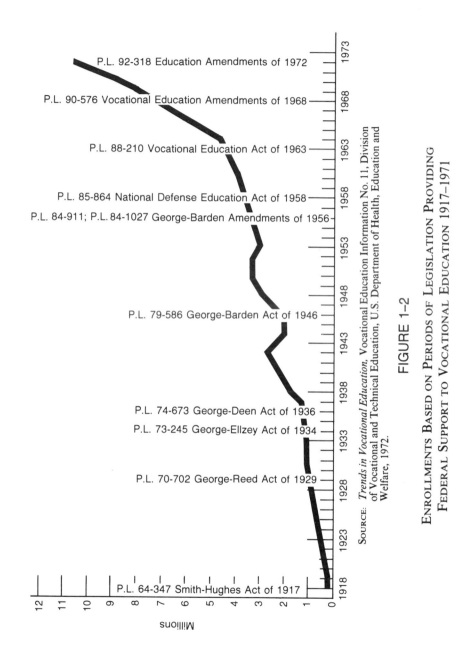

FIGURE 1-2

ENROLLMENTS BASED ON PERIODS OF LEGISLATION PROVIDING FEDERAL SUPPORT TO VOCATIONAL EDUCATION 1917–1971

SOURCE: *Trends in Vocational Education*, Vocational Education Information No. 11, Division of Vocational and Technical Education, U.S. Department of Health, Education and Welfare, 1972.

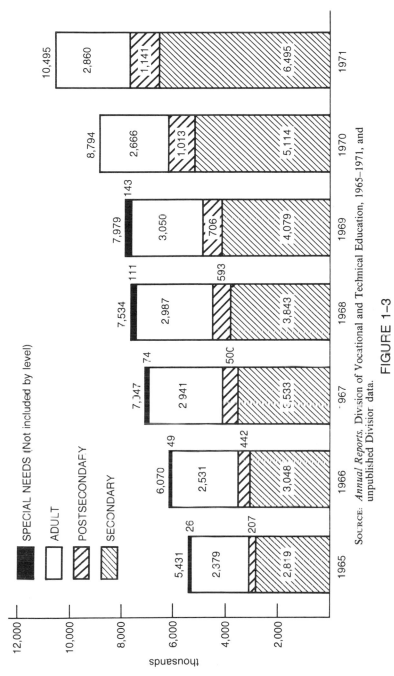

SOURCE: *Annual Reports*, Division of Vocational and Technical Education, 1965–1971, and unpublished Division data.

FIGURE 1-3

VOCATIONAL ENROLLMENTS BY BROAD PROGRAM CLASSIFICATIONS (1965–1971)

Summary

In this chapter the historical background of vocational education has been presented with emphasis on the background of trade, industrial, and technical education. Considerable emphasis has been placed on federal legislation because it is within this legislation and its administrative regulations that what might be considered a national policy has been established for vocational education. It is this national effort that has served as the unifying force for each state to provide programs for their youths and adults.

Continuous growth in programs has been illustrated by enrollment growth patterns. Also, the breadth of the progress has been suggested by showing enrollments by various program categories and by Office of Education instructional titles.

QUESTIONS AND ACTIVITIES

1. What factors have contributed to the sustained national concern for trade, industrial, and technical education over the years?

2. Suggest how the factors affecting the national concerns have tended to change over the years.

3. Discuss the major changes brought about in the vocational education programs as a result of the Vocational Education Act of 1963.

4. In addition to providing additional funding, what new program directions were brought about by the Vocational Amendments of 1968?

5. Discuss the need for trade, industrial, and technical programs to serve the needs by people vs. the needs of employers.

SOURCE MATERIALS

1. *Annual Report of the Federal Board for Vocational Education.* Washington, D.C.: U.S. Government Printing Office, 1917, p. 14.

2. *American Vocational Journal.* Washington, D.C.: American Vocational Association 35 (October 1960): 22.

3. *American Vocational Journal.* Washington, D.C.: American Vocational Association 35 (November 1960): 6.

4. Barlow, Melvin L. *History of Industrial Education in the United States.* Peoria, Ill.: Charles P. Bennett Co., Inc., 1967.

5. *Education for a Changing World of Work.* Report of the Panel of Consultants of Vocational Education, U.S. Office of Education. Washington, D.C.: U.S. Government Printing Office, 1963

6. Fitzpatrick, Edward A. *McCarthy of Wisconsin.* New York: Columbia University Press, 1944.

7. *Vocational Education: The Bridge Between Man and His Work.* Summary and Recommendations adapted from the General Report of the Advisory Council on Vocational Education. Washington, D.C.: Superintendent of Documents, U.S. Government Printing Office, 1968.

Chapter 2 TRADE AND INDUSTRIAL EDUCATION AND THE LABOR MARKET

A brief history of trade and technical education has been provided in chapter 1. This chapter will address itself to the past, present, and projected concerns and relationships of the program to manpower needs. It will also provide information on manpower projections for the years ahead in an attempt to suggest new program directions appropriate to addressing such needs.

Some contemporary writers would have us believe that the early vocational legislation was concerned exclusively with meeting employer demands and that beginning with the Vocational Education Act of 1963, legislation gave primary emphasis to meeting the needs of people. This position cannot be fully substantiated and is at best an oversimplification. It is undoubtedly true that World War I influenced the timing and tenor of the passage of the Smith-Hughes Act of 1917 and that the immediate concern of this legislation was to meet the country's manpower needs as they related to the war effort. Trade and industrial education was central to this thrust to increase the nation's industrial capacity. In contrast to this position, however, Hoík Smith, a congressman and coauthor of the Smith-Hughes Act, in a portion of a speech before the National Society for Promotion of Industrial Education provided a rationale for industrial education based both on the needs of industry and the needs of individuals. Smith said:

It is a great problem you have undertaken. I do not know that there is a greater problem, or so great a problem in our country. It reaches our position in national commerce. It will solve the question as to whether our manufactories and world's commerce to which our best resources entitle us.

No system of education or manufacture is logical which undertakes to carry a youth as far as he has to go through school and college and drops him without having done anything to teach him how to do that which will most probably aid him to make his daily livelihood (Barlow 1967).

The previous quotation selected from among many is exemplary of the fact that early leaders in vocational education had the needs of people in mind as well as the needs of employers. Trade and industrial education in the early legislation was directed primarily at preparation for skilled occupations which the Vocational Education Act of 1963 broadened and charged to include educational responsibilities for all levels of workers. Moreover, the 1963 Act related funding categories to people as contrasted to service areas such as trade and industrial education or agricultural education. At the same time, however, it was the 1917 vocational education legislation which made provisions and in fact required a working arrangement with state employment services with the idea in mind of making programs more responsive to employer demands.

It is evident that vocational education legislation and program developers have always been greatly concerned with meeting employer demands for skilled manpower. The added dimension in more recent legislation has been the objective of providing vocational educational opportunities to all persons including the disadvantaged who have never been in demand by employers except during periods where there was great need for manpower. Trade, industrial, and technical education, as in the past, should not only try to serve the needs of industry but also try to be continually aware of the needs of individuals in order that all may have the opportunity to gain skills that will give them the opportunity to compete in the labor market.

The Nature of the Work Force

"This Nation does not preplan the future of its working citizens. The Manpower future is shaped by tens of millions of individual decisions on the part of employers, students, workers, union officials, educators and government officials" (U.S. Dept. of Labor 1970).

The above statement was made by the United States Secretary of Labor in a preface to a publication on manpower projections for the '70s. Several facts are set forth by these statements which make forecasting of the nation's work force even on a gross national basis difficult. Even more difficult is the problem of forecasting for an individual state and for a district or local area of a state.

It would not be difficult to imagine a controlled type of society where employees had no options about the occupation in which they would spend their lifetime and the government controlled the economy completely including the determination of the natural resources to be used, the amount and kinds of products to be manufactured, and the kind and amounts of goods and services to be consumed by its citizens. In such a society or nation, forecasting could be quite concise. Also, the planning for the training of manpower could be relatively simple. This might suggest a utopian situation for manpower planners, but it certainly would be counter to all the principles of a democracy where individual choice of an occupation has been cherished along with the free enterprise system.

In spite of the difficulties involved in manpower planning in our society, most of us would not like to work in a tightly regulated society where individual options were not available and where a free enterprise system was not in operation. Therefore, educational planners must learn to cope with the uncertain ties that exist and will continue to exist while at the same time use the best information available for planning educational programs.

Labor Market Trends

This section will describe labor market trends using primarily sources documented from the U.S. Department of Labor.

It seems appropriate to look at the present and projected participation ratio in the labor market. Table 2-1 provides information on the total population 16 years and over, the labor force, and participation ratio by states. It can be noted that the population in the 16 years and over age range is expected to increase by more than 40 million between 1960 and 1980 and that the total labor force is expected to increase to more than 99 million by 1980. According to projections, participation rates are not expected to increase dramatically, rather the increase in the labor force is mainly due to the increase in the population.

It can be seen that for the nation between 1970 and 1980, the population increase in 16 years of age and older category will increase by 16.9 percent while for the same period the labor force will increase 18.3 percent. It will also be interesting to review the growth rates by regions of the country and by states. Not only are the population growth rates somewhat different among the states but also the growth in the labor force.

Table 2-2 provides information on the labor force and labor participation ratio by sex and age. For trade, industrial, and technical educators, such information is desirable in order to have a better idea of the nature of the potential clientele to be served in full or part-time programs. Small discrepancies will be noted comparing figures from one table to another. For example, the projected population for the year 1970 as shown in table 2-1 is slightly less than the actual figures shown in table 2-2.

Of particular interest in table 2-3 are the participation rates of women as compared to men in the various age categories. Table 2-4 summarizes the actual and projected changes in the labor force by occupational group. It is important to have information on not only the size of the labor force but also the numbers that are employed by occupational groups. Table 2-4 provides data by occupational groups for the years 1960 and 1970 with projected figures for 1980. It is seen that there will be a growth in all categories except nonfarm laborers and farmers and farm laborers. The highest rates of increase between 1970 and 1980 are expected to be in professional and technical workers and in service workers. Table 2-5 provides information on employment by industry divisions.

One is often led to believe that there were very rapid shifts (increases or decreases) in employment by industry divisions between the years 1960 and 1970 and even greater expected through 1980. This has not been the case and particular note should be taken of the actual and projected number changes and annual rate of change for industry division in table 2-5. For example, the relationship of growth between goods producing industries and service producing industries is not as dramatic as is suggested by some manpower planners. In the report by the U.S. Department of Labor, the belief is further substantiated that there will be a period of strong economic growth which would be accompanied by extensive workforce growth. Figure 2-1 shows that the GNP may increase three times the 1950 level, given high employment levels and expected productivity gains. The labor force, as shown in figure 2-2, is expected to number more than 100 million by 1980, growing by 15 million in the 1970s.

> This economic and labor force growth will help us to address such important national needs as:
>
> 1. Higher living standards.
> 2. Better education, health and housing.
> 3. Urban rebuilding, improved transportation and crime reduction.
> 4. Environmental quality improvement.
>
> (*U.S. Manpower in the 1970's—Opportunity and Challenge* 1970)

Of the number of positions available the largest number of employment opportunities will continue to be in the service producing industries as illustrated in figure 2-3.

> The United States entered the post World War II period with more workers producing goods than providing services. Service-producing in-

TABLE 2-1

Total Population, Total Labor Force, and Labor Force Participation Rates for Persons 16 Years and Over, by Region and State, 1960 to 1980

Region and State	Total population [1] Actual 1960 (April 1)	Projected 1970 (July 1)	Projected 1980 (July 1)	Total labor force [1] Actual 1960 (April 1)	Projected 1970 (annual average)	Projected 1980 (annual average)	Labor force participation rates (percent) Actual 1960	Projected 1970	Projected 1980	Percent change [2] Population 1960-70	1970-80	Labor force 1960-70	1970-80
United States	120,735	140,966	164,726	69,237	83,875	99,204	57.4	59.5	60.2	16.8	16.9	21.1	18.3
Northeast	31,289	35,235	39,747	18,144	20,852	23,488	58.0	59.2	59.1	12.6	12.8	14.9	12.6
North Central	34,636	38,571	44,377	19,829	22,981	26,918	57.2	59.6	60.7	11.4	15.1	15.9	17.1
South	36,062	43,002	50,500	20,217	25,161	30,080	56.1	58.5	59.6	19.2	17.4	24.5	19.6
West	18,744	24,157	30,099	11,046	14,873	18,721	58.9	61.6	62.2	28.9	24.6	34.6	25.9
New England	7,277	8,197	9,386	4,296	4,971	5,691	59.0	60.6	60.6	12.6	14.5	15.7	14.5
Maine	652	707	791	366	406	460	56.1	57.4	58.2	8.4	11.9	10.9	13.3
New Hampshire	415	486	569	249	303	359	60.0	62.3	63.1	17.1	17.1	21.7	18.5
Vermont	261	297	340	147	177	207	56.3	59.6	60.9	13.8	14.5	20.4	16.9
Massachusetts	3,594	3,948	4,478	2,112	2,398	2,726	58.8	60.7	60.9	9.8	13.4	13.5	13.7
Rhode Island	604	664	726	358	391	422	59.3	58.9	58.1	9.9	9.3	9.2	7.9
Connecticut	1,751	2,095	2,482	1,064	1,296	1,517	60.8	61.9	61.1	19.6	18.5	21.8	17.1
Middle Atlantic	24,012	27,038	30,361	13,848	15,881	17,797	57.7	58.7	58.6	12.6	12.3	14.7	12.1
New York	11,921	13,528	15,117	6,963	8,011	8,876	58.4	59.2	58.7	13.5	11.7	15.0	10.8
New Jersey	4,233	5,087	5,990	2,496	3,024	3,539	59.0	59.4	59.1	20.2	17.8	21.2	17.0
Pennsylvania	7,858	8,423	9,254	4,389	4,846	5,382	55.9	57.5	58.2	7.2	9.9	10.4	11.1
East North Central	24,282	27,390	31,837	13,995	16,354	19,298	57.6	59.7	60.6	12.8	16.2	16.9	18.0
Ohio	6,490	7,422	8,682	3,692	4,394	5,203	56.9	59.2	59.9	14.4	17.0	19.0	18.4
Indiana	3,108	3,497	4,056	1,783	2,117	2,526	57.4	60.5	62.3	12.5	16.0	18.7	19.3
Illinois	6,939	7,699	8,896	4,094	4,642	5,406	59.0	60.3	60.8	11.0	15.5	13.4	16.5
Michigan	5,122	5,823	6,761	2,913	3,416	4,036	56.9	58.7	59.7	13.7	16.1	17.3	18.2
Wisconsin	2,623	2,949	3,442	1,513	1,785	2,125	57.7	60.5	61.7	12.4	16.7	18.0	19.0
West North Central	10,354	11,181	12,540	5,834	6,627	7,620	56.3	59.3	60.8	8.0	12.2	13.6	15.0
Minnesota	2,238	2,506	2,943	1,283	1,508	1,801	57.3	60.2	61.2	12.0	17.4	17.5	19.4
Iowa	1,857	1,942	2,140	1,037	1,162	1,323	55.8	59.8	61.8	4.6	10.2	12.1	13.9
Missouri	2,991	3,178	3,543	1,659	1,810	2,055	55.5	57.0	58.0	6.3	11.5	9.1	13.5
North Dakota	403	440	490	226	261	297	56.1	59.3	60.6	9.2	11.4	15.5	13.8
South Dakota	440	492	543	248	292	331	56.4	59.3	61.0	11.8	10.4	17.7	13.4
Nebraska	952	1,044	1,145	546	635	718	57.4	60.8	62.7	9.7	9.7	16.3	13.1
Kansas	1,473	1,579	1,736	835	959	1,095	56.7	60.7	63.1	7.2	9.9	14.8	14.2
South Atlantic	17,162	20,939	25,017	9,880	12,476	14,979	57.6	59.6	59.9	22.0	19.5	26.3	20.1
Delaware	296	365	450	177	221	272	59.8	60.5	60.4	23.3	23.3	24.9	23.1
Maryland	2,060	2,571	3,121	1,234	1,575	1,900	59.9	61.3	60.9	24.8	21.4	27.6	20.6
District of Columbia	562	611	713	368	399	470	65.5	65.3	65.9	8.7	16.7	8.4	17.8
Virginia	2,623	3,180	3,732	1,522	1,900	2,248	58.0	59.7	60.2	21.2	17.4	24.8	18.3
West Virginia	1,227	1,251	1,319	584	661	722	47.6	52.8	54.7	2.0	5.4	13.2	9.2
North Carolina	2,951	3,459	3,963	1,739	2,112	2,410	58.9	61.1	60.8	17.2	14.6	21.4	14.1
South Carolina	1,485	1,766	2,043	884	1,086	1,246	59.5	61.5	61.0	18.9	15.7	22.9	14.7
Georgia	2,548	3,073	3,576	1,500	1,890	2,192	58.9	61.5	61.3	20.6	16.4	26.0	16.0
Florida	3,410	4,663	6,100	1,872	2,632	3,519	54.9	56.4	57.7	36.7	30.8	40.6	33.7
East South Central	7,830	8,965	10,178	4,205	5,101	5,972	53.7	56.9	58.7	14.5	13.5	21.3	17.1
Kentucky	2,005	2,216	2,453	1,026	1,200	1,394	51.2	54.2	56.8	10.5	10.7	17.0	16.2
Tennessee	2,376	2,757	3,109	1,304	1,594	1,836	54.9	57.8	59.1	16.0	12.8	22.2	15.2
Alabama	2,096	2,413	2,802	1,142	1,392	1,659	54.5	57.7	59.2	15.1	16.1	21.9	19.2
Mississippi	1,353	1,579	1,814	733	915	1,083	54.2	57.9	59.7	16.7	14.9	24.8	18.4
West South Central	11,070	13,098	15,305	6,132	7,584	9,129	55.4	57.9	59.6	18.3	16.8	23.7	20.4
Arkansas	1,181	1,366	1,520	604	756	880	51.1	55.3	57.9	15.7	11.3	25.2	16.4
Louisiana	2,050	2,465	2,973	1,064	1,355	1,689	52.9	55.0	56.8	20.2	20.6	27.4	24.6
Oklahoma	1,591	1,776	1,949	845	998	1,142	53.1	56.2	58.6	11.6	9.7	18.1	14.4
Texas	6,248	7,491	8,863	3,599	4,475	5,418	57.6	59.7	61.1	19.9	18.3	24.3	21.1
Mountain	4,364	5,679	7,052	2,520	3,491	4,443	57.7	61.5	63.0	30.1	24.2	38.5	27.3
Montana	435	496	573	249	301	353	57.2	60.7	61.6	14.0	15.5	20.9	17.3
Idaho	423	489	577	245	309	377	57.9	63.2	65.3	15.6	18.0	26.1	22.0
Wyoming	214	247	292	128	156	185	59.8	63.2	63.4	15.4	18.2	21.9	18.6
Colorado	1,156	1,473	1,780	670	911	1,137	58.0	61.8	63.9	27.4	20.8	36.0	24.8
New Mexico	573	711	936	324	425	578	56.5	59.8	61.8	24.1	31.6	31.2	36.0
Arizona	827	1,236	1,638	466	727	993	56.3	58.8	60.6	49.5	32.5	56.0	36.6
Utah	542	709	892	312	448	580	57.6	63.2	65.0	30.8	25.8	43.6	29.5
Nevada	194	318	364	126	214	240	64.9	67.3	65.9	63.4	14.5	69.8	12.1
Pacific	14,380	18,478	23,047	8,526	11,372	14,278	59.3	61.5	62.0	28.5	24.7	33.4	25.6
Washington	1,915	2,201	2,577	1,109	1,339	1,596	57.9	60.8	61.9	14.9	17.1	20.7	19.2
Oregon	1,194	1,392	1,588	676	810	931	56.6	58.2	58.6	16.6	14.1	19.8	14.9
California	10,726	14,221	18,094	6,379	8,784	11,251	59.5	65.9	62.2	32.6	27.2	37.7	28.1
Alaska	143	170	213	98	112	133	68.5	65.9	62.4	18.9	25.3	14.3	18.8
Hawaii	402	494	575	264	327	367	65.7	66.2	63.8	22.9	16.4	23.9	12.2

[1] Does not include the Armed Forces abroad.

[2] Changes for 1960–70 are not strictly comparable with those for 1970–80 because the 1960 data relate to the decennial census date of April 1, the population projections relate to July 1, and the labor force projections are annual averages based on the Current Population Survey.

Note: These labor force projections were prepared in 1965 and are not consistent with the revised labor force projections published in the preceding tables in this section. Revised projections will be prepared in the future incorporating the results of the 1970 census.

Source: *Manpower Report of the President,* 1973.

dustries—government, transportation, public utilities, trade, finance, services and real estate—took the lead in number of jobs in the '50's and raced ahead of goods in the '60's.

The trend is expected to continue—so that by 1980 service-producing industries will employ twice as many workers as goods-producing industries.

This trend will lead to greater overall job stability because employment levels in the service area are less affected by fluctuations in the economy (*U.S. Manpower in the 1970's—Opportunity and Challenge* 1973).

At the same time, because of the attainment of a higher level of education employment will continue to shift toward white-collar and service occupations. Although white-collar workers will outnumber blue-collar workers by more than 50 percent in 1980, 31 million workers will be employed in blue-collar jobs, an increase of more than 2 million over 1970 as shown in figure 2-4. The number of service workers will continue to increase, while the number of farm workers will decline still further. Yet the fastest growth will be in the professional, technical, and service occupational groups, as illustrated in figure 2-5.

TABLE 2-2

TOTAL POPULATION, TOTAL LABOR FORCE, AND LABOR FORCE PARTICIPATION RATES, BY SEX AND AGE, 1960 TO 1990

| Sex and age | Total population, July 1 | | | | | Total labor force, annual averages | | | | | Labor force participation rates, annual average (percent of population in labor force) | | | | |
| | Actual | | Projected | | | Actual | | Projected | | | Actual | | Projected | | |
	1960	1970	1980	1985	1990	1960	1970	1980	1985	1990	1960	1970	1980	1985	1990
BOTH SEXES															
16 years and over	121,817	142,366	167,839	175,722	183,079	72,104	85,903	101,809	107,716	112,576	59.2	60.3	60.8	61.3	61.5
MALE															
16 years and over	59,420	68,641	80,261	84,285	87,911	48,933	54,343	62,590	66,017	68,907	82.4	79.2	78.0	78.3	78.4
16 to 19 years	5,398	7,619	8,339	7,141	7,045	3,162	4,395	4,668	3,962	3,901	58.6	57.5	56.0	55.5	55.4
20 to 24 years	5,553	8,668	10,666	10,305	9,021	4,939	7,378	8,852	8,496	7,404	88.9	85.1	83.0	82.4	82.1
25 to 34 years	11,347	12,601	18,521	20,540	21,040	10,940	11,974	17,523	19,400	19,853	96.4	95.0	94.6	94.4	94.4
35 to 44 years	11,878	11,303	12,468	15,409	18,378	11,454	10,818	11,851	14,617	17,398	96.4	95.7	95.1	94.9	94.7
45 to 54 years	10,148	11,283	10,781	10,680	11,922	9,508	10,487	9,908	9,744	10,909	94.3	92.9	91.9	91.7	91.5
55 to 64 years	7,564	8,742	9,776	9,874	9,424	6,445	7,127	7,730	7,716	7,307	85.2	81.5	79.1	78.1	77.5
55 to 59 years	4,144	4,794	5,263	5,129	4,787	3,727	4,221	4,558	4,421	4,112	89.9	88.0	86.6	86.2	85.9
60 to 64 years	3,420	3,948	4,513	4,745	4,637	2,718	2,906	3,172	3,295	3,195	79.5	73.6	70.3	69.4	68.9
65 years and over	7,530	8,395	9,710	10,386	11,081	2,425	2,164	2,058	2,082	2,135	32.2	25.8	21.2	20.0	19.3
65 to 69 years	2,941	3,139	3,653	3,852	4,065	1,348	1,278	1,289	1,322	1,365	45.8	40.7	33.5	34.3	33.6
70 years and over	4,590	5,256	6,077	6,534	7,016	1,077	886	769	760	770	23.5	16.9	12.7	11.6	11.0
FEMALE															
16 years and over	62,397	73,725	87,078	91,437	95,168	23,171	31,560	39,219	41,699	43,669	37.1	42.8	45.0	45.6	45.9
16 to 19 years	5,275	7,432	8,057	6,910	6,777	2,061	3,250	3,669	3,203	3,188	39.1	43.7	45.5	46.4	47.0
20 to 24 years	5,547	8,508	10,401	10,049	8,801	2,558	4,893	6,592	6,523	5,826	46.1	57.5	63.4	64.9	66.2
25 to 34 years	11,605	12,743	18,442	20,301	20,750	4,159	5,704	9,256	10,339	10,678	35.8	44.8	50.2	50.9	51.5
35 to 44 years	12,348	11,741	12,903	15,741	18,524	5,325	5,971	6,869	8,560	10,219	43.1	50.9	53.2	54.4	55.2
45 to 54 years	10,438	12,106	11,625	11,407	12,695	5,150	6,533	6,537	6,542	7,364	49.3	54.0	56.2	57.4	58.0
55 to 64 years	8,070	9,763	11,307	11,492	10,934	2,964	4,153	5,057	5,213	5,003	36.7	42.5	44.7	45.4	45.8
55 to 59 years	4,321	5,257	5,966	5,804	5,396	1,803	2,547	3,055	3,033	2,853	41.7	48.4	51.2	52.3	52.9
60 to 64 years	3,749	4,506	5,341	5,688	5,538	1,161	1,606	2,002	2,180	2,150	31.0	35.6	37.5	38.3	38.8
65 years and over	9,115	11,433	14,343	15,537	16,687	954	1,056	1,239	1,319	1,391	10.5	9.2	8.6	8.5	8.3
65 to 69 years	3,347	3,780	4,595	4,942	5,267	579	644	758	814	864	17.0	16.4	16.5	16.5	16.4
70 years and over	5,768	7,653	9,748	10,595	11,420	375	412	481	505	527	5.4	5.0	4.9	4.8	4.6

Population Data from the Department of Commerce, Bureau of the Census, Current Population Reports, Series P-25: for 1960, No. 241; for 1970, unpublished estimates (prepared before availability of 1970 census results); for 1980 to 1990, No. 493, Series E. All other data from the Department of Labor, Bureau of Labor Statistics, forthcoming publication.

SOURCE: *Manpower Report of the President,* 1973.

TABLE 2-3

Changes in the Total Labor Force, by Sex and Age, 1960 to 1990

Sex and age	Actual		Projected		Number change			Percent change		
	1960	1970	1980	1990	1960-70	1970-80	1980-90	1960-70	1970-80	1980-90
BOTH SEXES										
16 years and over	72,104	85,903	101,809	112,576	13,799	15,906	10,767	19.1	18.5	10.6
16 to 24 years	12,720	19,915	23,781	20,319	7,195	3,866	-3,462	56.6	19.4	-14.6
25 to 44 years	31,878	34,466	45,499	58,148	2,588	11,033	12,649	8.1	32.0	27.8
25 to 34 years	15,099	17,678	26,779	30,531	2,579	9,101	3,752	17.1	51.5	14.0
35 to 44 years	16,779	16,788	18,720	27,617	9	1,932	8,897	.1	11.5	47.5
45 years and over	27,506	31,521	32,529	34,109	4,015	1,008	1,580	14.6	3.2	4.9
45 to 64 years	24,127	28,301	29,232	30,583	4,174	931	1,351	17.3	3.3	4.6
65 years and over	3,379	3,220	3,297	3,526	-159	77	229	-4.7	2.4	6.9
MALE										
16 years and over	48,933	54,343	62,590	68,907	5,410	8,247	6,317	11.1	15.2	10.1
16 to 24 years	8,101	11,773	13,520	11,305	3,672	1,717	-2,215	45.3	14.8	-16.4
25 to 44 years	22,394	22,792	29,374	37,251	398	6,582	7,877	1.8	28.9	26.8
25 to 34 years	10,940	11,974	17,523	19,853	1,034	5,549	2,330	9.5	46.3	13.3
35 to 44 years	11,454	10,818	11,851	17,398	-636	1,033	5,547	-5.6	9.5	46.8
45 years and over	18,438	19,778	19,696	20,351	1,340	-82	655	7.3	-.4	3.3
45 to 64 years	16,013	17,614	17,638	18,216	1,601	24	578	10.0	.1	3.3
65 years and over	2,425	2,164	2,058	2,135	-261	-106	77	-10.8	-4.9	3.7
FEMALE										
16 years and over	23,171	31,560	39,219	43,669	8,389	7,659	4,450	36.2	24.3	11.3
16 to 24 years	4,619	8,143	10,261	9,014	2,524	2,118	-1,247	76.3	26.0	-12.2
25 to 44 years	9,484	11,675	16,125	20,897	2,191	4,450	4,772	23.1	38.1	29.6
25 to 34 years	4,159	5,704	9,256	10,678	1,545	3,552	1,422	37.1	62.3	15.4
35 to 44 years	5,325	5,971	6,809	10,219	646	898	3,350	12.1	15.0	48.8
45 years and over	9,068	11,742	12,833	13,758	2,674	1,091	925	29.5	9.8	7.2
45 to 64 years	8,114	10,686	11,594	12,367	2,572	908	773	31.7	8.5	6.7
65 years and over	954	1,056	1,239	1,391	102	183	152	10.7	17.3	12.3

Source: *Manpower Report of the President,* 1973.

TABLE 2-4

Employment by Occupation Group, 1960, 1970, and Projected 1980 Requirements

Occupation group	Actual				Projected 1980 [1] requirements		Number change		Annual rate of change	
	1960		1970							
	Number	Percent distribution	Number	Percent distribution	Number	Percent distribution	1960-70	1970-80	1960-70	1970-80
Total employment [2]	65,778	100.0	78,627	100.0	95,100	100.0	12,849	16,473	1.8	1.9
Professional and technical workers	7,460	11.4	11,140	14.2	15,500	16.3	3,671	4,360	4.1	3.4
Managers, officials, and proprietors	7,067	10.7	8,289	10.5	9,500	10.0	1,222	1,211	1.6	1.4
Clerical workers	9,762	14.8	13,714	17.4	17,300	18.2	3,952	3,586	3.5	2.4
Sales workers	4,224	6.4	4,854	6.2	6,000	6.3	630	1,146	1.4	2.1
Craftsmen and foremen	8,554	13.0	10,158	12.9	12,200	12.8	1,604	2,042	1.7	1.8
Operatives	11,950	18.2	13,909	17.7	15,400	16.2	1,959	1,491	1.5	1.0
Service workers	8,023	12.2	9,712	12.4	13,100	13.8	1,689	3,388	1.9	3.0
Nonfarm laborers	3,553	5.4	3,724	4.7	3,500	3.7	171	-224	.5	-.6
Farmers and farm laborers	5,176	7.9	3,126	4.0	2,600	2.7	-2,050	-526	-5.2	-1.8

[1] These projections assume 3-percent unemployment and a services economy in 1980, as described in *The U.S. Economy in 1980* (Washington: Department of Labor, Bureau of Labor Statistics, 1970), Bulletin 1673.

[2] Represents total employment as covered by the Current Population Survey.

Source: *Manpower Report of the President,* 1973.

TABLE 2-5

Employment by Industry Division,
1960, 1970, and Projected 1980 Requirements

Industry division	Actual				Projected 1980 [1] requirements		Number change		Annual rate of change	
	1960		1970		Number	Percent distribution	1960-70	1970-80	1960-70	1970-80
	Number	Percent distribution	Number	Percent distribution						
Agriculture [2]	5,458		3,462		3,000		−1,996	−462	−4.7	−1.4
Total nonagricultural wage and salary workers [3]	54,234	100.0	70,616	100.0	86,600	100.0	16,382	15,984	2.7	2.1
Goods-producing industries	20,393	37.6	23,336	33.0	27,085	31.3	2,943	3,749	1.4	1.5
Mining	712	1.3	622	0.9	550	.6	−90	−72	−1.4	−1.1
Contract construction	2,885	5.3	3,345	4.7	4,600	5.3	460	1,255	1.5	3.2
Manufacturing	16,796	31.0	19,369	27.4	21,935	25.3	2,573	2,566	1.4	1.3
Durable goods	9,459	17.4	11,198	15.9	13,015	15.0	1,730	1,817	1.7	1.5
Nondurable goods	7,336	13.5	8,171	11.6	8,920	10.3	835	749	1.1	.9
Service-producing industries	33,840	62.4	47,281	67.0	59,515	68.7	13,441	12,234	3.4	2.3
Transportation and public utilities	4,004	7.4	4,504	6.4	4,740	5.5	500	236	1.2	.5
Transportation	2,549	4.7	2,689	3.8	2,900	3.3	140	211	.6	.8
Communication	840	1.5	1,121	1.6	1,130	1.3	281	9	1.9	(4)
Electric, gas, and sanitary services	615	1.1	695	1.0	710	.8	80	15	1.2	.2
Wholesale and retail trade	11,391	21.0	14,922	21.1	17,625	20.4	3,531	2,703	2.7	1.7
Wholesale	3,004	5.5	3,924	5.4	4,600	5.3	820	776	2.4	1.9
Retail	8,388	15.5	11,098	15.7	13,025	15.0	2,710	1,927	2.8	1.6
Finance, insurance, and real estate	2,669	4.9	3,690	5.2	4,260	4.9	1,021	570	3.3	1.4
Service and miscellaneous	7,423	13.7	11,630	16.5	16,090	18.6	4,207	4,460	4.6	3.3
Government	8,353	15.4	12,535	17.8	16,800	19.4	4,182	4,265	4.1	3.0
Federal	2,270	4.2	2,705	3.8	3,000	3.5	435	295	1.8	1.0
State and local	6,083	11.2	9,830	13.9	13,800	15.9	3,747	3,970	4.9	3.5

[1] See footnote 1, table E–9.

[2] Represents agriculture employment as reported in the Current Population Survey; includes self-employed and unpaid family workers in addition to wage and salary workers.

[3] Represents wage and salary employment as covered by the BLS monthly survey of nonagricultural payroll employment.

[4] Less than 0.05 percent.

Source: *Manpower Report of the President,* 1973.

Educational Attainment

It is important that trade, industrial, and technical educators have background on the educational levels of the population they will serve. Table 2-6 provides projections on educational level for the year 1980. Even though we are a highly educated nation, not all have had or will have the opportunity to fully participate. For example, by 1980 it is expected that only 16.9 percent of those over twenty-five will have had four or more years of college. The median years of school is expected to be 12.5 percent.

TABLE 2-6

PROJECTED EDUCATIONAL ATTAINMENT OF THE CIVILIAN LABOR FORCE 25 YEARS AND OVER, BY SEX, COLOR, AND AGE, 1980

Years of school completed, sex, and color	Total, 25 years and over	25 to 34 years	35 to 44 years	45 to 54 years	55 to 64 years	65 years and over
BOTH SEXES						
Total: Number	76,327	25,474	18,386	16,252	12,947	3,268
Percent	100.0	100.0	100.0	100.0	100.0	100.0
Less than 4 years of high school	28.7	17.8	25.6	35.2	39.5	53.1
4 years of high school or more	71.3	82.2	74.3	64.7	60.5	46.8
Elementary: Less than 5 years [1]	1.8	.7	1.4	2.4	2.8	4.4
5 to 7 years	4.0	1.3	3.1	5.5	6.7	11.0
8 years	6.1	2.2	4.3	7.9	10.8	19.3
High school: 1 to 3 years	16.8	13.6	16.8	19.4	19.2	18.4
4 years	42.4	47.3	44.7	39.4	37.8	24.4
College: 1 to 3 years	12.0	14.2	12.1	10.6	10.1	9.9
4 years or more	16.9	20.7	17.5	14.7	12.6	12.5
Median years of school completed	12.5	12.7	12.5	12.4	12.3	11.5
MALE						
Total: Number	48,665	17,054	11,682	9,995	7,844	2,090
Percent	100.0	100.0	100.0	100.0	100.0	100.0
Less than 4 years of high school	29.6	18.2	26.2	37.4	42.4	56.6
4 years of high school or more	70.4	81.9	73.8	62.6	57.6	43.5
Elementary: Less than 5 years [1]	2.1	.9	1.7	3.1	3.6	5.2
5 to 7 years	4.3	1.5	3.5	6.3	7.2	11.2
8 years	6.6	2.4	4.6	8.9	11.7	20.8
High school: 1 to 3 years	16.6	13.4	16.4	19.1	19.9	19.4
4 years	39.7	46.6	41.7	34.4	33.3	22.1
College: 1 to 3 years	12.1	14.0	12.2	10.8	10.3	8.7
4 years or more	18.6	21.3	19.9	17.4	14.0	12.7
Median years of school completed	12.5	12.7	12.6	12.4	12.2	11.0
FEMALE						
Total: Number	27,662	8,420	6,704	6,257	5,103	1,178
Percent	100.0	100.0	100.0	100.0	100.0	100.0
Less than 4 years of high school	27.0	17.1	24.8	32.0	35.1	47.0
4 years of high school or more	73.2	82.9	75.2	68.0	64.8	52.9
Elementary: Less than 5 years [1]	1.1	.4	.9	1.4	1.5	3.0
5 to 7 years	3.4	1.0	2.4	4.3	5.8	10.7
8 years	5.4	1.8	3.9	6.3	9.5	16.7
High school: 1 to 3 years	17.1	13.9	17.6	20.0	18.3	16.6
4 years	47.2	48.8	49.9	47.4	44.7	28.7
College: 1 to 3 years	12.0	14.5	11.9	10.3	9.8	12.1
4 years or more	14.0	19.6	13.4	10.3	10.3	12.1
Median years of school completed	12.5	12.7	12.5	12.4	12.2	12.1
WHITE						
Total: Number	67,631	22,153	16,256	14,491	11,742	2,989
Percent	100.0	100.0	100.0	100.0	100.0	100.0
Less than 4 years of high school	26.8	16.5	23.7	32.4	36.8	50.5
4 years of high school or more	73.4	83.5	76.4	67.6	63.2	49.4
Elementary: Less than 5 years [1]	1.3	.6	1.3	1.8	1.7	2.4
5 to 7 years	3.4	1.2	2.7	4.5	5.4	9.6
8 years	6.1	2.1	4.2	7.6	10.7	19.8
High school: 1 to 3 years	16.0	12.6	15.5	18.5	19.0	18.7
4 years	43.2	47.3	45.5	41.0	39.5	25.9
College: 1 to 3 years	12.4	14.4	12.5	11.0	10.5	10.4
4 years or more	17.8	21.8	18.4	15.6	13.2	13.1
Median years of school completed	12.5	12.7	12.6	12.4	12.3	11.9
NEGRO AND OTHER RACES						
Total: Number	8,696	3,321	2,130	1,761	1,205	279
Percent	100.0	100.0	100.0	100.0	100.0	100.0
Less than 4 years of high school	44.0	26.4	40.9	59.1	66.4	80.9
4 years of high school or more	56.1	73.6	59.1	40.8	33.6	19.0
Elementary: Less than 5 years [1]	5.4	1.6	2.5	7.6	13.1	25.4
5 to 7 years	8.7	2.3	6.2	13.8	19.0	26.5
8 years	6.7	2.6	5.6	10.4	12.7	13.6
High school: 1 to 3 years	23.2	19.9	26.6	27.3	21.6	15.4
4 years	36.3	47.4	39.0	26.5	21.6	9.3
College: 1 to 3 years	9.3	12.3	9.1	7.0	6.0	4.3
4 years or more	10.5	13.9	11.0	7.3	6.0	5.4
Median years of school completed	12.2	12.5	12.2	11.0	9.7	7.8

[1]Includes persons with no formal education.

Prepared by the Department of Labor, Bureau of Labor Statistics, consistent with projections of the educational attainment of the population published by the Department of Commerce, Bureau of the Census in Current Population Reports, Series P-25, No. 390. These projections are based upon the educational attainment of the population and labor force as reported in the monthly Current Population Survey. These projections are not consistent with the totals shown in table E-7 because they are based on earlier projections than those shown in that table.

Projections for 1975 and 1985 consistent with those shown here for 1960 are published in the Bureau of Labor Statistics' Special Labor Force Report No. 122.

SOURCE: *Manpower Report of the President, 1973.*

Billions of GNP (1969 dollars)   2-1

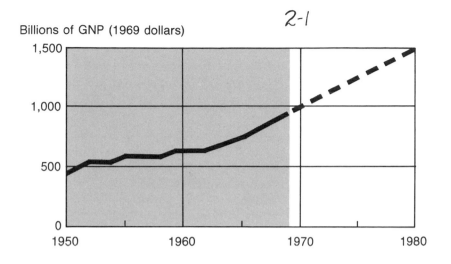

SOURCE: *U.S. Manpower in the 1970's—Opportunity and Challenge,* 1970.

FIGURE 2-1

Millions of total labor force

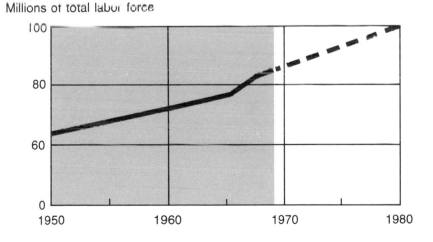

SOURCE: *U.S. Manpower in the 1970's—Opportunity and Challenge,* 1970.

FIGURE 2-2

51

Millions of workers

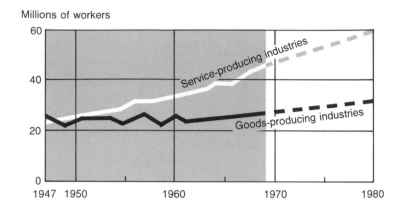

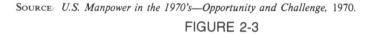

SOURCE: *U.S. Manpower in the 1970's—Opportunity and Challenge,* 1970.

FIGURE 2-3

Millions of workers

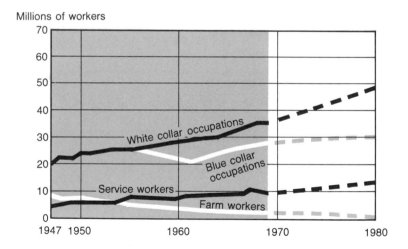

SOURCE: *U.S. Manpower in the 1970's—Opportunity and Challenge,* 1970.

FIGURE 2-4

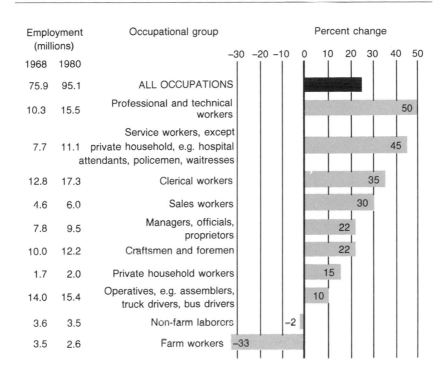

Employment (millions)		Occupational group	Percent change
1968	1980		
75.9	95.1	ALL OCCUPATIONS	
10.3	15.5	Professional and technical workers	50
7.7	11.1	Service workers, except private household, e.g. hospital attendants, policemen, waitresses	45
12.8	17.3	Clerical workers	35
4.6	6.0	Sales workers	30
7.8	9.5	Managers, officials, proprietors	22
10.0	12.2	Craftsmen and foremen	22
1.7	2.0	Private household workers	15
14.0	15.4	Operatives, e.g. assemblers, truck drivers, bus drivers	10
3.6	3.5	Non-farm laborers	-2
3.5	2.6	Farm workers	-33

Source: *U.S. Manpower in the 1970's—Opportunity and Challenge*, 1970.

FIGURE 2-5

Summary

Keen insights into the labor force, present and projected, are necessary for planning adequate trade and industrial education programs. There has always been a concern for both meeting the needs of people as reflected in vocational education legislation and for meeting manpower needs. While these two objectives are somewhat parallel, they may not be completely compatible. This fact is particulary challenging as trade, industrial, and technical educators accept the challenge of providing training for various categories of disadvantaged and handicapped persons and in fact become involved in the tasks of playing a key role toward making all individuals employable.

QUESTIONS AND ACTIVITIES

1. Contact the State Employment Service Office in your area to determine what state or local information is available on employment.

2. Discuss the question, "Is recent vocational education legislation directed more at serving the needs of people or meeting the needs of the labor force?"

3. From the table on projected levels of education by 1980, discuss the probable congruence of these differences between "white" and "other races." What specific implications do you see these differences having for trade, industrial, and technical education?

4. Identify and discuss the changes which have taken place in the labor force by occupational groups.

SOURCE MATERIALS

1. Barlow, Melvin L. *History of Industrial Education in the United States.* Peoria, Ill.: Charles A. Bennett Co., Inc., 1967.

2. *Manpower Report of the President.* Washington, D.C.: U.S. Department of Labor, U.S. Government Printing Office, 1973.

3. *U.S. Manpower in the 1970's: Opportunity and Challenge.* Washington, D.C.: U.S. Department of Labor, U.S. Government Printing Office, 1970.

Chapter 3 DEFINITION AND OBJECTIVES OF TRADE, INDUSTRIAL, AND TECHNICAL EDUCATION

The need has long existed for a common understanding—even within the profession itself—for a clear cut definition of trade, industrial, and technical education. It is the intent of this chapter to clarify many of the misunderstandings about these terms and to provide a sense of distinction of each by definition, actuality, and statistics. In an occupational "hands on sense," each of these areas, "trade," "industrial," and "technical," become quite different. Workers are employed in a trade or an industrial or technical occupation; they are so identified on the basis of their performances. One does not usually perform all of these occupations within a single employment opportunity.

Undoubtedly, the complexity of the distinction among the trade, industrial, and technical occupations, emerged in a historical sense from the advancements in technology as traced in chapter 1. The demand for the tradesman as a craftsman of the early days (then sometimes referred to as an artisan) proliferated at the times of the Industrial Revolution and the start of mass production of goods and services. The demands of the economy over the years relegated the tradesman (such as in the building trades) to a more and more custom role, and mass production drained off many of the craftlike (or artisanlike) competencies formally needed by a tradesman. The industrial employee consequently became usefully employed as more of a specialist of production and one whose skills were quite limited to the production of the product at hand.

55

In like manner, the technical occupations came into being when industry found it needed an employee who could function between the tradesman and the mass production worker and the engineer.

Although the distinction between what actually takes place in the employment world in terms of a trade, industrial, or technical occupation is quite clear, it is frequently not clear in the case in educational programs.

Definition

By definition, the terms trade, industrial, and technical have been defined in the American Vocational Association's publication, *Vocational-Technical Terminology* (1971), to mean:

Trade—An occupation which usually requires a period of apprenticeship as part of the learning process. Mastery can embody a well-defined cluster of skills, knowledge of physical sciences, mathematics, applied drawing and mechanical principles.

Trade and Industrial education—Instruction planned to develop basic manipulative skills, safety practices, judgment, technical knowledge, and related occupational information for the purpose of fitting persons for initial employment in (trade or) industrial occupations or upgrading and retraining workers employed in industry.

Technician—A person who is qualified by education, training, and experience to perform duties and/or services which require judgment skills equal to or greater than manipulative skills, and which involve knowledge of science, mathematics, manufacturing and construction processes, and human relations.

Technical education—The branch of education devoted to instruction and training in occupations *above the craftsman or trade levels,* but generally not professional in nature. Instruction may not be baccalaureate in content but is evaluated usually by credit criteria rather than by clock hours. The courses qualify persons for employment in paraprofessional positions and as technicians, engineering aides, and production specialists.

Industrial education—A generic term applying to all types of education related to industry including industrial arts education, vocational industrial education (trade and industrial education), and much technical education.

Probably the most confounding of these terms is that of *industrial education.* Few persons (including educators themselves) understand that industrial education embraces the areas of trade, industrial, and some technical education. Even fewer persons recognize that as such, there is no one educational program called industrial education that can teach all three occupational areas. The reason for this is that no one teacher can be competent occupationally in all trades or industrial and technical occupations.

The mere fact that schools have "shops" and the administrator refers to teachers as "shop teachers" often confuses students, parents, and the teachers themselves into thinking that the content taught in the "shop" is indeed all things to all people, without regard to the purpose for which that particular physical facility was designed and the accountability of that teacher to meet specific educational objectives.

The educational enterprise comes closest to meeting the many objectives of industrial education through the course called industrial arts. The AVA booklet on terminology defines *industrial arts education* as:

> An area of education that involves the preparation, growth, and guidance of the individual for modern living through individual or cooperative group experiences in working with industrial materials, tools, and processes and studying their social and economic significance to the individual and the nation. It involves a program of instruction organized to develop an understanding of the technical, consumer, occupational, recreational, organizational, social, historical, and cultural aspects of industry and technology. Learning experiences include activities such as experimenting, designing, constructing, evaluating, and using tools, materials, and processes which provide opportunities for creativity and problem solving. Also, sometimes used to mean the preparation of teachers in the field of industrial arts education.

Friese (1964), an early leader in the field, distinguished industrial arts from vocational industrial education (a term used also to describe trade and industrial education) in terms of aims by stating factors in industrial arts and vocational industrial education that are different:

> *Aims*—The single overall aim of any form of vocational industrial (trade and industrial) education is to prepare for advantageous entrance upon or progress in industrial type vocation. This work constitutes a *curriculum* and it therefore embraces courses of a related nature. It also includes the most essential units of general education, as English, social studies, and health.
>
> The several aims of industrial arts, . . . must meet the test of (a) being functionally valuable to *all* boys and girls in junior high school or (b) being particularly significant for *all* boys in junior high school, or (c) being of special interest, not vocational, to *any* boy or girl in senior high school. These are courses. They do not constitute a curriculum. Some are state mandated. Others are elected. The aims of each must reflect these conditions.
>
> *Related Information*—The related information of vocational industrial education, "related subjects" is essentially mathematics, physical science and drafting.
>
> In industrial arts the related part of the instruction falls into many categories, including art and design, technological phases of the physical sciences

and mathematics, some phases of botany, parts of sociology, economics and government (related laws and government regulations of workers and industry).

Describing further the differences between industrial arts and trade and industrial education, Friese stated:

> *Equipment*—In general, trade instruction requires equipment essentially similar to that encountered on the job. In industrial arts, in both junior and senior high schools, the hand tools are usually of standard size, the machinery of medium size and power operated hand machines for some handicrafts are, of course, small. Apparatus, as in electronics is either of trade standards in size or in somewhat smaller size, sometimes in school 'kits.'

> *Problem Organization*—The articles made in industrial arts frequently cross trade and handicraft lines. . . . Emphasis is placed, where possible, upon student development in interests, capacities and attitudes along with correct technical processes.

> In vocational industrial education the articles made and the processes drilled upon are restricted to one trade and at times closely related trades. The work is carried out 'on a useful and productive basis.' This condition cannot always be entirely achieved. Emphasis is placed upon the product.

> *Design*—In vocational industrial education the design of articles made is usually the work of others. In industrial arts the design may be that of another, be modified from that of others, or be the result of student creativity in 4-step projects.

> *Teachers*—The industrial arts teacher must be a college graduate in industrial arts, have considerable versatility in manual skills, be effective in drawing and design, have sufficient background in the sciences and mathematics, be effective in teaching techniques and be familiar with the humanities and arts.

> The vocational industrial teacher must first be an experienced and competent tradesman. In his collegiate preparation he must give emphasis to the sciences, drafting and design, mathematics, techniques of teaching and considerable contact with the humanities and arts.

> *Students*—The students in industrial arts, in both junior and senior high schools are 'all the children of all of the people' theoretically. In all too many instances they are only the boys. This is because industrial arts has lagged grossly in selecting from its vast reservoir of educative experiences (2) those which are functional in the lives of girls or (b) those which are equally applicable to both boys and girls.

> In vocational industrial education the students are selected who because of their interest, aptitudes, abilities and other circumstances elect to prepare themselves for a gainful occupation. The recent movement into our senior high schools of great numbers of post-war babies has again raised an old issue, that of assigning misfits in school to the vocational depart-

ment. This is wrong for the boy, the school, his parents and society which pays the bill.

For additional distinguishing differences between *industrial arts* and *trade, industrial, and technical education* see Appendix A.

Vocational Education

Just as the term "industrial education" is generic in that it includes industrial arts, trade and industrial and some technical education, so is the term vocational education generic. *Vocational education* in its broadest sense is defined as:

> Vocational or technical training or retraining which is given in schools or classes (including field or laboratory work and remedial or related academic and technical instruction incident thereto) under public supervision and control or under contract with a state board or local educational agency, and is conducted as part of a program designed to prepare individuals for gainful employment as semiskilled or skilled workers or technicians or subprofessionals in recognized occupations and in new and emerging occupations, or to prepare individuals for enrollment in advanced technical education programs, but excluding any program to prepare individuals for employment in occupations generally considered professional or which require a baccalaureate or higher degree (American Vocational Association 1971).

The key to this definition is the wording "designed to prepare individuals for gainful employment." When interpreted in this manner, much confusion can be eliminated about the differences between general education and vocational education, or for that matter differences between college preparatory education and vocational education. In other words, vocational education can be distinguished in an occupational sense as can the ingredients to provide it. For example, the physical facility to carry out the instruction ideally must be close to that found in the employment world. The teacher must possess the occupational competency of a successful practitioner of the occupation which usually stems from considerable employment experience in the particular occupation to be taught. The curriculum needs must reflect the content (usually derived from an occupational analysis) of the occupation being prepared for, and the instructional materials must portray the terminology and intended mastery as expected of a person employed in the occupational area. The lack of any one of these elements injects to the educational program the risk of turning out a product something different from that of a person prepared for gainful employment.

In a like manner, *vocational education* as a term is generic to the offerings of agricultural education, distributive education, health education, home economics, business and office education, technical education, and trade and industrial education. These discrete areas make up, at least at present, what is known as the whole of the vocational education offerings, both in terms of the philosophy of the field and the federal legislation which supports the total concept.

Career Education

More recently, the term *career education* has penetrated the educational enterprise. In the broadest sense, *career education* is "education itself" as stated by Hoyt, Evans, Mackin, and Mangum (1972):

> ... a total concept which should permeate all education, giving a new centrality to the objective of successful preparation for and development of a lifelong, productive career. Yet it must in no way conflict with other important education objectives. Its beneficiaries can still become good citizens, parents, and cultivated and self-aware human beings because career success can augment all other sound educational objectives.

> Career education should become part of the student's curriculum from the moment he enters school. It relates reading, writing, and arithmetic to the varied ways in which adults live and earn a living. As the student progresses through school, the skills, knowledges, and above all, the attitudes necessary for work success are stressed. This stress is phased into every subject for every student, not just in separate classes designed for those who are "going to work."

In support of this concept, Sidney P. Marland, Jr. has said:

> American schools are producing too many youngsters who qualify neither for a job nor for college. Many high school graduates go on to college only because they haven't the vaguest idea of what else to do.

> Career education is designed to give every youngster a genuine choice, as well as the intellectual and occupational skills necessary to back it up. Career education is not merely a substitute for "Vocational Education," or "General Education," or "College Preparatory Education." Rather, it is a blending of all three into an entirely new curriculum. The fundamental concept of Career education is that all educational experiences—curriculum, instruction, and counseling—should be geared to preparation for economic independence, personal fulfillment, and an appreciation for the dignity of work (Marland 1971).

CAREER EDUCATION AND VOCATIONAL EDUCATION

In this context, vocational education becomes but one of the components of the career education concept. As such, vocational education must be implemented at a point when occupational choices have been made and the desires to learn are self-recognized. At this point in time, the aims of the vocational educator—providing an individual with the knowledge and skills to enter gainful employment—should become clear. This should be a time for concentrating on an occupational area, and having experiences of a meaningful nature. The vocational education student should have opportunities to develop qualities which will distinguish him from an "employee applicant" who has not availed himself of vocational education. In high school, post high school, retraining, or any level, the end product of vocational education should be distinguishable by its quality.

Each component of vocational education—trade, industrial, and technical education—has a role to play in the continuum of educational offerings. Distinguishing definitions are important to the dialogue if one is to communicate the role of each and interpret this role as education designed to meet the needs of individuals.

Definition by Actuality

In order to further define trade, industrial, and technical education, it may be well to look at these terms as seen through the eyes of those engaged in each field.

TRADE AND INDUSTRIAL EDUCATION

It is often practice not to separate the term *trade and industrial education* into its discrete parts of (*trade*) and (*industrial*). That is to say, some of the occupations being taught are classified as trade while others are termed industrial occupations. As a separate division of the American Vocational Education, those concerned with the implementing and operating of trade and industrial education have banded together to provide an ongoing dialogue in terms of the challenges and missions of trade and industrial education. In this respect a task force of trade and industrial personnel have spelled out the future role of trade and industrial education in the following statement (American Vocational Association 1962):

INTRODUCTION

Trade and industrial education is a balanced program of studies and work experiences that have the common objective of producing competent workers. This program develops the skills, abilities, understandings, attitudes, and working habits and imparts knowledge or information needed by individuals who desire to enter and make progress in employment. The goal is an American citizen who as a worker is competent economically, socially, emotionally, and physically. The greatest asset of America is not its reserve of natural resources, but the skills and occupational competencies of the workers and the potential productivity of the youth preparing to enter employment. This asset is enhanced by trade and industrial education programs which assist individuals to increase their productive capacity and earning power.

It is of paramount importance that business, industry, and the general public be made aware of the increasing importance of this type of education and give active and unqualified support for its further development. The problems are many and varied but can be resolved through the full cooperation of educators, labor, management, and the general public.

This position statement presents a guide for trade and industrial education programs designed to meet the economic and industrial changes taking place today and for a period of time in which our present perspectives, values, and environment are still meaningul.

The authors* believe that this statement will help to mobilize the resources of America to provide trade and industrial education opportunities for all who have an interest in, who need, and who have the ability to profit from such programs.

". . . These truths to be self-evident . . ."

Education in a democracy is properly expected to meet the funadmental needs of the individual and of society.

The genius of American education has been its unity with diversity—a democracy must be concerned with providing for all people the kinds and levels of education most appropriate to their needs.

The wealth, strength, and safety of America depend chiefly on the economic and civic productivity of the educated man. Education should fit for total service to society.

Americans hold the conviction that man achieves his fullest self-realization and renders his greatest service through socially useful, effficient work.

Education continually faces change and new opportunities to expand its role in the society which it must sustain.

THE CHALLENGE . . .
CHANGE OR CRISIS

One consistent characteristic of trade and industrial education is its response to ever changing conditions and demands. The tempo of such changes is accelerating in this decade, and evidence points to even faster acceleration in the decade ahead.

---

*Authors consisted of: M. L. Barlow, E. M. Claude, James R. D. Eddy, J. F. Ingram, F. J. Konecny, Ernest G. Kramer, Ruth S. Lape, Gerald B. Leighbody, William G. Loomis, George W. Morgenroth, Joseph T. Nerden, Robert M. Reese, George L. Sandvig, and Byrl R. Shoemaker.

The rapidly changing scene brings complex problems and exerts pressures that have a profound effect on the American way of life. Some of these are: The international crisis facing our nation today is challenging our leadership and threatening our survival. The well being of this nation depends in large measure upon the quality of our work force.

The technological revolution is resulting in unprecedented demands for new knowledge, skills, insights, and understanding on the part of Americans.

By rapidly closing the gap between new knowledge and its direct application to daily life, progress in the next decade will make that of the past seem small.

New knowledge in all areas of human endeavor is accumulating to the extent that it is the most influential and vital force in the country, and the demand for education has become a national characteristic because of its vital need.

The growing population will require more skilled workers to produce its goods and serve its needs, but each must extend his skills and knowledge so that he can cope with change. Skill specifications and performance standards are more exacting, and many new demands are sure to come with new processes and inventions. Semi-skilled and unskilled jobs are diminishing, but those remaining require more education and training.

Changes in the labor force are a major problem as employment continues to grow faster in the service occupations than in the production industries; the work force remains highly mobile; the number of young people entering the work force increases annually; a larger proportion of women enter the labor market; and older workers remain in the labor market in greater numbers.

The economic, social, and political goals are changing for every American due to better transportation, communications, rising educational levels, amount of leisure time available, and the general upswing in the standard of living.

The movement of farm people to urban areas, especially young people, who need assistance in making transition to non-farm working and living situations is a growing problem.

The increasing demands on the natural resources by the rapidly expanding total population are altering the industrial and social patterns because of the crucial problems inherent where sustained yields are hard to maintain.

The trends in the age composition of our population indicate an increasing percentage in two extreme age brackets—too old for normal full employment and too young to be employed.

The growing number of youth 16 to 19 years old who fail to achieve successful integration into the labor force but who have the potential to perform in the skilled areas in demand represents a socio-economic loss the nation cannot afford to countenance.

Time is extremely important, and basic issues must be faced now. Positive and immediate action on all levels—federal, state, and local—is the first imperative.

THE MISSION

The mission of TRADE AND INDUSTRIAL EDUCATION in tomorrow's world is to continue the achievements of a skilled and progressive people. Its record of service to the nation in peace and in war can be mentioned with pride. Too few Americans understand or appreciate the scope of these accomplishments or how they have been brought about. Even greater accomplishments in trade and industrial education will be necessary to assist in providing the better life in the years ahead.

It is certain that technological change will continue at an accelerated pace. Productivity is the key to plenty, and trade and industrial education is essential to productivity. Yet the phenomenal record of the past does not ensure future progress. Productivity depends now, as always, on the wisdom and action of individuals.

The mission of trade and industrial education is the development of PEOPLE—not products; people who can produce; people with adaptability to the dynamics of the era; people whose occupational interest or employment is in trade, service, or technical pursuits—from the lowest to the highest positions; people who share the benefits and the responsibilities of a democratic society with all other people.

This mission is to ensure economic independence and to continuously improve the standard of living of a large majority of the work force. It must be in tune with the evolving social and increasingly complex technological pattern of the times.

There is virtually no limit to the kinds of trade and industrial education programs which may be offered except for the imagination of the educator, the vocational interests of the students, and the needs of industry for a skilled work force. To be effective, such programs must be occupation centered and provide a flexibility that will adapt to time, location, demands, and conditions.

Trade and industrial education is geared to the individual's needs, interests, and capacity rather than to a grade level. This means that emphasis must be placed on effective vocational guidance for youth and adults which includes occupational information, counseling, testing, placement, and follow-up. In more precise terms, the purposes of trade and industrial education are as follows:

> To prepare youth and adults for satisfying and productive employment.

> To assist employed workers to achieve greater satisfaction and success in present employment or to advance to more highly skilled jobs.

> To provide related instruction for apprentices.

> To provide retraining of workers who, due to personal reasons or economic changes, find it necessary to move to new employment.

To assist in the development and improvement of supervisory personnel in all areas served by trade and industrial education.

To provide an administrative organization, staff, and facilities which can be expanded rapidly for training in the event of a national emergency.

To complement the total program of public education so that it will best meet the varying needs of the people for making a living and making a life.

A major responsibility of trade and industrial education is to carefully evaluate what has been accomplished and analyze the true needs of business and industry for trade and industrial education. This must be done in cooperation with applicable governmental agencies, management, and labor.

This is a human mission—but the needs of individuals for occupational training to prepare for employment and the needs of industry and business for trained workers are positively related. Trade and industrial education recognizes both the needs of the individual and the economy of the nation, thus contributing to a wholesome economy, satisfactory employment, and a high standard of living.

In context with the challenge and mission of trade and industrial education, there exist some 140 instructional trade and industrial programs relating to over 2,200 titles in the *Dictionary of Occupational Titles* (Office of Education 1969) that can be offered throughout the nation's vocational enterprise. Such breadth of offering can be considered anything but narrow in its mission.

TECHNICAL EDUCATION

Technical education, on the other hand, has been viewed by most practitioners as different from trade and industrial education. *Technical education* is a generic term encompassing many and varied levels and types of technicians. A technician may work under a wide variety of titles, most of which do not include the term *technician*. It is apparent that a sharp line cannot always be drawn to differentiate semiprofessional activities such as computation, analysis, or laboratory testing from those that border on skilled labor, such as installation or trouble shooting on mechanical, electrical, or electronic equipment. The degree of technical ability required by these jobs varies considerably. Figure 3-1 shows this distinction in terms of several general characteristics as found in what might be called broad field-oriented versus more specific job-oriented technicians.

The concept of technical education has frequently been discussed in a number of U.S. Office of Education's publications. The following section has been liberally adapted from the U.S. Office of Education, *Criteria for Technician Education—A Suggested Guide* (1968).

Field-oriented versus Job-oriented Technicians

General Characteristics	Field-oriented	Job-oriented
Individual	Usually interested in a broad technical area	Usually wants a specific job or has a narrow field of interest
Training	Formal, field-oriented, received at institute of higher learning such as technical institute or junior college	Formal or informal, job-oriented, received in industry or at vocational-technical school
Knowledge and manipulative skills	Minimum manipulative skills, maximum knowledge; broader treatment of mathematics and science with development of value judgment in addition to information and skills	Varying degrees of manipulative skills, related knowledge, mathematics, and science depending on area of technology
Initial responsibility in industry	Specific, usually of orientation type	Specific, usually of productive type
Eventual responsibility in industry	Broad, usually supervision or design	Specific, charged with specified area, usually without supervisory responsibility
Supervision	Functions mainly on own initiative under direction of engineer or scientist	Requires supervision, reports to engineering technician or department head

FIGURE 3-1

CHARACTERISTICS OF FIELD-ORIENTED AND JOB-ORIENTED
TECHNICIANS

There are many kinds of technicians, just as there are many kinds of professional scientists. They are usually educated in rigorous two-year post-secondary programs designed to provide them with the knowledge, skills, and attitudes necessary for them to perform in a specific field of applied science. Many are employed in the physical sciences and related engineering fields such as chemical, metallurgical, mechanical design or production, civil, electrical and electronics, or architectural technicians. Others are employed in the applied biological sciences, particularly in the medical field and in the broad spectra of agricultural research, processing, and utilization. They may be medical laboratory, dental hygiene, dental laboratory, radiological, horticultural, food processing, oceanographic, crop and livestock production, soil science, or forestry technicians. Some combine biological and physical science disciplines. Examples of these workers are water and sanitation, pharmaceutical, or special clinical or hospital and equipment technicians.

Technicians are becoming an increasingly essential part of the scientific and management team for research, development, production, and the provision of special services in all fields of applied science. The team is comprised of professional scientists, specially trained technicians, and skilled production, laboratory, or service workers. The ratio of technicians to professional physical scientists or engineers at present is usually less than one to one, but the trend seems to be toward two or more for each engineer or physical scientist.

The increase in services in the health field requires from six to ten clinical, nursing, laboratory, and similarly specialized technicians to support the professional services and research of each medical doctor, podiatrist, dentist, laboratory technologist, or other professional health practitioner.

Agricultural production, service, and research technicians are needed in increasing numbers because of the impact of technology on agricultural production and processing. Knowledge of plant and/or animal science at the technician level is becoming increasingly necessary in the management of farms and in dairy production. Agricultural technicians excel in the distributive and service areas related to agriculture because they are technically competent and knowledgeable.

The explosion of new scientific knowledge has caused changes in education so that the recently graduated scientist or engineer, who often has had limited laboratory experience, now functions more as a theoretical, diagnostic, interpretive, creative, or administrative professional. He must delegate much of his scientific work to other skilled members of the scientific team. Thus, a serious shortage in trained manpower capable of giving the technical laboratory or clinical service formerly performed by the engineer or medical professional has developed. The number of new technicians of all kinds needed each year is estimated to be at least 200,000, and the needs for new kinds of technicians and for upgrading or updating employed technicians of all kinds will evidently continue to increase.

Programs for educating technicians have taken place in a number of institutions and settings. Figure 3-2 represents several of these efforts through different types of educational institutions.

Training Objectives			
Single Skill Occupations	Skilled Craftsmen	Technical Specialists	Engineering Technicians
			Technical Institute
	Community/Junior College		
	Vocational-Technical School		
Vocational-Industrial or Area Vocational School, Multiskill Centers, etc.			

FIGURE 3-2

OVERLAPPING FUNCTIONS OF DIFFERENT TYPES OF SCHOOLS

Examples of technical education programs as spelled out in a position paper on technical education by Shoemaker (1969) include:

Engineering

  1. Mechanical Technology
  2. Electrical Technology
  3. Electronic Technology
  4. Chemical Technology
  5. Metallurgical Technology
  6. Civil Technology

Home Economics

  1. Dietary Technology

Health

  1. Dental Hygiene
  2. Dental Laboratory Technology
  3. Medical Laboratory Technology

Business

  1. Computer Programming Technology
  2. Junior Accounting Technology
  3. Office Management Technology
  4. Executive Secretary Technology

Distribution

  1. Wholesale Management Technology
  2. Retail Management
  3. Restaurant Management Technology

Agriculture

  1. Agriculture—Business Technology
  2. Agriculture Equipment Technology
  3. Food Processing Technology
  4. Animal Science Technology
  5. Dairy Technology

If one accepts the concept of technical education as a level of education, it then becomes necessary to provide it a rightful place in the total program of education. Because of the evolutionary nature of technical occupations, some misconceptions have grown up which make it difficult for technical education to take its rightful place as a (new) level of educational service in our educational organization.

Since some people became technicians by reason of upgrading of certain skilled workers or craftsmen, and because of the highly skilled nature of certain of the craft occupations, technical education has sometimes been confused with vocational education and the concept presented that technical education is vocational education with a little more technical content. On the other hand, because of the relationship of technical education to the professional and the fact that some professional people are working in technical occupations or performing technical functions as a part of their occupations, some want to adjust downward the content of some professional programs and still give college credit for such courses in order to assure status and level, although it is not clear to what professional area the college credit would apply.

It is our belief that technical education emerging as a new field of education will prepare people who are related to both the skilled craftsman and the professional, but, should prepare the individual through a curriculum unique to his needs, rather than an upgraded or downgraded curriculum planned for another level of occupations.

There are some 72 instructional programs designed to prepare technicians in over 120 occupational titles as found in the *Dictionary of Occupational Titles* and listed in *Vocational Education and Occupations, 1969.* In addition to this number, there are some 53 programs and 59 occupational titles under Health Occupations Education which could be classified as technical since they carry the term technician in their titles.

Again, it is important to emphasize that technical education is not narrow, although in the health fields it is more specific than broad in that there are tighter standards, certifications, and accreditation of programs. It, therefore, behooves those in the profession to understand that no single technical education program can produce the basic understandings, skills, attitudes, and knowledge needed to produce an adequate supply of technicians for manpower needs.

One can summarize the actual differences between trade, industrial, and technical education by the various curricula themselves. Figure 3-3 shows graphically the differences in terms of manipulative skills and technical skills needed by the worker. It should be noted, as the classification of work progresses from laborer to engineer, the amount of technical skills increase and the manipulative skills needed decrease. The dashed lines in figure 3-3 indicate that at various points the distinctions are not abrupt but "fade" into one another. Nevertheless, they do appear and are quite distinguishable in various curricular offerings.

In keeping with the concept of manipulative versus technical skill needs, various curricula have been developed to reflect the degree of differences between trade, industrial, and technical education. Examples of this are apparent when comparing an Electronic Radio and Television Servicing curriculum with an Electronics Technology curriculum; see figures 3-4 and 3-5.

It should be noted that the Electronics, Radio and Television Service curriculum is one year in length while the Electronics Technology cur-

riculum covers two years. The content in the two curricula are quite different, and it should be apparent that they conform to a great extent to the
concept of variance of manipulative skills versus technical skills as seen in
figure 3-3. Other examples could be given in terms of the Practical Nursing

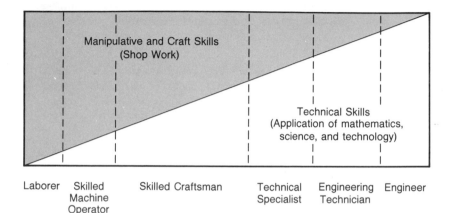

FIGURE 3-3

RELATIVE AMOUNTS OF MANIPULATIVE AND MENTAL EFFORTS
REQUIRED OF WORKERS

RADIO AND TELEVISION SERVICING
(One Year Diploma)

This program provides the student with the knowledge and
skills necessary to perform capably as a radio and television
service man. Instruction is also given in hi-fi and stereo
equipment and small appliances.

	CREDITS	
Course Name	*1st Sem.*	*2nd Sem.*
Radio and Television Servicing I	10	
Related Accounting	2	
Basic Salesmanship	2	
Human Relations	2	
Radio and Television Servicing II		10
Mathematics II		2
Science I		3
Communications I		2
	16	17

FIGURE 3-4

A ONE YEAR RADIO AND TELEVISION SERVICING CURRICULUM
REPRESENTING TRADE AND INDUSTRIAL EDUCATION

ELECTRONICS

ASSOCIATE DEGREE

The electronics industry offers the technician a wide range of job opportunities in manufacturing, research and development, communications, or installation and maintenance of electronic equipment. Communications and industrial electronics continues to expand at a rapid rate and the position of technician or engineering assistant within the industry is one of the fastest growing of the occupational classifications.

FIRST YEAR

FIRST SEMESTER

Course Name	Credits
Direct and Alternating Current Fundamentals	3
Direct and Alternating Current Fundamentals Laboratory	2
Technical Mathematics I	5
Technical Science I	4
Communication Skills I	3
College Orientation	0

SECOND SEMESTER

Electronic Circuits I	4
Electronic Circuits I Laboratory	2
Technical Mathematics II	4
Technical Science II	4
Communication Skills II	3

SECOND YEAR

FIRST SEMESTER

Electronic Circuits II	3
Electronic Circuits II Laboratory	2
Circuit Analysis	5
Electronic Instrumentation	4
American Institutions	3

SECOND SEMESTER

Economics	3
Psychology of Human Relations	3
Seminar	2
Job Orientation	0
Digital Computers	4
Electives	4–6

ELECTIVES

Electronic Drafting and Design	4
Basic Computer Concepts	3
Electronic Data Transmission	4
Digital and Analogue Control Circuits	4

FIGURE 3-5

A Two Year Electronics Curriculum Representing Technical Education

curriculum versus the Registered Nurse curriculum, Auto Mechanics versus Automotive Technology, and so forth. Curriculum then, distinguishes to a large extent the difference between trade, industrial, and technical education.

Definition by Statistics

In defining trade and industrial and technical education by statistics, as in table 3-1, one can see readily the thrust of the effort in terms of their differences.

In fiscal year 1970 (July 1, 1969-June 30, 1970) there were close to 9 million students enrolled in vocational education. Of this number, trade and industrial education represented approximately 22 percent and technical education only three percent of the total. If, however, health education is added to the technical classification, the percentage increases to approximately 6 percent of the total. In sum, trade, industrial, and technical education accounted for 28 percent of the total enrollment in vocational education during fiscal year 1970.

When examined in terms of program completion during the fiscal year 1970, trade and industrial students had a 20 percent program completion ratio, technical education students roughly a 14 percent ratio, while students enrolled in health programs had a 30 percent program completion ratio. Differences in length of program (time) and increases in total enrollment (approximately an 11 percent increase) are factors to be recognized in interpreting the statistics in this manner. For example, the health programs in practical nursing are usually one year programs as are many technical programs, whereas trade and industrial programs are mainly two and four year offerings.

When examining the program noncompletion ratio for the same time, and recognizing the discrepancies in the data because of the variance of the program length and the yearly increase of enrollments in different programs, it appears that overall there is approximately a 5 percent noncompletion ratio in the total vocational education effort.* More specifically and for only the fiscal year 1970, there was a 7.7 percent noncompletion ratio for trade and industrial students, about a 10 percent noncompletion ratio for technical education students, and only a 3 percent noncompletion ratio for health education students.

---

*There could be a number of reasons for noncompletions such as dropping out or receiving employment prior to completion. Computed on FY 1970 data of 1,685,739 completions and 93, 929 noncompletions. Source: Office of Education, *Summary Data, Vocational Education Fiscal Year, 1970.*

TABLE 3-1

ENROLLMENT IN TRADE, INDUSTRIAL, AND TECHNICAL EDUCATION
BY PROGRAM AND BY LEVEL, AND COMPLETIONS
FISCAL YEAR 1970[a]

Instructional Program	Total	Elementary and Secondary	Post-secondary	Adult	Completions	Left prior to completion
All Vocational	8,793,960	5,114,451	1,013,426	2,166,083	1,685,739	92,929
Trade and Industrial	1,906,133	692,396	261,182	952,555	343,116	26,268
Technical	271,730	34,386	151,621	85,723	38,188	4,036
Health[b]	198,144	31,915	102,515	63,614	61,746	2,383

Notes: [a]Source: Office of Education, *Summary Data, Vocational Education, Fiscal Year 1970.*
[b]Data provided since large portion of health occupations are technical.

As vague as these data may be, they are indicative of the overall holding power of the total vocational offerings as contrasted to any similar data of other educational offerings such as four year college noncompletors which is reported as high as 50 percent. The main point here is, that for many youth and adults, there appears to be a "holding power" to vocational education and its components of trade, industrial, and technical education.

Summary

In summary, trade, industrial, and technical education account for approximately one-fourth of the total federally reported enrollment in vocational education. These educational programs appear highly successful in terms of holding power when noncompletion data are compared with completions and they produce an output of approximately 90 percent of those who enter the programs. These data are a tribute to those who administer, supervise, and instruct these programs.

QUESTIONS AND ACTIVITIES

1. Discuss the definitions of trade; trade and industrial education; technician; technical education; industrial education; industrial arts education.

2. What are the similarities between vocational education and industrial arts education? What are the differences?

3. How does career education and vocational education interrelate?

4. The mission of trade, industrial, and technical education is clear in the minds of those who wrote *The Challenge*. Do you agree with this point of view?

5. Technical education can be defined in terms of field-oriented and job-oriented. Give the distinction as you see it.

SOURCE MATERIALS

1. *The Challenge—A Statement of the Trade and Industrial Division.* Washington, D.C.: American Vocational Association, 1962.

2. *Criteria for Technician Education—A Suggested Guide* (OE–80056). Washington, D.C.: U.S. Office of Education, 1968.

3. Friese, John F. *The Role of Industrial Arts in Education.* University Park, Pa.: The Pennsylvania State University, 1964.

4. Hoyt, K. B.; Evans, R. N.; Mackin, E. F.; and Mangum, G. L. *Career Education—What It Is and How To Do It.* Salt Lake City, Utah: Olympus Publishing Company, 1972.

5. Marland, Sidney P., Jr. "Career Education," an address before the thirty-third sessions of the International Conference on Education; Geneva, Switzerland: September 15–23, 1971.

6. Shoemaker, Byrl R. *A Position Paper on Technical Education.* Columbus, Ohio: State Department of Education, Division of Vocational Education, 1969.

7. *Summary Data, Vocational Education Fiscal Year 1970.* Washington, D.C.: U.S. Office of Education, 1972.

8. *Vocational Education and Occupations* (OE–80061). Washington, D.C.: U.S. Department of Health, Education and Welfare, Office of Education, 1969.

9. *Vocational-Technical Terminology.* Washington, D.C.: American Vocational Association, 1971.

Chapter 4 DETERMINING PROGRAM NEEDS

Trade, industrial, and technical education has often been criticized for not meeting current manpower needs within a particular community or setting. Chapter 2 has described labor market trends. This chapter will attempt to show how a specialist in trade, industrial, and technical education can determine and, at any particular time, assess the curricular needs of his program.

Let us assume in this instance, it is desired to start a new offering in one of the areas of trade, industrial, or technical education. Since the program director is initiating a new venture, he probably will call upon some expert advice as what to offer. Possibly a new building is being planned or a redistricting is taking place or at long last the school district has awakened to the need for some specific trade, industrial, and technical offerings. This is not an atypical situation faced by many school districts at the present time. What can be done to make the right decisions and plan for such offerings?

The Community Survey

Probably the most common approach to the problem of determining program needs is to conduct a community survey.

Keep in mind that the definition of trade, industrial, and technical education is one of specific occupational training and not of a cluster or general nature. Such a definition relates directly to the *Dictionary of Occupational Titles* of the U.S. Department of Labor (1965) which lists over 2,000 different occupations for which trade, industrial, and technical education can prepare. Appendix B provides a listing of the popular code titles as found in this publication.

The community survey approach to the problem utilizes the concept of involvement of a large number of persons. In essence the approach attempts to uncover job opportunities from every possible source including large and small employers within the community. It tries to project long-range employment opportunities for program graduates. Short-range employment opportunities are not conducive to the investment in elaborate facilities and training needs of students. The steps in making a community survey are as follows:

1. *Meeting with the local administrative officer of schools* (on secondary or postsecondary level)—The initial step is to meet with the local administrative officer. Items to be discussed include the following:
    a. Determine the predominate trade, industrial, and technical occupations to be covered.
    b. Discuss the tentative number of trade, industrial, and technical programs the school could justify. A general rule of thumb is one vocational curriculum for each 300 students in the upper three years of high school. This would be somewhat less for postsecondary offerings.
    c. Survey what is already in existence, e.g., what is being offered, how many students are enrolled. See figure 4-1 for a sample data form to record such information.
    d. Assess the general attitude toward such curricular offerings and if favorable recommend the conduct of a Community Survey.

2. *Identifying the community*—Probably one of the most difficult tasks is to identify the community to be served by the graduates from the potential trade, industrial, and technical program. The question to ask is, "Where do people from this educational area find employment?" The answer to this question may be far different than the boundaries of the school district or postsecondary institution itself. In other words, in making a community survey of this type, employment of potential graduates prescribes the boundaries of what is called "the community." It is not uncom-

State Department of Education
DIVISION OF VOCATIONAL EDUCATION
TRADE & INDUSTRIAL SERVICE
Columbus, Ohio

DATA ON LOCAL EDUCATIONAL PROGRAM

1. Total High School enrollment _____

2.

	9	10	11	12
Girls in grades				
Boys in grades				
Totals				

3. The High School is a ____3 yr.____4 yr. school. (Check one)

4. The High School program operates on a____period day. Each period is____ minutes in length.

5. ____ % of the High School graduates enter college.

6. Indicate the number of High School students enrolled in each of the courses listed

	Boys	Girls
Business Education	____	____
Home Economics	____	____
Agriculture	____	____
Distributive Education	____	____
Trade and Industrial Education	____	____

7. Approximately____% of the graduates leave the community for employment (do not include those entering college).

8. Check your industrial arts curriculum and the grades in which it is offered. Add any areas which are not listed.

8	9	10	11	12	Subject
					Machine Shop
					Auto Mechanics
					Electricity
					Cabinet Making
					Sheet Metal

8	9	10	11	12	Subject
					Foundry
					Carpentry
					Drafting

9. List any trade and industrial vocational education programs offered under the supervision of the Public Schools during this school year.
(a) In-school (b) Apprenticeship (c) Journeymen extension courses

(Use back of sheet for additional information)

FIGURE 4-1

SAMPLE DATA FORM ON A LOCAL EDUCATIONAL PROGRAM.
COURTESY: TRADE AND INDUSTRIAL EDUCATION SERVICE, OHIO
STATE DEPARTMENT OF EDUCATION.

mon to find a great deal of survey data actually being assembled from outside the immediate "community area." On some occasions all the data may be of this nature when it is found that the area serves as a "bedroom" community and people earn their living elsewhere.

To help prescribe the boundaries of the community, some sources of information are the local chamber of commerce (especially the manufacturers division), city or township planning committee or industrial development committee, personnel director's association, state employment service, and local telephone (yellow pages) directory. Where the number of employers are large, a representative sample will need to be taken of each, keeping in mind the small employer has as much if not more interest in any potential training program. In fact, the large employer can afford and often does his own training. Consequently, do not be surprised to find large employers less interested in the school's endeavors than the small employer.

3. *Selection of participants*—Once the boundaries of the survey are decided, the next step is to select the participants. From whatever directory is being used, the names and addresses of those individuals to be involved should be listed carefully. Work with names and not just titles such as president or personnel director. Try to engage the top decision-making person in the organization. It is all right if this individual delegates someone else to meet the survey obligation, but it is most important that the top individual be involved. After all, this is a community endeavor involving the school system and a future source of employees for the community's skilled manpower needs. Aim for top personnel involvement. It is not often that the school has an opportunity to confer with the community leaders in business and industry.

4. *Deciding the approach*—Without a doubt, the interview technique is the best approach, and anything else such as a mailed questionnaire will fall far short of achieving maximum results. Nothing takes the place of face-to-face interaction and if a school system is serious about making a substantial investment in a trade, industrial, and technical education program, this is the way to begin—direct involvement of industrial and business leaders in the decision-making process. Mailed questionnaires may be useful as follow-up instruments to collect data that need clarification, but they are no substitute for a good interview.

5. *Determining the interview teams*—Usually a minimum of two individuals make up a team. This could be a local school representa-

tive, such as a teacher, guidance counselor, student and a representative of the state department of education or any such combination. Plan for enough teams so that the entire survey can be completed in not more than a week's time. Orient the teams as to their task and caution them that they should not take more than 30 to 40 minutes per interview.

6. *The plan of action*—Keep in mind that it is desirable to get as many individuals as possible involved in the process. Therefore, the plan of action ideally should include the following:
    a. Involve the entire teaching staff. Set an in-service session aside for orientation and discussion of the trade, industrial, and technical education program. Discuss how the community survey can assist in determining the need for such a program. Secure staff involvement and cooperation right from the start.
    b. Organize a dinner meeting in the school cafeteria. Invite all those contacted or their representatives as well as those interested in education such as members of the local school board, trustees, PTA, key administrative staff, and teachers' association officers. See figure 4-2 for a sample invitation letter.
    c. Plan the dinner meeting program around the forthcoming community survey. Acquaint the audience with the problem and orient them as to the purpose of trade, industrial, and technical education. This could be accomplished by means of showing a movie; there are several good ones available on the topic.
    d. As part of the dinner program, pass out the data sheets and describe how the survey is to be conducted. Indicate that over the next few days a team from the school will visit their place of business to conduct an interview. Keep the whole dinner program short and to the point.

7. *Conducting the survey*—Use the mass media to let the community know a community survey is in progress. Write the news release to include the purpose of the survey, the amount of community involvement, what constitutes a survey team, and the like.
   Keep in mind that the interview form is structured to record all pertinent data. This should be a well thought-out instrument taking no more than 30–40 minutes to complete. See figure 4-3 for a sample interview form.
   Compile the data and write the report. It may be that a prereport news release may be appropriate to keep interest alive until the report is ready for release.

8. *The final report*—The final report of the survey including the findings and recommendations should be made to the local secondary or postsecondary administrative officers. In turn, the report (whether printed or oral) should be disseminated broadly to the teaching staff and community as a whole.

At this point a decision should be made by the board and/or administration as whether or not to proceed with reorganization and/or expansion of a trade, industrial, and technical program. If

---

Dear Mr. _____:

You are cordially invited to dinner at ___ p.m. on _____ at the

_____.
                    (name of dinner place)

The purpose of this dinner is to acquaint you with the plan for a survey of vocational trade and industrial education needs in _(city)_, and enlist your assistance in the conducting of this survey. Those in attendance will be the heads of local industries and labor organizations, members of the Board of Education, and representatives from the State Department of Education, Division of Vocational Education. A postal card for your convenience of reply is enclosed.

The survey of vocational education needs will be conducted on _(date)_, following this dinner meeting. During the survey, a representative of both the State Department of Education and the local public school system will call upon each of the major employers to obtain the following information.

1. Number of persons employed in the occupations included in the survey.
2. Average yearly turnover in each trade.
3. Number of apprentices or learners in each trade.
4. Employment practices as regards to the entrance of workers into the skilled trade technical fields.

Enclosed I am sending you some information on trade and industrial education that will enable you to better understand this type of program in order that you can more adequately assist us with the survey.

In the event it is definitely impossible for you to attend this dinner meeting, please suggest the name of a person as near the top of your organization as possible to represent your firm.

                                        Cordially,

                                        _____
                                        Superintendent of Schools

Encl.

FIGURE 4-2

SAMPLE LETTER OF INVITATION TO TAKE PART IN COMMUNITY
SURVEYS. COURTESY: TRADE AND INDUSTRIAL EDUCATION SERVICE,
OHIO STATE DEPARTMENT OF EDUCATION.

SURVEY FORM
FOR
TRADE AND INDUSTRIAL VOCATIONAL EDUCATION

Name of Company _____

Address of Company _____ Date of Interview _____

Types of Products Manufactured or Services Sold _____

Name(s) of Person(s) Interviewed   Name   Position

                                _____   _____

                                _____   _____

A. EMPLOYMENT DATA

Skilled & Technical Occupations Only (those that take 2,000 hrs. or more to learn)	Number Employed	Average No. Employed per Year as Replacements or for expansion	Number Apprentices or learners	Indicate if Employment is likely to increase, decrease or remain steady
1.				
2.				
3.				
4.				
5.				
6.				
7.				
8.				
9.				
10.				

B. EMPLOYMENT PRACTICES

Check
one

( ) 1. Employee may be employed and placed directly into a skilled position or a person may be upgraded to a skilled position regardless of seniority.

( ) 2. Any skilled position open must be posted in order that present employees can bid for the position but ability not seniority is the basis for selection.

( ) 3. Trade positions open must be filled on the basis of the seniority of the applicant employed by the company regardless of competency.

( ) 4. All persons employed must enter at the lowest level of work and progress on basis of seniority.

      5. The minimum age of employment is _____.

FIGURE 4-3

SAMPLE INTERVIEW FORM. COURTESY: OHIO TRADE AND INDUSTRIAL EDUCATION SERVICE, OHIO STATE DEPARTMENT OF EDUCATION.

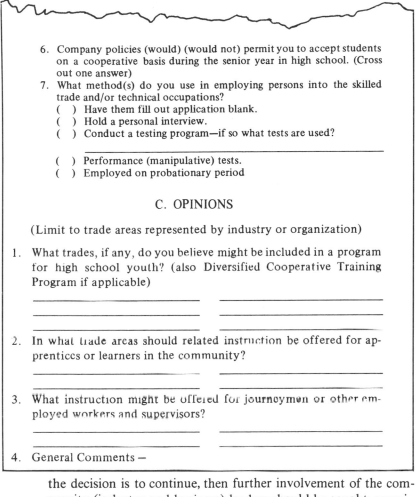

6. Company policies (would) (would not) permit you to accept students on a cooperative basis during the senior year in high school. (Cross out one answer)
7. What method(s) do you use in employing persons into the skilled trade and/or technical occupations?
   ( ) Have them fill out application blank.
   ( ) Hold a personal interview.
   ( ) Conduct a testing program—if so what tests are used?

   _____

   ( ) Performance (manipulative) tests.
   ( ) Employed on probationary period

C. OPINIONS

(Limit to trade areas represented by industry or organization)

1. What trades, if any, do you believe might be included in a program for high school youth? (also Diversified Cooperative Training Program if applicable)

2. In what trade areas should related instruction be offered for apprentices or learners in the community?

3. What instruction might be offered for journeymen or other employed workers and supervisors?

4. General Comments —

the decision is to continue, then further involvement of the community (industry and business) leaders should be sought, especially in the form of advisory committees.

In summary, the community survey procedure can be outlined as follows:

CONDENSED OUTLINE FOR CONDUCTING A TRADE AND INDUSTRIAL EDUCATION COMMUNITY SURVEY

1. Preparation steps prior to the survey
   a. Initial meeting with the local administrative officer
      I. Assistant supervisor for the district
      II. Superintendent and other key personnel, from the local school staff and community
      III. Endorse or reject idea of survey

IV. Determine trade and industrial occupations to be included.
   b. Administration of a student interest questionnaire
      I. Local guidance personnel assisted by the Guidance Services, State Department of Education
   c. Public relations activities
      I. Letter of invitation to dinner meeting—follow up with telephone check
      II. Use of printed material
         A. Brochures from State Trade and Industrial Education Services
         B. Pamphlets from State Trade and Industrial Education Services
      III. Newspaper and radio publicity
   d. Orientation of local staff
      I. Discuss purpose of survey
      II. Show film or slides to give them necessary background
   e. Information to be gathered prior to survey
      I. Results of student interest questionnaire
      II. Data on local education program—statistical report on enrollment, etc. See figure 4-1.
2. Visitation of team to community
   a. Meeting with local administrative officer—3:30 P.M. on day of dinner meeting
   b. Faculty meeting for orientation—directly after school
   c. Dinner meeting—evening prior to survey
   d. Program of visitation in community
3. Evaluation of survey results and recommendations for future action
   a. Evaluation of survey results and formulation of recommendations by members of State Staff of Trade and Industrial Education Service participating in survey
   b. The report—returned in approximately three weeks
   c. Review of recommendations and final action by local board of education or governing board.

The Student Interest Survey

The interest of students in trade, industrial, and technical as well as other type vocational programs should be measured at the same time as the survey is being conducted. One of the outstanding pieces of work in this area has been the development of the Ohio Vocational Interest Survey (D'Costa, Winefordner, Odgers, and Koons 1970).

The OVIS is an outgrowth of an interest inventory developed by the Division of Guidance and Testing, Ohio Department of Education. As such, it combines an information questionnaire with an interest inventory. Twenty-four interest scales are included, and each student completing the instrument receives an individual profile of his strengths as to job and occupational choice. The entire spectrum of occupations as defined by the *Dictionary of Occupational Titles* (U.S. Department of Labor 1965) are represented in the twenty-four interest scales.

The format of the OVIS consists of a 7-item "Student Information Questionnaire" and a 280-item "Interest Inventory" in a machine scorable package. The reading level makes the instrument ideal for the eighth grade level and above, and there is no set time limit. High school students usually take between 60–90 minutes to complete the package.

Advisory Committees

Although the use of advisory committees is covered more completely in chapter 7, their role in determining program needs should be mentioned. Advisory committees can be of substantial assistance not only in assessing the need for specific trade, industrial, and technical education programs but also in organizing and implementing these programs. From an organizational standpoint, the involvement of persons employed in the occupational pursuit itself provides up-to-date input in a unique manner. Not only can such individuals answer questions as to the status of the occupation in terms of employment and promotional opportunities, but also they can serve as an accurate barometer in terms of future trends. Relative to program implementation, the advisory committee members can help in determining physical facility needs, equipment and hardware requirements, teacher qualifications and selection, instructional materials and teaching aides, and curriculum content. Moreover, through their wide contacts within the occupational area, advisory committee members can assist with student placement after graduation (or as part of a cooperative program) and assessment of the program and the "end-products." The use of advisory committees in program determination and planning should by no means be overlooked.

Summary

By combining student interest with community need, a substantial case can be built to support the organization and/or expansion of trade, industrial, and technical education among the offerings of an educational system. The community survey entails detailed planning, involvement of a large number of people, and data collection through either the interview technique or the use of a questionnaire. The "public relations" aspect of the community survey adds an unanticipated benefit. A student interest survey should be an integral part of the process so as to provide a total picture.

QUESTIONS AND ACTIVITIES

1. Why make a community survey of trade, industrial, and technical education needs?

2. What are the constraints (problems) faced in attempting to conduct a community survey?

3. Why is it desirable to couple the community survey with a student interest survey?

4. Who should be designated to lead the community survey?

5. What should be the role of the teacher in the conduct of a community survey? Student interest survey? Organization of an advisory committee?

6. Practice the interview technique by role playing in the classroom.

7. Duplicate copies of the questionnaire instrument and conduct an interview with an employer.

8. Discuss the *Ohio Vocational Interest Survey* with guidance personnel.

SOURCE MATERIALS

1. D'Costa, A. G.; Winefordner, D. W.; Odgers, J. G.; and Koons, P. B., Jr. *Ohio Vocational Interest Survey.* New York: Harcourt, Brace, Jovanovich, Inc., Test Department, 1970.

2. *Dictionary of Occupational Titles,* Volumes I and II. Washington, D.C.: U.S. Department of Labor, 1965.

3. *Let's Find Out Through a Trade and Industrial Education Community Survey.* Columbus, Ohio: State Department of Education, Division of Vocational Education, 1969.

Chapter 5   TRADE, INDUSTRIAL, AND TECHNICAL EDUCATION PROGRAMS

Trade, industrial, and technical education is quite broad in terms of (1) the variety of occupations for which training is provided, (2) the age levels of persons served, and (3) the types of programs provided. Prior to the Vocational Education Act of 1963, funding under the federal acts was organized under such categories as trades and industries, agriculture, distributive education, and home economics. Federal regulations spelled out in rather specific terms definitions and requirements for various types of programs within each of the broad categories. The more recent federal legislation for purposes of fund allocation has tended to blur what were discrete program types, by allocating funds on the basis of categories of persons to be served as opposed to the traditional service areas such as trades and industry and agriculture. The federal regulations under which programs are administered have also become more general, leaving the specific program specifications up to the state. While there is much merit in providing or allowing greater flexibility in program definition and requirements, the fact remains that there is not the uniformity of definition of programs that once existed throughout the various states.

For students who wish to explore in more depth the traditional program definitions, it is suggested that they refer to Vocational Education Bulletin No. 1 (U.S. Office of Education 1946).

Types of Programs and Classes

As mentioned earlier, federal acts beginning with the Vocational Amendments of 1963 do not specify the types of classes but do specify the types of individuals for which training is to be provided. Included are (1) full-time students in secondary or postsecondary institutions, (2) persons who have entered the labor market and who need training or retraining to achieve stability or advancement in employment, and (3) students who are disadvantaged or handicapped.

In the following paragraphs is a description of the types of programs necessary to meet the needs of these groups of people. The challenge to trade, industrial, and technical educators is to provide training that will meet the needs for all persons who can benefit from training of a trade or technical nature.

DAY TRADE CLASSES

"Day Trade Classes" has been the traditional designation for classes serving full-time students in trade, industrial, and technical education. Such classes or programs are provided at the high school level in regular or "comprehensive" high schools, in specialized vocational or technical high schools, or in area high schools. In the case of area high schools, a common pattern is for the students to attend the area facility for a portion of the day and to remain for a part of the day in their home high school.

At the postsecondary level, programs are conducted in junior or community colleges, in trade schools or technical institutes, or colleges. A limited number of classes are conducted in four year institutions of higher education.

Traditionally classes have been designated as Type A, Type B, or Type C classes. These distinctions exist in a number of states for reporting or reimbursement purposes; they have disappeared in other states.

In Type A classes, related instruction is given in separate classes outside of the workshop or laboratory. In Type B classes, related instruction is provided as an integral part of the shop or laboratory instruction. The Smith-Hughes and George-Barden Acts called for a minimum of thirty hours per week of instruction with at least one-half of the total time of instruction to be on a "useful or productive basis, i.e., field, shop, laboratory, cooperative or other occupational experience."

A typical schedule of a student in a machine shop program in a Type A program would be one-half day in machine shop practice, one or two periods of related instruction, and one or two periods of general subjects such as English or history which is often required to meet graduation requirements. Such a program is often two or three years in length. In the case of a Type B program, a student would be in the shop for a half day with related instruction being provided by the shop teacher within that half day time period. The remainder of the day is spent in other high school subjects.

Class schedules for typical Type A, and Type B programs are shown in figures 5-1 and 5-2 respectively.

SIXTY MINUTE PERIODS	MONDAY	TUESDAY	WEDNESDAY	THURSDAY	FRIDAY	FORTY-FIVE MINUTE PERIODS
1st PERIOD	GENERAL SUBJECT(S)					1st PERIOD 2nd PERIOD
2nd PERIOD 3rd PERIOD	RELATED TECHNOLOGY INCLUDING TECHNICAL AND OCCUPATIONAL INFORMATION					3rd PERIOD 4th PERIOD
	LUNCH PERIOD					
4th PERIOD 5th PERIOD 6th PERIOD	MANIPULATIVE INSTRUCTION IN SHOP OR LABORATORY WORK					5th PERIOD 6th PERIOD 7th PERIOD 8th PERIOD

SOURCE: *Manual of Operation* (Ohio: State Board of Education, 1970), p. III-6.

FIGURE 5-1

SAMPLE SCHEDULE FOR PROGRAM TYPE A

SIX PERIOD DAY	MONDAY	TUESDAY	WEDNESDAY	THURSDAY	FRIDAY	EIGHT PERIOD DAY
1st PERIOD 2nd PERIOD 3rd PERIOD	GENERAL ACADEMIC SUBJECTS					1st PERIOD 2nd PERIOD 3rd PERIOD 4th PERIOD
	LUNCH PERIOD					
4th PERIOD 5th PERIOD 6th PERIOD	MANIPULATIVE INSTRUCTION IN SHOP OR LABORATORY WORK					5th PERIOD 6th PERIOD 7th PERIOD 8th PERIOD

SOURCE: *Manual of Operation* (Ohio: State Board of Education, 1970), p. III-10.

FIGURE 5-2

SAMPLE SCHEDULE FOR PROGRAM TYPE B

Post high school full-time programs vary in length and in content emphasis. Figure 5-3 shows a curriculum for a one year machine tool operation diploma program. The program places heavy emphasis on shop work and directly related content. This is quite typical of one year postsecondary vocational programs.

An outline for a two year mechanical design curriculum is shown in figure 5-4. It will be noted that the content of this curriculum is much broader than the one year vocational program curriculum. It includes a greater percentage of technical content as compared to shop work, as well as classes that might be considered general education.

Type C classes have been defined as special classes for out-of-school youth or adults, or classes to prepare for single-skilled or semiskilled occupations. Federal regulations formerly permitted a school week of less than

FIRST SEMESTER						
Course Number	Course Name	Class Hours	Lab Hours	Total Week Hours	Total Sem. Hours	Course Value
809–300	Orientation	1	0	1	18	0
420–357	Machine Shop I	0	15	15	270	5
420–388	Machine Shop Related I	4	0	4	72	4
421–339	Blueprint Reading	4	0	4	72	4
804–303	Shop Mathematics I	3	0	3	54	3
801–305	Communications Improvement I	3	0	3	54	3
442–313	General Welding	3	0	3	54	3
	TOTAL	18	15	33	594	22
SECOND SEMESTER						
809–300	Orientation	1	0	1	18	0
420–358	Machine Shop II	0	15	15	270	5
420–389	Machine Shop Related II	4	0	4	72	4
804–304	Shop Mathematics II	3	0	3	54	3
801–306	Communications Improvement II	3	0	3	54	3
806–375	Applied Science	3	0	3	54	3
809–327	Human Relations	3	0	3	54	3
	TOTAL	17	15	32	576	21
	GRAND TOTAL	35	30	65	1170	43

FIGURE 5-3

Curriculum for a One Year Machine Tool Operation Diploma Program

FIRST SEMESTER

Course Number	Course Name	Class Hours	Lab Hours	Total Week Hours	Total Sem. Hours	Course Value
606-101	Mechanical Drafting I	2	6	8	144	4
606-131	Materials of Industry	2	0	2	36	2
606-160	Manufacturing Processes I	2	2	4	72	3
804-151	Mathematics I	5	0	5	90	5
801-151	Communication Skills I	3	0	3	54	3
809-100	Orientation	1	0	1	18	0
	TOTAL	15	8	23	414	17

SECOND SEMESTER

606-103	Mechanical Drafting II	1	6	7	126	3
606-162	Manufacturing Processes II	2	2	4	72	3
806-151	Technical Science I	2	2	4	72	3
804-152	Mathematics II	5	0	5	90	5
801-152	Communication Skills II	3	0	3	54	3
809-100	Orientation	1	0	1	18	0
	TOTAL	14	10	24	432	17

THIRD SEMESTER

606-110	Descriptive Geometry	1	2	3	54	2
606-118	Basic Mechanism	2	2	4	72	3
606-130	Strength of Materials	3	0	3	54	3
806-152	Technical Science II	2	2	4	72	3
809-151	Psych of Human Relations	3	0	3	54	3
809-153	American Institutions	3	0	3	54	3
809-100	Orientation	1	0	1	18	0
	TOTAL	15	6	21	378	17

FOURTH SEMESTER

606-116	Machine Design	3	0	3	54	3
606-125	Design Problems	1	6	7	126	3
606-112	Tool Design	1	4	5	90	3
606-153	Electronic Drafting	2	2	4	72	3
612-100	Fluid Power & Pneumatics	1	2	3	54	2
809-110	Economics	3	0	3	54	3
809-100	Orientation	1	0	1	18	0
	TOTAL	12	14	26	468	17
	GRAND TOTAL	56	38	94	1692	68

FIGURE 5-4

CURRICULUM FOR A TWO YEAR MECHANICAL DESIGN
ASSOCIATE DEGREE PROGRAM

thirty hours; less than half of the time had to be spent in vocational training. It should be emphasized again that this designation by type of class or the definition as provided is no longer a requirement of the federal acts and may or may not be used in a given state.

The strict time requirement for classes prior to the Vocational Education Amendments of 1968 for day trade classes came under constant attack by many general school administrators. Likewise, it was strongly defended by many vocational educators. Arguments continue to persist relative to the time that should be devoted to occupational preparation at the high school level. In terms of use of federal funds, the decision is now up to each individual state. The danger that existed in the eyes of many trade, industrial, and technical educators is that time provided would not be adequate to acquire the specific skills and knowledge necessary to successfully enter and progress in a chosen occupational field.

Obviously the time requirements for a given level of occupational proficiency will vary with the occupational area. Also, programs may have different objectives related to the breadth or depth to be provided in a given program. The time requirement is only one of the factors which make a program vocational, but it seems obvious that the time must be adequate to meet expected objectives.

COOPERATIVE CLASSES

A cooperative education program may be considered a type of day trade class. However, in a cooperative education program the student spends a part of his regular school day in an employment situation. See figure 5-5 for two different program schedules. Programs are known by different titles in various states; the two most common titles are industrial cooperative training (ICT) and diversified occupations (DO). The term diversified has sometimes been misunderstood. It should be made clear that it refers to the fact that students in a class may be involved in training for different occupations, rather than a single student being exposed to training for more than one occupation.

Cooperative education classes have been used very effectively in smaller cities where the student interest or the employment opportunities in an occupational field do not justify setting up an in-school program. Cooperative education classes are used also in larger school population areas for occupations where there are not large numbers of employees.

The program provides for a written agreement between an employer, the school, the student, and the parents. The student works a minimum of fifteen hours per week, usually one-half of his school day being employed in conformity with all federal and state laws. The training agreement developed by the school teacher-coordinator and the employer spells out such

Sample 1

SIXTY MINUTE PERIODS	MONDAY	TUESDAY	WEDNESDAY	THURSDAY	FRIDAY	FORTY-FIVE MINUTE PERIODS
1st PERIOD	GENERAL SUBJECT(S)					1st PERIOD 2nd PERIOD
2nd PERIOD 3rd PERIOD	SUPERVISED OCCUPATIONAL STUDY AND RELATED TECHNOLOGY					3rd PERIOD 4th PERIOD
	LUNCH PERIOD					
4th PERIOD 5th PERIOD 6th PERIOD	COOPERATIVE EMPLOYMENT					5th PERIOD 6th PERIOD 7th PERIOD 8th PERIOD

Sample 2

SIXTY MINUTE PERIODS	MONDAY	TUESDAY	WEDNESDAY	THURSDAY	FRIDAY	FORTY-FIVE MINUTE PERIODS
1st PERIOD	Group A SPECIFIC RELATED STUDY					1st PERIOD
2nd PERIOD	Group B GENERAL SUBJECTS Group A GENERAL SUBJECTS					2nd PERIOD
3rd PERIOD	Group B SPECIFIC RELATED STUDY					3rd PERIOD
	A & B GENERAL SUBJECTS					4th PERIOD
	LUNCH PERIOD					
4th PERIOD 5th PERIOD 6th PERIOD	COOPERATIVE EMPLOYMENT					5th PERIOD 6th PERIOD 7th PERIOD 8th PERIOD

SOURCE: *Manual of Operation* (Ohio: State Board of Education, 1970), p. V-6.

FIGURE 5-5

SAMPLE SCHEDULES FOR PROGRAM IN COOPERATIVE CLASSES

provisions as the hours of employment, wage rate, the skills and knowledge to be learned with a proposed time plan for training in the various operations or on specific equipment.

Related instruction is provided in the school, usually an hour a day or more, by the teacher-coordinator. (Instruction typically includes information which may be generally related to all occupational areas and which is taught to the group as a whole.) Trade knowledge is provided through the use of individualized instructional materials. Examples of content for generally related instruction are labor-management relations, social security provisions, and workman's compensation.

The teacher-coordinator, as a part of his schedule, has release time from school to supervise trainees on-the-job. The teacher coordinator maintains a close working relationship with the students' on-the-job instructor.

It should be mentioned that other scheduling plans exist. In at least two states a "week-about" schedule is common where a student spends alternate weeks in school and on the job.

The cooperative program offers the advantages of a close school-employer relationship over other training methods. Also, for many students the opportunity to earn a wage is important. This program also provides the opportunity for training in occupations where the purchase of equipment by the school would not be feasible.

Primary disadvantages lie in the fact that placement in good training situations is often difficult when the labor market is tight. Also, for maximum effectiveness the teacher-coordinator to student ratio must be kept small. Less than 20 students is optimum, and the number should not exceed 25. The instructional cost compared to academic classroom instruction is somewhat greater.

CLASSES FOR APPRENTICES

Classes for the related technical training of apprentices are provided as a part of most trade and industrial programs. Traditionally, the federal apprenticeship standards which include an "indenture" have called for related instruction of at least 144 hours per year for all apprentices. Figure 5-6 displays a typical Apprentice Indenture agreement. State or local standards may require additional hours. The practice in some states is 288 hours per year. In some areas apprentices attend related classes at night and/or on Saturdays, but it is becoming increasingly common to give instruction during the regular work day with apprentices being paid while they attend school.

Classes are usually taught by a journeyman in the trade area who is employed by the school. The content for the training is agreed on by the apprenticeship committee and the school. In philosophy, related instruction should be comprised primarily of classroom type work, although in practice it has been found that it is often desirable to provide some training in skills since many can be more efficiently taught in school than on-the-job.

Effective programs are dependent upon the schools' ability to work with the joint apprenticeship committee made up of workers and employers of the responsible employer groups.

A somewhat typical course outline for apprentice-related instruction for auto mechanics is shown in figure 5-7. It is noted that in this curriculum most of the instruction is of a classroom nature. However, good instruction

WISCONSIN DEPARTMENT OF
INDUSTRY, LABOR AND HUMAN RELATIONS
Division of Apprenticeship and Training
Box 2209   Madison, Wisconsin 53701

Emp. No. _____

Cty.-City _____

App. Dist. _____

Insp. Mo. _____

APPRENTICE INDENTURE

School Dist. _____

This Indenture
prepared by _____Date _____

Trade Code _____

THIS INDENTURE Made in quadruplicate between _____
(Name of Employer)

hereafter called the first party, and _____
hereafter called the second party,   (Name of Apprentice)

WITNESSETH, That the first party agrees to employ the second party as an apprentice
in the trade, craft or business of _____
upon the terms and conditions in this indenture.   (Trade or Craft)

That the apprenticeship term begins on the ___day of _____, 19 __
and terminates upon the completion by the apprentice of _____
of employment for said employer in said trade, craft,   (Term of Apprenticeship)
or business.

That the said apprentice agrees to diligently and faithfully fulfill all the obligations of
this apprenticeship.

Social Security No. _____

Date of Birth _____

_____   _____
(Apprentice—Print or Type)   (Name of Firm or Corporation)

_____   _____
(Street Address)   (Street Address)

_____   _____
(City)   (Zip)   (City)   (Zip)

The provisions binding on the parties hereto as to probationary period, school attendance,
hours of employment, processes, wages and the methods or plans of instruction are contained in exhibit "A" which said exhibit is made a part hereof.

The Department of Industry, Labor and Human Relations may annul this indenture
upon application of either party after a satisfactory showing of good cause.

The Department of Industry, Labor and Human Relations shall issue a certificate of apprenticeship to the apprentice who has satisfactorily completed the terms of this indenture.

IN WITNESS WHEREOF, The parties have caused this indenture to be signed as required by Chapter 106.01 of the laws of Wisconsin.

_____   _____
(Apprentice Signature)   (Signature and Title of Official)

_____
(Signature of Parent or Guardian if a Minor)

FIGURE 5-6

SAMPLE OF AN APPRENTICE INDENTURE

EXHIBIT "A"—MACHINIST

TIME: 8320 Hours

EXTENT OF PERIOD OF APPRENTICESHIP: A total of 8320 hours shall constitute the period of apprenticeship. The first 400 hours of employment shall constitute the probationary period.

SCHOOL ATTENDANCE: Approximately 144 hours per year of the above time shall be devoted to school instruction, for which the apprentice shall be paid at his regular rate.

SCHEDULE OF PROCESSES TO BE WORKED: The schedule of processes to be worked shall be as follows, but not necessarily in this sequence.

	APPROXIMATE HOURS
Tool Crib (40); Tool Grinding (40); Inspection (40)	120 hours
Drills (Spindle and Radial)	400 hours
Milling Machines (Vertical and Horizontal)	520 hours
Engine Lathes	400 hours
Turret Lathes (Vertical, Horizontal, & Boring Mills)	1040 hours
Layout	520 hours
Misc. Mach. (Keyseater & Broach, Gear Hobber, Shaper, Etc.)	520 hours
Grinders (Surface, Internal, External)	600 hours
Planer Type Mill	520 hours
Boring Bars (Small, Large, & Jigborer)	1040 hours
Numerical Controlled Machines (when available)	1040 hours
Advanced Training & Specialization (Tool Design, Lab. Work, Process Engineering, Production Control)	1050 hours
Related Instruction	550 hours
TOTAL HOURS	8320 hours

COMPENSATION TO BE PAID: The apprentice shall receive wages in accordance with the provisions for such pay as set forth in the currently prevailing contract with the union (AFL-CIO, U.S. Steelworkers, Local 1533). The pay schedule is divided into 8 pay periods of 1040 hours per period.

SPECIAL PROVISIONS: In the first six (6) months, the apprentice shall purchase a tool box and acquire the tools of his trade. By the completion of his apprenticeship he is to have accumulated the necessary tools of a machinist.

At the completion of the required period of apprenticeship, the graduate indenture apprentice shall receive a bonus of one hundred dollars ($100.00).

The Company reserves the right to review at anytime this contract for the purpose of granting time credit for previous experience, education or outstanding performance, with the approval of the Industrial Commission.

FIGURE 5-6—*CONTINUED*

Course Name	Weekly Class Hours	Total Semester Hours
FIRST SEMESTER		
Auto Math I	1	9
Basic Electricity	1	9
Engine Rebuilding I	3	27
Brakes and Power Train.	3	27
TOTAL	8	72
SECOND SEMESTER		
Auto Science	1	9
Auto Communications (written)	1	9
Tune-up and Diag. I (Electrical)	3	27
Welding	3	27
TOTAL	8	72
THIRD SEMESTER		
Auto Math I or Auto Math II	1	9
Auto Salesmanship	1	9
Body Repair	3	27
Engine Rebuilding II	3	27
TOTAL	8	72
FOURTH SEMESTER		
Auto Bookkeeping and Accounting	2	18
Auto Transmission	3	27
Tune-up and Diag. II (Carburetion)	3	27
TOTAL	8	72
FIFTH SEMESTER		
Auto Math I or Auto Math II or Auto Math III	1	9
Auto Communications (oral)	1	9
Auto Machine Shop	3	27
Power Accessories	3	27
TOTAL	8	72
SIXTH SEMESTER		
Human Relations	2	18
Automotive Chassis	3	27
Diesel Engines	3	27
TOTAL	8	72
GRAND TOTAL	48	432

FIGURE 5-7

AUTOMOTIVE MECHANICS APPRENTICE CURRICULUM

would dictate using actual components for demonstration and to a limited degree for testing the students' abilities to apply the technology learned.

Part-Time and Adult Education

Persons served in part-time classes in trade, industrial, and technical classes number approximately twice the number served in full-time programs. Classes may be provided in any trade, industrial, or technical occupation for purposes of upgrading present skills or of learning new, employment-related skills. Programs may vary from a few hours of instruction to programs designed to be carried out over a year or more. Content may include skill training in a shop or laboratory or related learning in a classroom, or a combination of both.

The success of an effective program is quite dependent upon the schools' ability to respond rapidly to identified needs for training of local business and industry or groups of individuals. Therefore, the schools' offerings vary greatly from one year to another. Classes are usually conducted in the evening hours when school facilities are more available than during the regular school day. However, many classes are provided, specifically, to accommodate persons working night shifts.

Program flexibility is enhanced by the fact that part-time staff from business and industry are used extensively for instruction. This makes possible the staffing of a great variety of classes. Employees in industry are usually available to teach part-time with short notice since the teaching does not interfere with their jobs.

General Adult Education

Trade, industrial, and technical educators are often involved with providing non-occupation-related classes for adults. These classes are usually self-supporting or nearly so through enrollment fees and/or local school system financing. These types of classes, although not contributing to employment competence, do provide a community service to the citizens and are effective public relations media.

Classes are extremely varied in their content. Some fairly typical ones requiring facilities of a trade and industrial nature would include woodworking, plastics, art metal working, and auto mechanics.

Summary

In this chapter the breadth of trade, industrial, and technical offerings has been illustrated—in terms of the occupations for which training is provided as well as in terms of the kinds of needs served. Classes are provided for full-time students at both the secondary and post-secondary levels. The unique needs of apprentices are served through related instruction classes to supplement the skills and technical knowledge obtained on-the-job.

In addition, industrial cooperative training programs have been discussed. Some typical course outlines have been shown which serve to contrast the nature of the content for the several types of programs.

QUESTIONS AND ACTIVITIES

1. Outline what might be an optimum program of trade, industrial, and technical education for a medium sized school district in your state.

2. Explain how the apprentice program operates in your state. Do you have a state apprenticeship law?

   What is the relationship to the Bureau of Apprenticeship and Training (BAT)?

   How is the related apprenticeship instruction provided?

3. Contrast the differences between technical education curricula and vocational education curricula.

4. Explain the advantages of a good cooperative program.

5. Discuss the rationale for having trade, industrial, and technical education programs provided in your state at both the secondary and post-secondary levels.

SOURCE MATERIALS

1. *Administration of Vocational Education—Rules and Regulations.* Washington, D.C.: U.S. Government Printing Office, 1967.

2. Barlow, Melvin, ed. *Vocational Education.* National Society for the Study of Education, Sixty-Fourth Yearbook. Chicago: University of Chicago Press, 1965.

3. Bowler, Earl M. "Adult Programs," in *Encyclopedia of Education,* pp. 486–494. New York: MacMillan Press, 1971.

4. Burt, Samuel M. *Industry and Vocational Technical Education.* New York: McGraw-Hill Co., 1967.

5. ———. "Vocational Education Advisory Committees," in *Encyclopedia of Education,* pp. 494–498. New York: MacMillan Press, 1971.

6. *Education for a Changing World of Work.* Report of the Panel of Consultants on Vocational Education, U.S. Department of Health, Education and Welfare. Washington, D.C.: U.S. Government Printing Office, 1963.

7. Evans, Rupert N. *Foundations of Vocational Education.* Columbus, Ohio: Charles E. Merrill Publishing Co., 1971.

8. Gillie, Angelo C., and Miller, Aaron J. *A Suggested Guide for Post-Secondary Vocational and Technical Education,* Leadership Training Series No. 29. Columbus, Ohio: Center for Vocational and Technical Education, Ohio State University, 1970.

9. Law, Gordon F., ed. *Contemporary Concepts in Vocational Education.* First Yearbook of the American Vocational Association. Washington, D.C.: American Vocational Association, 1971.

10. Leighbody, Gerald B. *Vocational Education in America's Schools: Major Issues of the 70's.* Chicago: American Technical Society, 1972.

11. *Manpower Report of the President.* Transmitted to the Congress, March, 1972. Washington, D.C.: U.S. Government Printing Office.

12. *Organization and Operation of a Local Program of Vocational Education.* Washington, D.C.: U.S. Department of Health, Education and Welfare, 1968.

13. Rhodes, James A. *Alternative to a Decadent Society.* Indianapolis, Indiana: Howard W. Sams and Co., Inc., 1969.

14. Roberts, Roy W. *Vocational and Practical Arts Education.* New York: Harper and Row, 1965.

15. *Vocational Education, Bulletin 1.* Washington, D.C.: Department of Health, Education and Welfare, U.S. Office of Education, 1946.

16. *Vocational Education: The Bridge Between Man and His Work.* Summary and Recommendations adapted from the General Report of the Advisory Council on Vocational Education. Washington, D.C.: Superintendent of Documents, U.S. Government Printing Office, 1968.

Chapter 6 THE ADMINISTRATION OF TRADE, INDUSTRIAL, AND TECHNICAL EDUCATION

During fiscal year 1970 approximately two million individuals participated in secondary, postsecondary, and special needs trade, industrial, and technical education programs. Obviously this vast student body studied under some type of administrative organization. It is the purpose of this chapter to examine the various administrative structures of trade, industrial, and technical education and to delineate a number of administrative roles necessary for carrying on the day-by-day operation of these educational offerings.

The Administrative Structure

Public education is usually under the general management of a governing board, such as a board of education for kindergarten through high school and a board of trustees for postsecondary or higher education. The composition of such boards, their powers, and their duties are defined by state and local law. To run the day-by-day operation there is usually some type of executive head such as a superintendent or president. These individuals are directly responsible to their respective governing boards. To assist them, they are provided with subordinate staff to perform various duties. Staff members accept specific assignments and report to their superiors who report in like fashion along the organizational continuum. Ultimately the superintendent or president reports to the board; for it is he who accepts responsibility for the actions of his staff.

The chief administrator of a local vocational school or program must function within the framework of the administrative organization and within the policies established by his board. If the chief administrator is the superintendent or president, he is responsible for every phase of the educational program under his jurisdiction. A typical organizational chart for an area or county vocational-technical school system appears in figure 6-1.

It should be noted from figure 6-1 that the area or county vocational school superintendent reports directly to the vocational board of education. The superintendent's staff includes assistants of various kinds (administrative, business manager, adult evening director, subject matter supervisors, etc.), an assistant (or deputy) superintendent, principals of separate schools and the like. Although an overall advisory committee is shown, this committee may or may not be used. Undoubtedly there will be other advisory committees used throughout the system for specific purposes such as curriculum, facilities planning, and apprenticeship training.

Another and possibly more common administrative structure is found when the vocational-technical offerings are part of a comprehensive school system. Figure 6-2 shows such a typical organization:

In figure 6-2, the director of vocational education answers to the school superintendent. He serves as a specialist in this area and may also be assigned the adult education program within the system. To carry out these functions he may have several assistants or supervisors under him. If the school system is large and has several high schools, there may be subject matter supervisors or assistant directors for each, such as trade, industrial and technical; business and office education; home economics; and distributive education.

Usually the line of authority is maintained through the high school principal. This is indicated by the solid line in the organization chart. The dotted line indicates indirect authority—access to the high school staff for special events and communications, in-service training, and the like.

Still another administrative pattern places the vocational director under the respective high school principal. In figure 6-3, it can be readily seen that the vocational director acts much the same as an assistant principal in that he is responsible for all the vocational offerings and may be responsible for all the vocational students as well. A vocational director at this level is handicapped to a large degree unless he is given considerable freedom to operate in the community as an agent of the principal or superintendent to promote the full spectrum of vocational offerings. The better plan, and the one which is now taking shape in the United States Office of Education, is to have the person in charge of vocational-technical education be a deputy superintendent.

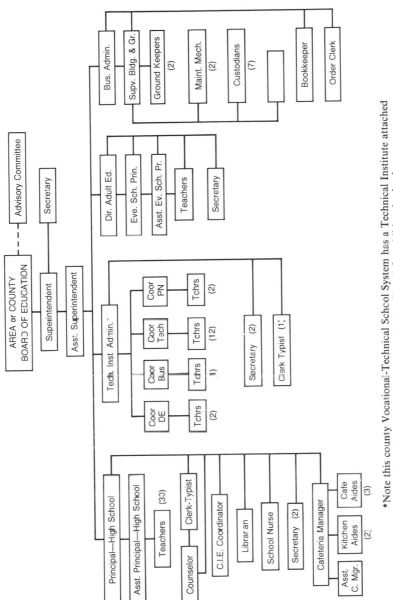

*Note this county Vocational-Technical School System has a Technical Institute attached to it. The High School organization can be duplicated for additional schools.

FIGURE 6-1

A TYPICAL AREA OR COUNTY VOCATIONAL-TECHNICAL SCHOOL SYSTEM

103

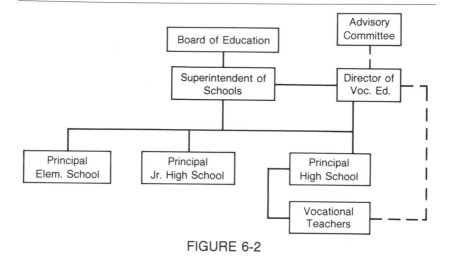

FIGURE 6-2

VOCATIONAL-TECHNICAL ORGANIZATION OF A COMPREHENSIVE
SCHOOL SYSTEM

ADMINISTRATIVE ROLES IN TRADE, INDUSTRIAL, AND TECHNICAL EDUCATION

The person whose speciality is trade, industrial, and technical education may not be the chief school officer, but it behooves one to look at the kinds of administrative qualities such individuals should possess.*

The Director (Supervisor) of Trade, Industrial, and Technical Education. This individual usually will be found in the larger school systems. He is responsible to the vocational director and is accountable for full-time, part-time, and special needs programs of trade, industrial, and technical education. He must possess unusual capacity and should have a broad knowledge of the structure of occupations, curriculum development, the use of advisory committees, physical facility development, the use of instructional materials and devices, and assessment of manpower training needs and techniques, as well as a sound preparation in administrative and supervisory skills. Moreover, he must meet the requirements of certification as set forth by the state plan of the state in which he serves.

Vocational Principal or Vice Principal. Although one rarely finds a principal of trade, industrial, and technical education (except in a special-

---

*It should be noted that the trade, industrial, and technical specialist holds national prominence as one often selected for the chief school officer, especially of area or county vocational school districts.

ized school), it is well to be aware that there exist administrative opportunities in this area for those who are qualified. The vocational principal must possess all of the qualifications of the director-supervisor. In addition, he will have to deal to a great extent with students, parents, faculty, and other school officials.

The principal (or vice-principal) faces many more day-by-day problems than do most other staff members. In a sense, he is the "works manager"—the one responsible for the everyday operation of the physical plant and the successful operation of the program. Upon the shoulders of the principal fall the immediate problems and decisions. It is he whose judgments are critical in terms of the relationships and interactions of students, faculty, and parents. Thus, the principal must be an individual who is first and foremost respected for his fair decisions and for his calmness, recognized for his leadership, and admired for being a good educator.

Teacher-Coordinator.   The position of teacher-coordinator is becoming more and more emphasized with the expansion of part-time cooperative programs. Teacher-coordinators of trade, industrial, and technical education offerings represent potential future higher administrative types, and the coordination function of this position provides a good deal of visibility of the individual involved. This position entails the responsibility for generating enthusiasm in the community for a cooperative trade, industrial, and technical program, locating training stations for placing students, supervising students while on the job, organizing and operating an advisory commit-

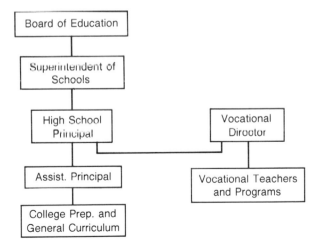

FIGURE 6-3

COMPREHENSIVE SCHOOL SYSTEM WITH VOCATIONAL DIRECTOR
UNDER HIGH SCHOOL PRINCIPAL

tee, and doing considerable public relations work for the entire school system. In addition, the teacher-coordinator is expected to help secure permanent employment for his graduates and to conduct follow-up studies to determine their success. Moreover, as a teacher the coordinator has the opportunity to motivate co-op students to master their academic and related subjects. All of these challenges prescribe precise qualifications for this individual. For example, he must be highly dedicated, energetic, aggressive, public-relations-minded, and knowledgeable about the total school system. The trade, industrial, and technical coordinator has a unique role in the administrative structure.

Apprentice Coordinator.   A unique position in the trade, industrial, and technical education field is that of apprentice coordinator. This staff member is held responsible for working with unions and industries that take part in the apprenticeship program of the United States Department of Labor. The apprentice coordinator represents the school's effort to assist in the development of journeymen-type mechanics for apprenticeable trades. The vocational schools that take part in this offering supply related instruction to those selected apprentices by joint apprenticeship committees. The coordinator is the individual charged with developing the curricula, securing the instructors, and providing the facilities and instructional materials necessary to carry on the learning activity. Frequently, the apprentice coordinator is delegated the responsibility of serving as secretary to each of the joint apprentice committees. In such a role, the individual must be knowledgeable about apprenticeship, have the respect of the unions and management alike, know curriculum development, and be able to deal with mature adults in a multitude of situations.

Director of Adult Education.   The school system that ignores the vocational needs of adults is not recognizing a major and highly important function. Although the director of adult education need not come from the ranks of trade, industrial, and technical education, it should be apparent to any superintendent that an individual with this background may possess many of the qualifications needed to serve in such a position. For example, the coordinator of apprenticeship obviously deals with adult education, and such an individual is well equipped to become an adult education director for the entire program. It is not surprising to find that in most instances the enrollment in part-time adult courses is greater than in full-time day school courses. Therefore, the person who directs these courses must be a good administrator.

Many of the qualifications needed for a director of adult education have already been mentioned for other positions. However, the outstanding characteristic of any successful adult education director is his ability to recognize the specific needs of his clientele. There is an old saying among those engaged in the direction of adult education: "Adults want what they want, and in as short a time span as possible." Adults do not return to school just to be going to school. They want good instruction by teachers who understand adult learning, with no extemporaneous material; and if they do not get what they are interested in, they merely fail to attend any more classes. The director of adult education must have a grasp of the occupational and general education needs of adults. He should know how to organize and promote the offerings, have the ability to work with community groups and to identify and enlist good teachers in the program, and should be accountable for the entire adult school operation.

State Supervisor of Trade, Industrial, and Technical Education.
Most likely, this position will be one of state supervisor of trade and industrial education or state supervisor of technical education within a state vocational division of a state department of education. Either position involves considerable leadership and administrative responsibility. The individual holding such a position is responsible for the promotion, development, and implementation of the total program within the state. Usually, as the head or chief of the service, he has a staff of subordinates who do most of the field work and carry out specifically assigned responsibilities. For example, one such subordinate may be designated the operating head of the vocational industrial clubs; another, head of the cooperative aspects of the program; and still another, head of the apprenticeship or adult responsibilities.

The supervisor will be expected to lead his staff and those in the field toward the goals of improving and maintaining the quality of trade, industrial, and technical education; expanding the offerings; and assisting in problem-solving and the like. From his vantage point in the state department of education he should lead through persuasion and not coercion and should administer in a fair and just manner. These characteristics contribute to success or failure in a relatively short period of time.

Job Descriptions

Probably one of the most neglected aids to the good administrator of education is adequate job descriptions. Too frequently the exact job qualifications and specifications describing the role of an individual in the administrative structure are missing. This is especially critical for the new or prospective employee who wants to know immediately what qualifications he must possess to fill a certain job and what his role will be if selected for it. Mere certification (the holding of the appropriate certificate) is not enough.

An example of a well written job description for the position of State Supervisor of Trade and Industrial Education (Ohio 1952) follows.

JOB QUALIFICATIONS AND SPECIFICATIONS FOR STATE
SUPERVISOR OF TRADE AND INDUSTRIAL EDUCATION
(EDUCATION SPECIALIST IV)
Salary Range: Open.

Job Description.   This is highly responsible professional educational and administrative work in supervising and directing an extensive program of financial and technical assistance to local public school districts in the field of vocational trade and industrial education. The work involves responsibility for the distribution of federal and state funds as reimbursement to local school districts for a portion of the costs of approved courses of instruction which meet reimbursement standards. This employee is responsible for developing standards for courses, qualifications for teaching personnel, and procedures for inspecting, approving, and evaluating local programs to determine compliance with established standards. An employee at this level renders service on a much broader scope than educational specialists II or III. They also have considerable responsibility for contacting and establishing cooperative relationship with such community and state agencies and organizations as trade, employee, employer, education and industrial groups. Educational specialist IV is responsible directly to the director of vocational education.

Types of Positions Covered.   State Supervisor, Vocational Trade and Industrial Education.

Qualifications (General).   *Age*—preferable 30–45; *Education*—(a) a graduate of a four-year course from an approved college or university, or (b) a Master's degree with a major in industrial education, and courses in school administration.

Occupational Experience.   (a) A minimum of three years of approved trade or industrial experience; (b) at least two years of successful teaching in trade and industrial education; or (c) three years of successful experience in supervising or administering a program of trade and industrial education or of training trade and industrial teachers.

Other.   An educational specialist IV must have the highest professional respect of those with whom he works and must have demonstrated his ability to plan and implement a program of democratic supervision in either industrial or educational areas of work. Dependability, honesty, enthusiasm, and a sincere interest in helping others are essential to success.

He shall have demonstrated ability as a supervisor as shown by his record in dealing with school officials, teachers, educational institutions, other supervisors, and leaders in trade and industrial areas of endeavor.

Role Description

The role or duties of positions should also be documented. The role of the State Supervisor of Trade and Industrial Education is clearly spelled out in the following example (Ohio 1952).

ROLE DESCRIPTION OF THE STATE SUPERVISOR OF TRADE
AND INDUSTRIAL EDUCATION

GUIDING PRINCIPLES

Supervision functions at the state level are based upon principles and policies conceived through the democratic process with the individuals or groups served. Principles and policies so determined are administered through the cooperative efforts of state and local personnel.

The plan for state supervision is based on the premise that programs of trade and industrial education should be operated by qualified and competent personnel employed by local boards of education. The aim of all supervisory services at the state level is to provide services that will assist the local community to provide quality instruction of the proper type at the appropriate time to meet the trade and industrial education needs of youth and adults in the community.

Funds available for distribution to promote trade and industrial education will be distributed on an impartial and equitable basis. Since legislation establishing funds for vocational education emphasizes promotion and the further development of vocational education, special assistance will be given to new programs in those communities where such programs can be justified.

In the promotion, organization, and operation of programs of trade and industrial education, assistance available from industrial, community, or other educational sources will be utilized.

OBJECTIVES

1. To promote trade and industrial education in Ohio for youth and adults in accordance with student, community, and industrial needs.

2. To provide a teacher improvement service that will enable qualified tradesmen to provide effective, efficient, and individualized instruction for persons enrolled in trade and industrial programs.

3. To provide assistance to persons in charge of trade and industrial programs in the local communities in evaluating and improving facilities, instruction, and community and school relations.

4. To distribute funds made available through state and federal appropriations for vocational education in a manner which will promote the

maximum opportunities for youth and adults in trade and industrial education.

5. To maintain such statistical and financial records as will be needed to promote the program and to justify the expenditure of state and federal funds.

6. To provide information to, and maintain good relations with, those organizations representing the groups served by trade and industrial education.

7. To provide report forms and consulting services to the school administrators in the local communities to enable them to claim reimbursement for their trade and industrial programs.

8. To determine that each phase of the program receives adequate consideration and emphasis.

9. To encourage the development of instructional materials on a state wide basis for use in local programs.

10. To promote the total program of vocational education.

DUTIES AND RESPONSIBILITIES

1. Administrative
   a. Direct the handling of all correspondence either through general instruction or by dictation.
   b. Direct the organization and management of the State Office for Trade and Industrial Education Service.
   c. Prepare state budget of Trade and Industrial Education Service for the Director of Vocational Education.
   d. Allocate state reimbursement funds to various trade and industrial services.
   e. Prepare recommendations to the director on needs of trade and industrial education as to equipment, staff, materials, supplies, and services required of other agencies.
   f. Prepare prospective annual program of activities for the Director of Vocational Education.
   g. Direct the preparation of a state plan of operating policies, procedures, and practices for use by all persons working in the trade and industrial education area.
   h. Attend staff conferences called by the director.
   i. Handle office contacts with representatives of the U.S. Office of Education, local boards of education, industry, labor, and other interested parties.
   j. Direct the in-service training of staff members.
   k. Direct the work of all staff personnel in trade and industrial education, and make special arrangements as required to provide services of this educational area.

2. Supervision

   a. Direct and/or carry out in cooperation with local school authorities an evaluation of available facilities for trade and industrial education when an application is made for a program, and make recommendations to the Director of Vocational Education.

   b. Direct and/or make visits to operating schools and classes to determine whether standards are maintained with reference to plant, facilities, curriculum, quality of instruction, etc.

   c. Review and evaluate the work of approved teacher-training institutions with reference to curriculum, courses of study, operating plans, staffs, students enrolled, etc., approve courses for reimbursement, and see that programs of teacher training approved by the State Board of Vocational Education are conducted as planned.

   d. Direct and/or review recommendations for qualified teacher applicants, supervisors, coordinators, and others, for certification.

   e. Direct and/or visit vocational schools and classes for the purpose of improving instruction, carrying recommendations to local school authorities for the correction or improvement of their program.

   f. Direct the development and operation of a program of teacher-training in cooperation with approved teacher-training colleges and universities for the purpose of improving instruction by providing in-service training for teachers.

   g. Direct such studies and investigations as may directly affect the quality of local instruction, such as courses of study, visual aids, progress records systems, etc.

   h. Direct and/or conduct conferences, workshops, or other programs designed to improve the services and personnel engaged in supervising, coordinating or teaching at the local level, as well as for teacher trainers, specialized field service instructors, and consultants.

   i. Evaluate the educational services rendered by the program, and develop future plans in accordance with the results.

   j. Direct the work of all consultants, specialized field instructors, and area supervisors, making any special assignments necessary to bring about the improvement of instruction in any educational situation.

   k. Prepare an overall plan for a continuous program of supervision at all levels of the program.

   l. Approve itineraries of teacher trainers, area supervisors, and consultants.

   m. Direct the preparation of and/or develop standards for the operation of reimbursed vocational schools and classes.

   n. Direct and/or prepare releases, bulletins, and other materials that contribute to a better understanding of the relationships existing in trade and industrial education with the end result in improved instruction.

3. Promotion
   a. Give talks to various groups, i.e., industrial groups, such as employer associations, trade associations, and labor groups; civic organizations, such as Kiwanis, Rotary, and chambers of commerce; educational and professional groups, such as guidance associations, school administrators, and commencement classes.
   b. Meet with small working committees representing industry, labor, trade associations, advisory committees, and survey groups for the purpose of planning various types of training programs in trade and industrial education.
   c. Serve as consultant in meetings called by local school administrators for purpose of planning educational program.
   d. Serve as guest instructor for classes and training programs conducted at universities and colleges.
   e. Prepare or direct the publication of bulletins, newsletters, and reports to acquaint industry, school authorities, and lay public with trade and industrial education.
   f. Prepare newspaper articles and take necessary photographs to provide information to the general public on various aspects of the program.
   g. Prepare or direct the writing of magazine articles.
   h. Prepare radio scripts and appear on radio or television programs.
   i. Serve on national committees for the purpose of studying new developments in trade and industrial education.
   j. Attend regional conventions of states and participate in panel discussions, conferences, etc.
   k. Participate in conferences called by State Superintendent of Public Instruction and Director of Vocational Education for local school administrators.
   l. Serve in advisory capacity to professional organizations such as Ohio Vocational Association, American Vocational Association, and Ohio Education Association.
   m. Participate in conferences with state supervisors of other vocational areas, such as distributive or agriculture education for the purpose of developing new programs of service that may overlap more than one area.

4. Teacher Training
   a. Direct the scheduling and operation of a short pre-service program for all beginning instructors semiannually.
   b. Direct the provision of systematic individual on-the-job instruction for new instructors during their first year of employment. Note: Considerable emphasis and importance is placed on the teacher training program since trade and industrial education is the only area of secondary education where occupational competency is paramount and takes precedence over college teacher-training work. Most all trades instructors begin teaching with no profes-

sional training, but are selected on the basis of their skill and knowledge of their trade or occupation.

c. Plan and direct a program for determining, through observation and evaluation, each instructor's weaknesses.

d. Plan for and direct the operation of a program to meet the needs covered in Item c above, either through individual or group instruction, whichever may most adequately meet the needs of the instructor.

e. Direct the study of new developments, and carry out investigations in the teacher-training field.

f. Direct and/or conduct vocational education courses for school administrators.

g. Direct the planning for short, intensive, technical courses.

h. Approve all courses offered in the trade and industrial education teacher-training program.

i. Direct the development of teacher training courses to meet evident needs.

j. Direct and develop cooperatively a state program of teacher training so that institutions may interchange credits for work completed by instructors.

k. Keep in close contact with the deans and teacher training personnel of the following cooperating colleges and universities:

Toledo University   Ohio State University
University of Cincinnati   Kent State University

5. Audits and Approvals

a. Audit and approve budget requests from local boards of education and cooperating universities to determine whether requests are in conformity with existing reimbursement policies.

b. Audit affidavits from local boards of education and cooperating agencies to determine whether expenditures are justifiable and approve such affidavits for payment.

c. Audit and approve all class schedules for students engaged in trade and industrial education.

d. Audit and approve training schedules for apprentice and adult classes conducted by local boards of education.

e. Audit, approve, and make recommendations to the Division of Certification on the qualifications of teachers engaged in trade and industrial education.

6. Financial

a. Determine annually the reimbursement rates to be made for the various programs, based upon the available funds and the cost factors involved, such as growth of the program, increased salaries, etc.

b. Make an equitable allocation of funds to the various services provided through trade and industrial education, making allowance for funds to promote and encourage new centers and programs.

c. Audit and approve affidavits for payment. (See Audits and Approvals Section).

d. Keep necessary records of reimbursements for auditors and for use in preparing financial reports. (See Reports Section).

e. Develop plans that will provide the greatest amount of use for every dollar of money available, especially aiming at assisting local schools in specifically improving their programs and at the expansion of programs in new work areas and new communities.

f. Determine salaries of consultants, assistant supervisors, etc., and plan for the economical use of travel budgets.

g. Make and maintain cost analysis of various aspects of the program.

h. Prepare annual budget request for the U.S. Office Of Education.

7. Reports

a. Direct and/or prepare financial, statistical, and descriptive reports to the U.S. Office Of Education in justification of the expenditures of local, state, and federal funds as they apply to trade and industrial education.

b. Prepare and submit reports with recommendations to the Director of Vocational Education, setting forth future plans for the improvement of the program.

c. Prepare and submit progress reports to the Director of Vocational Education to be included in the composite State Department of Education report to the Governor.

d. Prepare miscellaneous statistical and descriptive reports for agencies and individuals, such as Ohio Publicity Commission, publishers of educational literature, questionnaires from other states, and graduates engaged in writing theses and doctoral dissertations.

e. Call for such financial, descriptive, and statistical reports from boards of education, superintendents, directors, supervisors, coordinators, and teachers, as will provide a complete and accurate picture of the program.

f. Prepare and/or direct the development of reporting forms, either individually or through committee work, on which date is to be submitted.

g. Review field reports of consultants, area supervisors, teacher trainers, and others, and make recommendations concerning problems indicated.

8. Research Studies and Investigations

a. Establish experimental centers for the study of new programs, methods, and techniques in trade and industrial education.

b. Direct and/or coordinate research studies on pertinent aspects of the program not requiring establishment of experimental centers.

c. Cooperate with graduate students in outlining and counseling research studies in trade and industrial or allied areas.

d. Serve in advisory capacity to other groups conducting research such as the Ohio Education Association, universities and colleges.

9. Specialized Service

a. *Industrial Supervisory and Leadership Training.*This includes: (1) directing the overall plan of supervisory and leadership training; (2) planning types of services to be made available in this area; (3) selecting personnel; (4) evaluating the efficiency of the services provided.

b. *Apprenticeship Training.* This includes: (1) directing the overall plan of related instruction for apprenticeship training; (2) planning and/ or approving services to be made available in this area; (3) selecting and training personnel to serve on a consultant basis; (4) evaluating the service being rendered.

c. *Public Service Training.* This includes: (1) directing the overall plan of public service training for public service occupations, such as peace officers, custodians, fire-fighters, school cafeteria personnel, etc; (2) planning and/or approving the types of services available in this area; (3) selecting and training personnel or trainers in this area.

d. *Instructional Materials.* This includes: (1) directing the overall plan of preparation, duplication, and dissemination of instructional materials for trade and industrial education; (2) planning types of services to be made available in this area; (3) selecting and training personnel in this area; (4) evaluating services rendered.

e. *Special Areas.* This includes: (1) directing the overall plan of providing training services in specific areas, such as coal mining, rural electrification, power engineering, etc; (2) planning types of services to be made available in this area; (3) selecting and training personnel to serve as trainers in various programs; (4) evaluating the service being rendered.

POLICIES AND PROCEDURES

1. Promotion of trade and industrial education opportunities for youth and adults shall be the main concern of state supervision.

2. The democratic process and democratic action will be followed in program organization and operation.

3. Full use will be made of staff committees and advisory committees of trade and industrial personnel from the local communities in the

promotion, organization, and operation of the trade and industrial education services.

4. Local school administrators shall be consulted on any changes in program policies or procedures which affect the program at the local level.

5. An advisory committee including representatives for labor, management, and parent groups at the state level shall be organized to advise the state supervisor concerning program improvements.

6. Craft committees shall be maintained for the rural electrification and fire-fighting instruction programs. Such committees may be organized for other phases of the trade and industrial program.

7. Each state staff member shall be visited during the time he is performing the duties of his office at least once each year.

8. Good judgment shall be used in interpreting the program standards established in the Ohio Plan for Trade and Industrial Education. In no instance, however, shall a local school be given approval for an activity which is in violation of the standards set forth in the agreement with the U.S. Office of Education.

9. Every effort shall be made to promote the total vocational education program and the State Department of Education in all public relations materials and activities.

10. Area supervisors shall be notified each time a visit is made, by the state supervisor or his assistant, to a program in his area. A written report will be made concerning the visit for the benefit and use of the area supervisor.

11. Copies of all correspondence with local programs will be forwarded to the area supervisor concerned. Copies of correspondence of interest to the teacher-trainer will be forwarded to the teacher-trainer concerned.

12. All correspondence with teacher-trainers and area supervisors will be sent directly to the person concerned.

13. Whenever a local school is visited the administrative head of the school will be contacted.

14. No person shall be recommended for a position in a local program. Names of qualified persons shall be furnished upon request but without any recommendation.

15. Plans for organized class instruction as a part of the teacher-training program shall be submitted for approval by the teacher-trainer in charge prior to the opening of the class.

16. Reports, plans and recommendations requested by the State Director of Vocational Education or the U.S. Department of Education shall be submitted promptly. Reports requested from state staff and local program personnel will be expected to be on time.

17. State staff positions which have been vacated shall be filled promptly in order to maintain the proper services to the local programs.

18. Close contact shall be maintained with all workshops and meetings for state staff and local personnel.

19. Travel itineraries for teacher-trainers, area supervisors, supervisory training instructors, and consultants shall be required and reviewed weekly.

20. Reimbursement rates shall be established on the basis of service rendered to youth and adults and not upon the salary of the instructor. A special reimbursement rate may be established to encourage the organization of new programs.

21. Leaves of absence shall be granted only for professional improvement or military service. Such leaves of absence for professional improvement shall be denied when the services to local communities would suffer.

22. Summaries of reports received from local communities shall be returned to the supervisor and/or teacher in the local trade and industrial program.

23. Frequent consultation meetings will be held with the consultant for instructional materials to assist him to establish priorities on the material under development.

Summary

In summary, there exist a number of trade, industrial, and technical administrative positions on the local, county (area), and state level. Such administrative roles require specific qualifications. The job description is an important document to consider. It answers the questions of qualifications and background needed. Too frequently it is lacking in detail, and one finds it difficult to assess personal qualifications with those needed for job success. Another document of importance is the "role or duties description." In this description all the duties of the position are spelled out so one can see the functions expected of the position. Such a document is of special value to the new employee.

QUESTIONS AND ACTIVITIES

1. Draw an organizational chart for the school system in which you are employed. Indicate the lines of authority.

2. Modify the organizational chart in item 1 above to reflect what you consider the most "ideal."

3. Discuss the advantages of having the administrator of vocational education as high up in the organizational chart as possible.

4. Describe six positions, other than teacher, that may be held by those who possess backgrounds in trade, industrial, and technical education.

5. Assume you aspire to the position of Apprentice Coordinator. Write a job description for this position which includes those aspects you feel important.

SOURCE MATERIALS

1. *The Ohio Plan of Professional Services.* Columbus, Ohio: Trade and Industrial Education Service, Division of Vocational Education, State Department of Education, 1952.

2. U.S. Office of Education. *Organization and Operation of a Local Program of Vocational Education.* Distributed by the Instructional Laboratory, Trade and Industrial Education Service, The Ohio State University, Columbus, Ohio, 1968.

Chapter 7 LABOR, MANAGEMENT, AND COMMUNITY RELATIONS

One of the most important positions in any educational institution, in terms of community relations, is the person in charge of the trade, industrial, and technical education program. This individual, supported by his staff, can often make the difference in securing adequate support for the total school in cases where bond or operating levees must be voted on. This is particularly true for school systems or districts in which there is a strong industrial base. It is the industrial-related staff of the school that has frequent and continuous contact with industry and the work force in the community that makes the difference between good and poor community relations. For within this industrial sector is found representation of a sizeable part of the community power structure in most communities.

This chapter will deal with the specific relationships which trade, industrial, and technical education staff should have with groups and agencies outside of the school for the benefit of the school and the youth and adults it serves.

Obviously it is not possible to be all-inclusive in terms of the individuals or groups with whom the school staff should interact. However, an attempt will be made to identify the more important ones.

Advisory Committees

Advisory committees are the vehicles whereby business, industry, government, and service organizations can have an active input in planning and decision making at every level. At local levels, they have long been a part of the educational scene. One can examine the history of advisory committees and find their origins forming in the guilds during the Middle Ages and maturing in the apprenticeship movement in the beginning of this century (American Vocational Association 1969).

Trade and industrial educators have led the way among educators in their utilization of advisory committees. This has been the result of their close relationship with industry and their dependence upon the industrial sector for assistance in all phases of the program. The fact that many instructors and much of the leadership in trade and industrial education have strong ties with industry because of their experience as former employees in industry has strengthened this school-industry relationship resulting in the continued use of advisory committees.

Today citizen involvement is becoming very common in education. Advisory committees provide a means of obtaining significant suggestions or recommendations. School administrators have found that citizens can provide valuable assistance in determining the need for curriculum changes; in securing financial support for expansion and improvement of the school; in evaluating educational programs; and in dealing with many other problems facing educators.

Advisory committees exist on all the various levels of decision making and with various degrees of statutory authority. *Webster's New World Dictionary* defines "advise" as to "offer as advice" or "to inform." As such, activities of advisory committees are performed under different circumstances and from a different rationale at each level.

NATIONAL ADVISORY COUNCIL ON VOCATIONAL EDUCATION

The National Council was created by the Vocational Education Amendments of 1968, but two National Advisory Groups of consultants led the way for its establishment. The President's Panel of Consultants on Vocational Education was appointed by President Kennedy in 1961 and was commonly referred to as the Willis Commission (named after its chairman Benjamin Willis, former Chicago Superintendent of Schools). Its report, *Education For A Changing World of Work,* provided a framework for the Vocational Education Act of 1963. As stipulated in the 1963 Act, another group, the Essex Commission (named after Martin Essex, State Superintendent for Ohio), transmitted its report, *Vocational Education: The Bridge*

Between Man and His Work, on December 11, 1967, and its recommendations were incorporated in the Vocational Education Amendments of 1968.

The 1968 Act requires this national council to meet at least four times a year, advise the U.S. Commissioner of Education concerning the effectiveness and administration of new vocational education programs that are mandated by legislation, and submit annual reports and recommendations to the Secretary of Health, Education and Welfare for transmittal to the Congress. The twenty-one-member council is also authorized to conduct independent evaluations of programs and distribute the results.

STATE ADVISORY COUNCILS ON VOCATIONAL EDUCATION

The 1968 Amendments called for the establishment of State Advisory Councils for any state desiring to receive federal funds administered under this act. Section 104 of Part A labels their specific responsibilities:

> (B) advise the State Board on the development of and policy matters arising in the administration of the State Plan submitted pursuant to Part B of this title, including the preparation of long-range and annual program plans pursuant to paragraphs (4) and (5) of Section 123(a);
>
> (C) evaluate vocational education programs, services, and activities assisted under this title, and publish and distribute the results thereof; and
>
> (D) prepare and submit through the State Board to the Commissioner and to the National Council an annual evaluation report, accompanied by such additional comments of the State Board as the State Board deems appropriate, which (i) evaluates the effectiveness of vocational education programs, services, and activities carried out in the year under review in meeting the program objectives set forth in the long-range program plan and the annual program plan provided for in paragraphs (4) and (5) of Section 123(a), and (ii) recommends such changes in such programs, services, and activities as may be warranted by the evaluation.

To assure their independence, federal funds were made available to hire staff and make the necessary evaluations and studies. At least once a year, the State Advisory Council must provide the general public the opportunity to express its views on vocational education by holding a public hearing.

While the State Advisory Council is a somewhat new addition within the policy recommending structure of vocational education, it should not be inferred that the use of occupational-related advisory committees has been neglected at the state level nor that they have been replaced by the State Advisory Council. A number of states have utilized a statewide committee to advise on the total trade, industrial, and technical programs in the state; and even more common state committees to deal with a single occupational area such as electronics, machine trades, and automotive trades or the health occupations have been used throughout the years.

LOCAL ADVISORY COMMITTEES

The majority of advisory committees falls under this third category as defined by Samuel M. Burt:

> It is estimated that over 100,000 business and industry leaders throughout the United States are voluntarily serving on some 20,000 advisory committees established by secondary and post-secondary schools to assist in the development of vocational and technical education programs. In Wisconsin alone there are over 4,000 representatives of management and labor on the advisory committees of local and area vocational schools and technical institutes. Both the Los Angeles Trade-Technical College and Denver's Opportunity School have over 600 industry representatives on their advisory committees (Burt 1967).

The use of local advisory committees in vocational education has always been strongly encouraged but has been on somewhat of a voluntary basis. A recent survey by the American Vocational Association shows that thirty-four states stipulate the use of local advisory committees, and fifteen states, while not stipulating their use, recommend their utilization.

In May, 1969, the American Vocational Association contacted the state directors of vocational education and asked if their states stipulated the use of local advisory committees (stipulated being defined as called for by the State Plan). As early as 1913, Indiana law contained the following provision:

> Boards of education or township trustees administering approved vocational schools and departments for industrial, agricultural, or domestic science education shall, under a scheme to be approved by the state board of education, appoint an advisory committee composed of members representing local trades, industries and occupations (Acts 1913—Indiana).

Advisory committees, especially on the local level, vary in type and purpose and are known by a variety of names. A common and accepted way of categorizing advisory committees is the following:

1. General advisory committees

2. Occupational or craft advisory committees

3. Joint apprenticeship committees

General advisory committees may serve an area vocational center, a community or junior college, an entire school system, or a single school within the school system. As can be deduced from their name, general advisory committees are concerned with the total educational program of a district, a school, or a major program segment. Community and public relations, labor market requirements, and long-range goals are all concerns of this type of committee.

Occupational or craft advisory committees serve a single occupational area in a given school, a given school system, or sometimes in an entire state. The benefits accrued from such a committee are obvious. Information flow in the work world is a necessity for any effective vocational or technical program. As Riendeau puts it:

> The manpower needs of industry call for a long look at the work force of the future. These employment patterns signal a change in occupational education programs. Lines of communication must be maintained by schools and colleges with the industries which they seek to serve. Team work by the educational institutions and the sources of employment, through the medium of advisory committees is imperative if these changes are to be met (Riendeau 1967, p. 9).

The final classification of local advisory committees is the joint apprenticeship committee. It functions in a dual role in that it is the committee that actually is responsible for the administration of the apprenticeship program in a given occupation. Apprentices are often indentured to this committee. The committee is responsible for apprentice selection, placement with an employer, the supervision of their on-the-job training through the agreement or indenture, advice regarding the related instruction, evaluation of their training progress, and recommendation throughout the program (which is frequently given as part of the adult vocational offering) of apprentice advancement through wage increase.

The role of the joint apprenticeship committee in helping the school provide related instruction for apprenticeship is a most important one. Here the joint apprenticeship committee serves as an occupational or craft advisory committee to the school in matters related to providing an effective instruction program.

While previous discussion has had much to do with what is similar among advisory committees, what follows describes some of the functions for which these committees may be utilized. It is noteworthy that various committees may be in varying stages of implementing these activities.

The following list is representative of some of the functions served by advisory committees:

1. Assisting the school/district administration in interpreting developments in the economy and therefore the educational needs of the community to be served;

2. Assisting the school with community surveys by helping to determine what data is to be gathered and by gaining community support for such surveys;

3. Developing community support and understanding of the educational program of the school district;

4. Playing an important public relations role by representing and informing the business community;

5. Offering encouragement and aid to instructors to help them relate instruction to the particular occupational needs of the community;

6. Involving the resources of the committee members to identify potential teachers for quality vocational-technical programs;

7. Recommending and helping to establish local training standards;

8. Providing financial assistance in the form of scholarships, awards, equipment, and supplies;

9. Providing the technical expertise in teacher, facility, and equipment selection;

10. Assisting in placement of graduates of the programs.

Labor Organizations

Organized labor has played a key role in the growth and direction of trade, industrial, and technical programs in our nation. This is not to depreciate the support and assistance from individuals or occupational groups who are not a part of the union movement. In general, however, unorganized groups have not had the impact that is possible through a group that is organized at least in part so that its members might present a collective voice. Trade, industrial, and technical educators, as a group among educators, are certainly most knowledgeable of the past and potential contributions to educational programs by organized labor, since many members of the staff have been members of industrial or trade unions. However, for those persons preparing to become trade, industrial, or technical teachers who have not had that experience, it seems appropriate to provide in this chapter some background of the organized labor movement, its present status, and suggestions for developing a closer working partnership.

THE IMPORTANCE OF ORGANIZED LABOR

The organized labor movement is a very substantial economic and political body in our society. A large percentage of Americans subscribe to its principles and are dues-paying members. Both political parties are concerned with the support of organized labor and considerable time is spent at both the federal and state levels on legislation directly affecting unions. While the overriding purpose of labor unions is to improve the working conditions and raise the living standards of its members, the movement's political, social, and economic influence extends far beyond its membership. In fact, organized labor greatly influences many aspects of the American way of life.

The worker has progressed through history rather dramatically in his status in society. In Roman times the worker was a slave; his master, a free citizen. In feudal times the worker was a serf; his master, a lord. At present it can be said the worker is a free man. He does not in any way belong to his employer. He works for his employer, often under an agreement or a contract. It has only been in the last 300 years (depending upon the country) that political changes took place that made men free and equal before the law, which in turn brought changes in the legal and theoretical bases of the employment relationship. Once the worker became a free man, he was free to accept or reject; the employer likewise was free to spell out the conditions and the expectations of the employment. This employment contract became enforceable by law.

In this time of collective agreement it seems unusual to talk about an individual employment contract, since through collective bargaining most contracts arc for a group of individuals. However, in the case of apprentices, apprentice agreements are still on an individual basis. This represents one of the last vestiges of an individual employer-employee contract that is in common use today. The limitations of an individual bargaining with an employer are quite obvious. The employer owns the materials, machinery, or tools, while the worker owns nothing and has little influence except through his physical strength or the individual skills that he has learned. The employer has training and experience in handling sums of money, keeping records, accounting, and negotiating, while the worker has no such skills. It is obvious that the outcome of the individual employment contract between two free but unequal partners usually does not result in the employee faring too well.

The history of the labor movement is extremely interesting, and as trade, industrial, and technical educators you will wish to delve further into this topic. Even those most critical of the labor movement will admit that through organized labor the working man has gained social stature, dignity, and a wage level which has contributed greatly to his general well-being.

A healthy struggle continues to persist at both state and federal levels relating to labor laws and regulations designed to bring some balance in the bargaining powers between employers and employees. Historically, the principles of organized labor and collective bargaining are related primarily to manufacturing and other industrial pursuits. However, today they are being applied more broadly in terms of occupations and occupational groupings in which collective bargaining is being exercised. The fact that teachers and other public employees are coming under bargaining arrangements in increasing numbers is perhaps the most dramatic element of labor unions and collective bargaining of this decade.

UNION PURPOSES

In this discussion we are concerned primarily with industrial-type unions. While the AFL-CIO (American Federation of Labor, and Congress of Industrial Organization) does not represent in its membership all the industrial-type unions, it seems appropriate to use it as the largest and perhaps most representative of the union organizations.

The present purposes of the AFL-CIO include and reflect the general purposes which unions have had through history. However, as may be suspected, its purposes have been broadened through time. The concept of collective bargaining for "improved wages, hours, and working conditions" is listed first in the AFL-CIO constitution. This was a central purpose of unions historically and it tends to remain so today. However, many other purposes have been included. The purposes of the AFL-CIO constitution are listed as follows:

> To aid workers in securing improved wages, hours, and working conditions with due regard for the autonomy, integrity, and jurisdiction of affiliated unions.

> To aid and assist affiliated unions in extending the benefits of mutual assistance and collective bargaining to workers and to promote the organization of the unorganized into unions of their own choosing for their mutual aid, protection, and advancement, giving recognition to the principle that both craft and industrial unions are appropriate, equal, and necessary as methods of union organization.

> To affiliate national and international unions with this Federation and to establish such unions; to form organizing committees and directly affiliated local unions and to secure their affiliation to appropriate national and international unions affiliated with or chartered by the Federation; to establish, assist, and promote state and local central bodies composed of local unions of all affiliated organizations and directly affiliated local unions; to establish and assist trade departments composed of affiliated national and international unions and organizing committees.

> To encourage all workers without regard to race, creed, color, national origin, or ancestry to share equally in the full benefits of union organization.

> To secure legislation which will safeguard and promote the principle of free collective bargaining, the rights of workers, farmers, and consumers,

and the security and welfare of all the people, and to oppose legislation inimical to these objectives.

To protect and strengthen our democratic institutions, to secure full recognition and enjoyment of the rights and liberties to which we are justly entitled, and to preserve and perpetuate the cherished tradition of our democracy.

To give constructive aid in promoting the cause of peace and freedom in the world and to aid, assist, and cooperate with free and democratic labor movements throughout the world.

To preserve and maintain the integrity of each affiliated union in the organization to the end that each affiliate shall respect the established bargaining relationships of every other affiliate and that each affiliate shall refrain from raiding the established bargaining relationship of any other affiliate and, at the same time, to encourage the elimination of conflicting and duplicating organizations and jurisdictions through the process of voluntary agreement or voluntary merger in consultation with the appropriate officials of the Federation, to preserve, subject to the foregoing, the organizing jurisdiction of each affiliate.

To aid and encourage the sale and use of union-made goods and union services through the use of the union label and other symbols; to promote the labor press and other means of furthering the education of the labor movements.

To protect the labor movement from any and all corrupt influences and from the undermining efforts of communist agencies and all others who are opposed to the basic principles of our democracy and free and democratic unionism.

To safeguard the democratic character of the labor movement and to protect the autonomy of each affiliated national and international union.

While preserving the independence of the labor movements from political control, to encourage workers to register and vote, to exercise their full rights and responsibilities of citizenship, and to perform their rightful part in the political life of the community, state, and nation.

STRUCTURE OF AFL-CIO

Figure 7-1 shows the structural organization of the AFL-CIO. It is made up of more than 100 national and international unions which in turn have more than 60,000 local unions. The combined membership as of January 1, 1972, was 13,600,000 workers. In addition to the national and international unions, the AFL-CIO has state and city central bodies and trade and industrial departments. There are 50 state central bodies composed of and supported by local unions in their particular state.

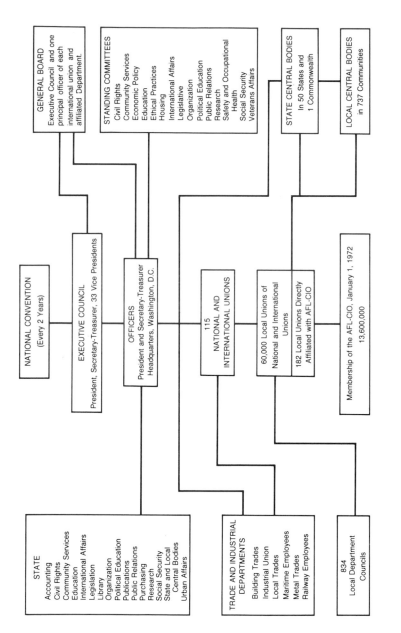

FIGURE 7-1

STRUCTURAL ORGANIZATION OF THE AFL-CIO

Basic policies of the AFL-CIO are set by its convention, which is its highest governing body. The convention meets every two years, although a special convention may be called at any time to consider a particular problem. Each national and international union is entitled to send delegates to the convention, its number being determined by the size of the union. The Executive Council serves as the governing body between conventions.

Although the national and international union has been presented first, the basic and most important unit is the local union. Local unions obviously are where the dues-paying members exist to support the district, state, and national bodies.

Local unions elect officers to administer their affairs and are somewhat independent organizations. A business agent is one who usually works full-time on union affairs, and, as his title implies, he carries on the routine business of the union, coordinates the work of the officers of the various committees, and supervises employees hired directly by the union.

As professionals in trade, industrial, and technical education, you will want to become acquainted with the unions in your district or city and with the leadership of these unions. You will not only gain considerable personal satisfaction from these new acquaintances, but they are highly essential for the conduct of efficient or effective programs. While you may have some relationship with union representatives as members of advisory committees, it is important that you relate in a much broader way and become known by the union leaders. The trade, industrial, and technical program is primarily for the purpose of educating potential workers, therefore these workers, as represented by organized labor, have the potential to be of considerable assistance to you in your program, whether you are concerned with a program for a single occupation or a range of occupations in the trade, industrial, and technical area.

Employers

Earlier in this chapter the desirability of trade, industrial, and technical educators working with advisory committees and labor groups was pointed out. It is obvious that employers and employer groups are also extremely important to your program. As a teacher in a specific occupational area you should, as soon as possible after becoming employed, get to know as many of the employers of persons in the occupations for which you are preparing as possible. Preferably, this would be done through actual visitations to their places of business. However, this may not be possible. The important thing, however, is to identify such employers and develop some plan to get to know many of them personally and to establish a climate through which dialogue related to your program may continue.

Administrative and supervisory personnel should place high on their priority of activities time for visitation and interaction with industrial employer representatives. Industrial leaders are usually anxious to become involved and to assist in school programs. Often, however, they are not sure what they can do or contribute. Also, they are quite hesitant at being aggressive in making the initial contact with the school. School personnel should take the lead to become acquainted and to involve them with the school. In the day-to-day pressures of operating a school, program, or individual class, meaningful contact with employers often is not given the priority it deserves. The employer segment of any community is not only central to the development and support of the vocational program but to the total educational program as well. Thus support of the total school program by the employer segment may result from their knowledge and perhaps involvement with the vocational program. As a vocational educator you need to know what employers expect of you, your program, and the school. In turn, employers are often willing to assist you to get the job done.

In most communities there are employer organizations with whom school personnel should consider relating. While it is not possible to mention all of them, several will serve as examples. Among the most important in many areas is the Chamber of Commerce, which has as part of its organization of structure a manufacturers or industrial division. Most of the industrial-type businesses will hold membership in an active Chamber of Commerce. While these local Chambers are very much autonomous from the state or national organization and therefore may vary greatly in their activities, many will have a committee on education and, in fact, may have education or training as one of their highlighted concerns. Examples across the nation are almost limitless in ways that Chambers of Commerce have contributed to vocational education which obviously make this organization an important one with which to become acquainted.

An industrial-related personnel club or personnel directors organization is found in many areas. Often, courtesy memberships are available to vocational education personnel. Whether through membership or some less formal arrangement, such organizations are usually anxious to become better acquainted with the vocational education program and to support it.

Automotive dealers' organizations are examples of an organization related to a particular occupational area. The involvement of this organization has been found to be extremely beneficial in automotive programs in identifying instructional staff, securing equipment, assisting in curriculum content, and in placing students on a cooperative basis and in full-time employment. It may be found that other parallel organizations exist in a community related to other occupational groups.

Other Community Involvement

Instructors in trade, industrial, and technical education should not be unaware of the potential for their programs through their contact with groups other than those of a strictly industrial nature. Membership in a service club, for example, provides the opportunity for meaningful dialogue with a broader range of community leaders. The technical institute director who is aware of the benefits of community involvement will encourage his staff members to participate in community groups as a way of increasing, on a broad base, understanding of his school and its mission. Staff will find that such involvement adds greatly to their community understanding and satisfaction; and the important outcome to the school is a greatly increased interest, involvement, and understanding of the school which affects actual monetary support and enrollment.

Summary

Success as a trade, industrial, or technical educator will depend to a large measure on your ability to work effectively with community groups and individuals. One of these groups will be the occupational or craft advisory committee for the particular occupational area in which you are involved. Since in most cases your students will become members of unions, it is important that you work closely with the organized labor group in the occupation or occupations for which you are training.

Likewise, it will be important to have frequent contact with employer and employee groups. While trade, industrial, and technical educators (as compared to other faculty in the school) will be uniquely related to industrial, labor, and employer groups, advantage should be taken of opportunities to participate in groups representing a broader segment of the community.

QUESTIONS AND ACTIVITIES

1. What types of advisory committees does your school or the school in which you expect to be employed have?

2. What are the key functions of each of the committees?

3. Specifically, what responsibilities and relationships do you presently have or expect to have with advisory committees?

4. What is the organizational structure of the union which is most closely related to your vocational or technical field?

5. What are ways in which you can effectively involve organized labor in your program or school?

6. What employer groups do you consider most important to your occupational area? In what ways are they important?

7. What plans do you have to work with employer groups?

SOURCE MATERIALS

1. *Acts of 1913-Indiana.* Chapter 24, Section 9.

2. American Vocational Association. *The Advisory Committee and Vocational Education.* Washington, D.C.: 1969.

3. Burt, Samuel M. *Industry and Vocational-Technical Education.* New York: McGraw-Hill Book Company, 1967.

4. *Education for a Changing World of Work.* Report of the Panel of Consultants on Vocational Education, U.S. Department of Health, Education and Welfare. Washington, D.C.: U.S. Government Printing Office, 1963.

5. Riendeau, Albert J. *The Role of the Advisory Committee in Occupational Education in Junior Colleges.* Washington, D.C.: American Association of Junior Colleges, 1967.

6. Strong, Merle E. *Industrial, Labor, and Community Relations.* Albany, New York: Delmar Publishers, 1969.

7. U.S. Department of Health, Education and Welfare. *Education for a Changing World of Work,* OE-80021. Washington, D.C.: U.S. Government Printing Office, 1963.

8. *Vocational Education: The Bridge Between Man and His Work.* Summary and Recommendations adapted from the General Report of the Advisory Council on Vocational Education, Superintendent of Documents. Washington, D.C.: U.S. Government Printing Office, 1968.

Chapter 8 GUIDANCE AND COUNSELING: PLACEMENT AND FOLLOW-UP

A critical need in trade, industrial, and technical education today is that of guidance and counseling placement and follow-up. Those involved in trade, industrial, and technical education must understand their role in this all-important function. It is the purpose of this chapter to review some of the theory behind guidance and counseling; to suggest several practical approaches to the problem; and to explore some techniques used to follow-up graduates.

The bridge between the functions of guidance counseling and vocational education has long been established. Vocational education first issued a challenge to guidance counselors to work cooperatively in the interests of those to be served by vocational education through the provisions for occupational information and guidance contained in the 1938 version of the George-Dean Act. Additional vocational education support for guidance and counseling can be traced through numerous other pieces of legislation. This support is also exemplified in the development of career education, which in part attempts to integrate the goals and functions of guidance counseling and vocational education into our schools' curricula. Upon analysis, it is evident that a major source of the financial support for career education has emanated from vocational education funds.

The fact that guidance counseling services and vocational education are "partners in the career development of youth" is a theme which is interwo-

133

ven throughout this chapter. With the advent of the career education movement, educators are being asked to rethink their philosophies and refocus their efforts. As John Moullette indicates:

> Within this movement both opportunity and challenge confront vocational education and vocational educators. The opportunity exists in the form of helping to bring more relevant education to the students involved. The challenge lies in knowing our field better. To participate in this new era, it is absolutely essential that the vocational education movement identify its beliefs, understand its strengths, and make known its distinctive characteristics and contributions to the field of American public education. This calls for introspection, a hard look at our part of the educational field. It may require, on our part, the discharge of unfounded myths, and it may lead to new or strengthened philosophies, renewed efforts, and improved strategies for vocational education consistent with the dawning of the 21st Century (Moullette 1973, p. 3).

One aspect of such an introspection would be the study of the purposes of guidance and counseling in an effort to determine the roles of vocational education in such services. As a starting point, let us review and focus upon guidance counseling: its body of theory, its personnel, its services, and particularly placement and follow-up.

The Theory Behind Guidance and Counseling

To understand guidance and counseling, one must review the theory of career development. How do careers unfold? What is the process of career development? A considerable body of theoretical and empirical research has been conducted in recent years in an effort to increase the understanding of the nature of intellectual and vocational development. Such research has been conducted in various fields including vocational guidance, career development, manpower economics, and career education. Although no single career development theory has gained total acceptance (from an eclectic viewpoint), several theories combined help to explain much about the attitudes, knowledge, and skills which tend to facilitate or inhibit career development (Taylor 1972).

Numerous classifications of career development theory exist. There is a consensus at this time that we can distribute the theories among the following: trait-factor, sociological, personality, and developmental. Budke (1971) has used these four dimensions in his survey of the appropriate literature in this area. Although this chapter will not treat the various theories in depth, a synopsis provides a background from which to compare past, present, and future trends.

Self-Concept or Developmental.   Theories which possess a developmental emphasis are usually comprehensive in that they are concerned with the expressions of vocational behavior over a long time span. In addition, such theories tend to focus on the individual's picture of himself (self-concept), which, as one develops, is compared with one's image of the occupational world (Herr 1972). Therefore, when the individual develops self-concept theories, he views occupational choice as being composed of various comprised choices and adjustments (Taylor 1972). As one begins to mature and refine the self-concept and the image of the wide world, one attempts to achieve a satisfactory union between "what I am as a person" and one's chosen occupation.

Personality Theories.   A basic assumption of those who place the individual's personality as the focus for career development is that people choose occupations to satisfy needs. Therefore different personality structures reflect different need priorities which are satisfied through one's occupational choice. In addition, various theorists have categorized occupations on the basis of personality types which tend to gravitate towards certain occupations. For example, Holland (1966) has classified occupations according to the following: realistic, intellectual, social, conventional, enterprising, and artistic. Ultimately, personality theory attempts to underscore the individual's conscious or unconscious attempt to relate his personality to career development in his expression of the desire for individual involvement, expression of interests, and satisfaction of personal needs.

Trait-Factor.   The origins of this approach can be traced to the time of Frank Parsons in the early twentieth century when a primary decision facing most individuals was which occupation to enter. This decision was usually placed in a point-in-time frame. Basically, the process involves two dimensions: analysis of an individual's abilities, interests, etc.; and characteristics of occupations. Therefore, satisfaction with one's career choice is a function of the accuracy of individual assessment and the occupational opportunities available.

Sociological Theories.   This approach is posited on the notion that there exist numerous influences which affect an individual's career decision-making process. Circumstances such as chance, path of least resistance, state of economy, and one's environment often play a direct role in the individual's career choice. Although many such influences may be beyond the control of the individual, the theory does cite the development of strategies to effectively cope with one's environment as a major task in the decision-making process. Therefore the individual's impressions of desirable jobs reflect their exposure to occupations in a particular social class (Taylor 1972).

Unified and Composite Theories.   Many people fail to see individual career development as falling within a particular theory but rather view career development from various perspectives, including the dimensions of several theories. As Taylor states:

> Composite theories address themselves to the conflict among the various classifications of theories and suggest the possibility that there may be some truth in all of them. One theory may satisfactorily explain the behavior of one person but not another (Taylor 1972, p. 12).

Studies of career development theory are numerous. Probably one of the best known is that of Ginzberg et al. (1951). This study identified three stages of career choice and asserted that career choice is a process (frequently an irreversible one) that can be identified over periods of life. The first of these is called the *Fantasy* period which is concerned with childhood vocational interests—most of which are fairly unrealistic. The Fantasy period takes place from birth to age eleven and is essentially nonvocational but includes dreaming and playing. The second period is called *Tentative.* Beginning at or near ages eleven to twelve, the individual shows not only interest but capacity, value, and transition stages. During the interest stage the youth devotes his time and talents to certain areas which may border on careers. His capacities and potential capabilities become more apparent as do his values and concerns. It is during the Tentative period that interests, capacities, and values begin to blend and some sort of composite view starts to emerge. The third period in this theory is that of *Realism.* This period sees the individual coming to grips with his total being and realizing his potential and abilities. It is during the period of realism that vocational direction is implemented. Since findings indicate that the individual must begin active participation in the career development process early—even from the day of birth—the next ten to fifteen years are critical in terms of activities and experience that contribute to vocational choice.

Studies by Donald Super (1953, 1963) elaborate on the developmental periods that the Ginzberg group suggested. Super and his colleagues identified five stages of vocational development beginning at about age fourteen: crystallization, ages fourteen to seventeen; implementation, twenty-one to twenty-five; stabilization, twenty-five to thirty-five; and consolidation, thirty-five and older. Super did not study the first of the five stages, early childhood years, but concentrated on the more mature stages of career development. He emphasized that career development is not a "once and for all" choice and that there are career patterns in vocational development made through one's life.

John Holland (1968) has contributed to the study of individual characteristics and corresponding careers. His six types are identified as (1) *realistic* —essentially an aggressive, strong-minded individual who prefers problems of a concrete nature rather than abstract theory; (2) *investigative*—an individual who likes to think and who avoids interpersonal relationships and contacts; (3) *social*—one who likes to work with people, such as teachers and social workers; (4) *conventional*—one who concerns himself with order and rules and regulations; (5) *enterprising*—one having verbal skills and the desire to manipulate other people, and (6) *artistic*—one who seeks self-expression through creative and artistic media.

The various research reports in sum tell us:

1. Career development is a life-long process beginning with elementary school experiences and continuing through adulthood; therefore, teachers and staff at all grade levels and in all subject areas have a role to play.

2. Career growth is a sequential pattern of decision making.

3. Individuals' career development may be influenced by such factors as self-concept, personality-need patterns, environment, and circumstance.

4. Often the career preferences of adolescents are broad, undefined, and changeable.

5. As the individual matures, it is projected that his career preferences will become more differentiated, defined, and realistic.

6. Career development can be facilitated via educational programs and activities within the individual classroom.

7. Since individuals' career development is modifiable, it is important that the educational system be flexible to accommodate students' altered plans, and that it offer a variety of educational choices and opportunities.

8. Career development theory has direct implications for education, both in general and vocational areas and for guidance counseling in particular.

Recent writings and research indicate that the developmental, self-concept theory is the most appropriate conceptual approach to contemporary education efforts. The developmental approach to career choice depicts career development as a logical, systematic process consisting of discreet phases which can be incorporated into a comprehensive educational program.

An attempt to integrate such a developmental approach into educational programs is reflected in the Comprehensive Career Education Model being developed at the Center for Vocational and Technical Education at The Ohio State University. This model utilizes such dimensions as awareness, orientation, exploration, and preparation stages for program emphasis. In addition, the model summarizes a number of the desirable elements needed in a K–12 career education offering. In figure 8-1 it can be readily seen that the program must extend throughout the K–12 program. Moreover, it is anticipated that the K–6 level will emphasize the broad world of work, the man-made environment, technology, and the social contributions made by various occupational groups and professions. At the 7–9 level there should be an opportunity to systematically explore occupations; at grades 10–12 the emphasis should target on narrower career choices and the initiation of occupational preparation. It is hoped through this "overall" scheme that the separate curricula of vocational education and academic education will diminish and the concept of career education will emerge.

The career education concept finds as one of its strengths career development theory. Since the career education concept begins in kindergarten, it parallels the accepted tenets of developmental theory. It attempts to allow individuals to become aware of their interests, aptitudes, and skills within their elementary school experiences. As the individual matures, more intensive exploration can take place and in the latter years of secondary education some specialization for those who reach this level of career choice can be provided. For others, the postsecondary years will constitute such specialization, and for still others, changes or multiple and secondary careers will be recognized and will need mastery. Career development, then, becomes a lifelong process.

GUIDANCE AND COUNSELING

One of the most criticized areas of education today is that of guidance and counseling. Those who make up this discipline are blamed for numerous ills of the educational enterprise when in fact they are often, by convenience or circumstance, mere pawns in the hands of school administrators. Guidance and counseling personnel are frequently given responsibilities that extend far beyond their primary roles and then are blamed for various shortcomings extending from not being able to place graduates into colleges of their first choices to not responding to the needs of school dropouts and the like. In addition, they often are delegated routine tasks of taking daily attendance, managing the office personnel, ordering books and supplies, and other such routines. Considering that the average student to counselor ratio ranges from 400–500 to one, when all is said and done, guidance personnel are inundated with far too many tasks and are often placed in an almost impossible situation.*

*A study by Kaufman et al., 1967, indicated that the typical counselor was involved 10 percent of the time in keeping records, 50 percent in conducting interviews, 8 percent in administering tests, 2 percent in handling disciplinary problems, 19 percent in consulting with teachers, and 11 percent in other general activities. The average ratio was 441 students to one counselor in the senior high school, and 497 to one in the junior high school (pp. 4–13).

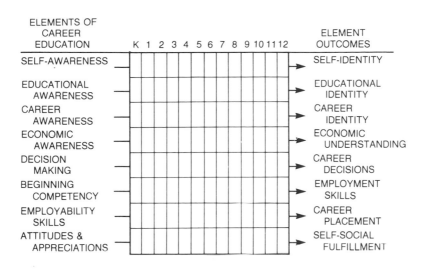

FIGURE 8-1

EXPERIENCES TO BE CONSIDERED AT ALL GRADE LEVELS WITH
SPECIFIED OUTCOMES.

Many of the criticisms of guidance and counseling have a basis of truth
in that too frequently guidance personnel have been college-oriented and
have de-emphasized occupational counseling. The fact that too many counselors have had *no* first hand occupational experience, view themselves as
pseudopsychologists, and do not understand the work ethic, prevents them
from coming to grips with their real role: that of assisting individuals in
their own career development. As the Honorable Kenneth McKay, Jr.,
Florida House of Representatives, put it:

> . . . We discovered two or three things that we didn't like about counseling.
> *One,* there weren't enough counselors. *Two,* the ones that were there were
> in the wrong place. *Three,* they were doing the wrong thing.

> Let me give you an idea of what it was like in Florida. We had 200
> elementary school counselors for 800,000 students. That's a ratio of 1 to
> 4,000. In the secondary area, we had 1,450 counselors for 650,000. Then
> they asked, "Well, where are they?" We discovered that just like voca-
> tional programs, they are concentrated in the tenth grade and up, which
> once again presents an ironic situation. The people who need the counsel-
> ing weren't there so it certainly makes the counselors' life easier and also
> makes them available for the other things that they are given to do in the
> school system like being the disciplinarian, and a few other things. They
> were in the wrong place; and they perceived their role as being to counsel

those who were going to graduate and, primarily, those who were going to go on to college.

They are educated wrong. In Florida, I do not know how it is in other states, counseling is offered as a course at a graduate level only. That is to say you can take it as a master's and doctor's degree program but you can't take it at the baccalaureate level. You can't take even a paraprofessional course at the junior college level. So what is the profile of the typical counselor being graduated in Florida, we ask ourselves. Well, he has 12 years of high school—public schools, primarily academic; four years of baccalaureate work, primarily academic. In fact, it probably is solely academic if he means to go under a graduate program because he's got to compete scholastically to get in. And then he has two years at least at the graduate level. (McKay 1971).

What Florida did about this situation was to create the "Occupational Specialist." School districts may hire individuals who are without academic attainment but who have the ability to relate to the needs of the students in a particular community. Other factors taken into account for this paraprofessional are: work experience, moral character, compassion, and many things that are considered necessary for the individual to function as an occupational specialist. The pay in Florida for such employees is at the same rate as a beginning teacher.

Another research effort which underlies the unmet needs of students was conducted by the Center for Vocational and Technical Education at The Ohio State University. The survey was designed to:

(1) describe the present status of guidance in public secondary schools in terms of services, functions of counselors, and student contact; (2) provide a reference point for future surveys; (3) compare the viewpoints of school administrators, counselors, teachers, students, and parents on guidance issues; (4) compare guidance programs by type of secondary school; (5) identify needed changes in the professional education of the counselor; and (6) identify needed research and program planning (Campbell 1968).

The study surveyed six types of public secondary schools, ranging from urban comprehensive to rural general academic. In addition, principals, counselors, teachers, parents, and students representing 353 schools from 48 states returned a total of 6,484 completed questionnaires. Some of their findings were the following:

1. When asked in which services they felt they could assist counselors, the majority of teachers saw themselves as being able to assist students with their course selection and choice of occupation.

2. Students understood that "learning about the world of work" was a most needed service within the schools.

3. Both students and parents reported that teaching about the world of work was one of the least available and most needed services in the schools.

4. Significant individuals and groups within schools held different opinions about such matters as the proper goals of the guidance program, the immediate needs to be met, the proper roles of participants, and the resources available and needed.

These findings coupled with the previously mentioned counselor "constraints" indicate that teachers have *direct* involvement in the guidance counseling function. Table 8-1 identifies specific roles teachers could play in the guidance service.

Another example of the "partnerships" between guidance-counseling and vocational education in action is the "capstone" concept utilized in Wisconsin's secondary level vocational education programs. The following basic guidelines are utilized by each school in analyzing its developmental position relative to the implementation of vocational programs:

1. Analysis of employment opportunities for high school graduates.

2. Development and/or implementation of vocational guidance that will lead qualified and interested students into the respective programs.

3. Courses which provide job competency or which lead into advanced post-high school programs must be identified and set up.

4. Teachers must be qualified and licensed.

TABLE 8-1

CAREER GUIDANCE RESPONSIBILITY ASSIGNMENT: SOME EXAMPLES

	Counselors	Teachers
Indirect Functions	Career guidance curriculum planning Teacher and parent consultation Inservice training programs	Career curriculum for basic education Parent-teacher conferences Development of instructional materials
Shared Functions	Joint vocational education instructor-counselor-student planning/contracting Joint employer-vocational education instructor-counselor planning Testing and evaluation	Joint teacher-counselor-student planning/contracting Team teaching of career concepts/units Joint teacher-parent student planning/contracting
Direct Functions	Individual counseling Group instruction/orientation Group counseling	Individualized instruction Classroom and group instruction Student organization and club

SOURCE: Norman C. Gysbers and Earl J. Moore, "Career Guidance: Program Content and Staff Responsibilities," *American Vocational Association Journal,* March, 1972, p. 7.

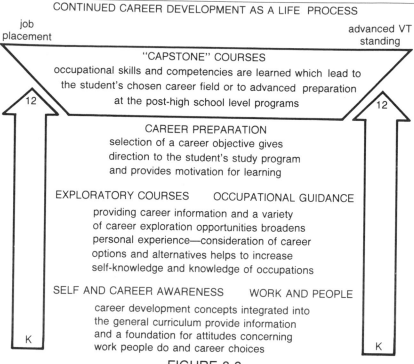

FIGURE 8-2

THE "CAPSTONE CONCEPT" WITHIN THE K–12 SYSTEM

5. Assistance in obtaining jobs must be available to students who complete the programs.

6. Provision must be made for follow-up of students as part of a continuous evaluation of the program in terms of job performance of graduates and success in meeting demands of employment markets (Strong 1970).

Figure 8-2 is a schematic representation of the "capstone" concept.
What is being said is that guidance and counseling personnel, as their jobs are presently structured, need help—the help of the total education profession—if they are to function as intended. Possibly too much is expected of counselors and too little assistance is obtained from teachers in general in the attempt to help students in their career development. The ability to relate to students is every teacher's responsibility; and if anyone thinks otherwise, he should try to remember which teachers had impact on *his* career choice. Ineffectual teacher-student relationships are what the education profession must try to prevent through formalized guidance and counseling and the individual classroom teacher.

ACTIVITIES

As a professional, the trade, industrial, and technical educator can take part in—and in some cases be responsible for—a multitude of guidance activities such as the the following.

- Plan school-wide program of guidance for course selection; start with what now exists.
- Hold special faculty meeting:
  - explain plans and schedules
  - distribute descriptive information
  - identify staff responsibilities
- Publicize meeting of students who may be interested in vocational education. Use:
  - bulletin board
  - school paper
  - local paper
  - exhibits
- Conduct assembly for all students considering enrolling in a vocational course.
  - explain program (what it is, who can profit, job outlets, fact that program is terminal but college is possible if plans change, differences and similarities between vocational education and other courses, club programs, etc.).
  - might use panel of vocational students or grads
  - distribute descriptive materials for take-home.
  - use appropriate visual aids.
  - provide time for discussion.
- Utilize regular group guidance programs. If school has a guidance course, guidance units in other courses, or a homeroom guidance program, course selection should become a topic for consideration. Activities listed elsewhere in this outline may be included in the regular group guidance program, if there is one.
- Develop Student Information.
  - utilize cumulative records in compiling student data.
  - have all interested students complete a personal appraisal form to study themselves in terms of educational and vocational choice.
  - administer an interest checklist or inventory.
  - have each complete a vocational planning questionnaire.
- Conduct "Vocational Education Visitation Day." Arrange for all students who *think* they may choose a vocational course to spend one day

in the program they are considering. Schedule no more "potential" students on any one day than present enrollees. Operate program "as usual" with time at end for discussion.

- Conduct field trips.
  Arrange for all potential vocational students to make a planned and guided visit to at least one employer's establishment to observe workers in the occupation they are considering.
- Conduct "Open House" or "Family Night" for potential students and/or their parents. Provide for:
  - explanation of program.
  - observation of classes in operation.
  - showing of appropriate visual aids.
  - discussion.
  - distribution of descriptive material to those who want it. (Should have reached parents at time of Student Assembly.)
  - opportunity for brief personal conference between parents and vocational teachers, principal, or counselor.
- Conduct individual counseling conferences for all students and/or parents who desire them.
  - publicize opportunities for conferences.
  - schedule interviews.
  - utilize all pupil data.
- Gear actual course scheduling into regular scheduling program of the school. Vocational teachers should be part of the faculty team responsible for the course selection and scheduling program. Provision should be made for faculty understanding of the objectives of vocational courses and the qualifications of students who can best profit by vocational training.

If more students sign up for a vocational course than can be accepted:
- all personal data on each applicant should be studied.
- individual counseling conferences should be arranged for all students whose choice seems to be at all questionable.
- teachers who know the student well should be consulted for clues to alternate programs.
- second choice courses should be considered.
- in certain cases (Vo. Ag., D.E., D.C.T.) the availability of opportunity for cooperative work experience will be one major factor to consider.
The practice of either accepting or rejecting those with the best scholastic record or the highest intelligence test score is *not* recommended. If possible, all decisions to change to a nonvocational course should be acceptable to the student and his parents.

- Vocational teachers may visit potential students at home to:
  - discuss program in more detail.
  - make preliminary decisions on project activities.
  - arrange cooperative job placement.
  - plan alternate program if necessary.

In other words, guidance and counseling is not a single person's job, but an integral part of the educational process. No greater reward can befall an educator than to be known for the impact he or she has had on the career development of a student.

PLACEMENT AND FOLLOW-UP

The lack of relevance in many of our educational programs is often defined as the void of any relationship between a student's school experiences and an identifiable *next step* beyond school. From another perspective, "the next step" can be viewed as an accountability tool to evaluate education at any level in terms of the extent to which students are prepared for, and are assisted in, taking the *next step*. Therefore, whether one emphasizes relevance or accountability as a rationale for the increased importance on placement and follow-up functions in our schools, it would be acknowledged by most that it must become a priority if we are to build a bridge between the *announced* purposes and the *actual* purposes of public education.

As we have seen with the other guidance counseling functions, vocational education teachers and staff members have a direct role in the placement and follow-up function in schools. As Bottoms and Matheny (1969) note:

> Guidance and vocational education must be merged if full value of such experiences is to be realized by the student. A team approach involving the counselor and other teachers, particularly the industrial arts teacher and the work experience coordinator, offers great potential for enhancing the career development of students.

Although much is said about the placement of graduates from trade, industrial, and technical education programs, documentation is scarce regarding the means by which this is accomplished. For example, the process of placing graduates in jobs often is left to the expertise of guidance and counseling personnel. Yet frequently counselors claim that placement is not one of their duties. This is often reflected in the absence of counselors' close articulation with business and industry as well as with the state employment service. The question then becomes, "How do graduates from trade, industrial, and technical education programs get placed in gainful wage-earning occupations?"

As near as can be determined at this time, placement of graduates is carried on in an informal, nonstructured manner involving the vocational teacher and his contacts with businessmen and employers. To some extent, advisory committees become involved in the placement process, but this is to the exclusion of guidance personnel because they are not usually involved with the operation of advisory committees. Through this more or less informal placement effort, the trade, industrial, and technical programs have been highly successful. According to the data gleaned over the years, placement of graduates has been one of the "hard data" figures that attests to the worth of these programs. For example, at one time and for almost forty years, the North Atlantic region, through its program specialist of the United States Office of Education Division of Vocational and Technical Education, carried on a yearly study of placement of graduates with its thirteen states (including the District of Columbia). The last of these studies was conducted relative to the June graduates of 1963 and indicated that 72 percent of those available from "all day" preparatory programs were employed in jobs related to their training. In contrast to the "all day" preparatory graduates, 90 percent of the cooperative program graduates were employed in job-related placement. Interestingly, girls showed a higher relationship between training and placement than did boys. The study of the 1963 graduates concluded, "These young people, primarily in the crucial 17–19 age group, not only have a diploma, but a salable skill—they have proved it by finding employment in occupations for which they were trained" (U.S. Office of Education 1964, p. 4).

Although the reporting of the placement effort for trade, industrial, and technical education graduates terminated (as a North Atlantic region effort) in 1963, several states have maintained the procedure through the years. One of these is Connecticut. In 1969, for example, Connecticut reported an overall vocational placement of 81 percent, a placement of 84 percent for trade and industrial, and 94 percent for technical graduates (Connecticut State Department of Education 1970).

At the time of the discontinuance of the North Atlantic Region placement studies it was the intent of the United States Office of Education to assume reporting of national placement figures. However, as is characteristic of most federal data systems, the reporting procedures lag far behind, and therefore when the information is released it is out of date. Placement data of this type is important as a measure of success or worth of trade, industrial, and technical offerings. The most important place to initiate placement data collection is not at the federal level but rather at the local level where the employment of graduates becomes the most meaningful.

A study (Schaefer and Kaufman 1971) indicates that approximately one out of two of all high school graduates, both female and male, are assisted by their schools in finding a job. This proportion is far too small when one considers the maximum effort that is put forth by guidance personnel to locate and place graduates into institutions of higher education. The role of guidance *must* include job placement if such personnel are to be looked upon as functional to the needs of all youth. The disproportionate amount of time that is typically devoted to the college-bound youth is a critical problem since the "next step" after termination of an educational program for nearly 60 percent of the nation's youth is work. According to Bottoms (1969, p. 2), this transition to the next step is too important to be left to chance:

> Activities provided by the school to facilitate the student's transition to *the next step* must be more than a simple matching of student with employer. Each student must be assisted in gaining those skills, attitudes, and understandings which will aid him in locating the most appropriate job. The school must assume responsibility for assisting a student in the clarification of his goals; providing him with knowledge about the labor market; helping him in evaluating his qualifications and abilities in terms of job opportunities; assisting him in developing the flexibility needed for adjusting to a fluctuating society; and, for many students, special assistance in adjusting to and retaining a job. Assisting each individual in making the best possible transition will require a total school effort on a fully organized basis.

In the case of follow-up of graduates from trade, industrial, and technical education programs, the lack of interest on the part of guidance personnel is even more apparent. Too few studies have been compiled to answer the question, "What happens to graduates three, five, and ten years later?" One exception to this is a study (Coe and Zanzalari 1964) which followed up vocational students from the Middlesex County Vocational Schools ten years after they had graduated. The purpose of the study was to find out the occupational, educational, marital, and armed service experiences of those who graduated in June 1953 through June 1963. Ninety-one percent responded to the brief questionnaire (See figure 8-3 for questionnaire).* Among the interesting findings were:

1. The percentage of trained graduates being placed in the trades was 81 percent in 1953. After 10 years, 60 percent of those available for employment were working at their trade.

2. The wage among male graduates on a hourly rate ranged from a low of $2.40 per hour to a high of $5.00 per hour. The mode was $3.00 per hour and the mean, $2.80 per hour.

3. Those employed in the trade had a turnover of 2.2 jobs while those not in the trade had an average turnover of 3.2 jobs.

*Another example of a follow-up questionnaire appears in Appendix C.

MIDDLESEX COUNTY VOCATIONAL AND TECHNICAL HIGH SCHOOLS
GRADUATE QUESTIONNAIRE

ANSWERS WILL BE KEPT CONFIDENTIAL   Date _____

Your Name: Mr., Miss, Mrs. _____
    If "Mrs." give your maiden name here: _____
Present Address _____ Telephone _____

1. Are you   A. __Single   C. __Divorced or Separated
           B. __Married   D. __Widowed (Check one of these)

      If married, how many children do you have? _____
      If married, year of marriage. _____

2. What trade did you study in school? _____

3. What are you doing now? (Check one or more)

    A. __Working for pay, full-time   G. __In Armed forces
    B. __Working for pay, part-time   H. __Not working; but looking
    C. __In school, full-time   I. __Not working; not looking
    D. __In school, part-time   J. __Other; (please describe)
    E. __Housewife   _____
    F. __In business for self   _____

4. Please list below any additional education you have had since leaving high school. (Check)

    A. __College or University   Graduate Yes __No __ Year _____
    B. __Business School   Graduate Yes __No __ Year _____
    C. __Correspondence Course   Graduate Yes __No __ Year _____
    D. __Evening School   Graduate Yes __No __ Year _____
    E. __Post Graduate High School Graduate Yes __No __ Year _____
    F. __Other _____

5. Please identify any institution shown in statement #4.

6. Please describe the jobs you have held since leaving high school:

Employer or firm	Title of Job	Date you Started	Months on Job	Approximate Weekly Salary

7. To what extent has your vocational and technical high school training helped you on the job?

    A. __A great deal   B. __Some   C. __Little or none   D. __Not certain

FIGURE 8-3

8. Have any specific high school courses or activities been of special value to you on your present job? (Check the blanks of those which have helped you.)

A. __English
B. __Mathematics
C. __Shop
D. __Science
E. __History

F. __Drawing and Art
G. __Student Government
H. __Student Activities
I. __Home Economics
J. __Other (Please specify)
_____

9. Which of the following helped you most in getting your first steady job after leaving high school? (Please check one or more)

A. __Parents or Relatives
B. __Friends
C. __Newspaper Ad
D. __Public Employment Agency

E. __School Placement Office
F. __My Own Efforts
G. __Other (Please specify)
_____

10. We would like to know how you rate the help your vocational and technical high school gave you on the following problems: (Please check the proper column for each item.)

PROBLEM	The High School Helped Me			
	A Great Deal	Some-what	Little or none	(I'm not certain)
A. Using your spare time				
B. Taking care of your health				
C. Taking part in community and civic affairs				
D. Marriage and family affairs				
E. Getting a job				
F. Getting along with other people				
G. Preparing for further education				
H. Understanding your abilities and interests				
I. Ability to read well				
J. Using good English				
K. Using mathematical skills				
L. Using your money wisely				
M. Conducting your business affairs				
N. Thinking through problems				

11. List the addresses of the homes in which you lived since leaving school (Number, Street, City, State, Length of time in house).

_____

_____

_____

_____

12. Please list your service experiences below:

Branch of Service	Dates	Highest Rank	Type of Work

13. Write below any suggestions you have concerning ways the Middlesex County Vocational and Technical High School could have helped you.

THAT'S ALL—AND THANK YOU FOR YOUR HELP AND COOPERATION

4. Approximately 25 percent of those working in the trade reached the foremen or supervisory category.

5. Graduates tended to live in the county after graduation. A total time of 88 percent of the possible time was lived in the county; 75 percent of the group lived their entire ten years in the county.

Obviously, follow-up studies such as this are useful in providing evidence and direction for future planning. Just how often they are undertaken and what role guidance personnel should assume in making them is a matter for consideration. Nevertheless, it would appear that the guidance staff should have an interest in such studies, and certainly the school can profit from the continuing involvement and interest of its graduates.

The data available indicate that the following principles might be considered in meeting the guidance needs of youth.

The Guidance Function Must Permeate the Entire School Environment.
Guidance can not be viewed as a function unique to the counselor and the guidance suite. Rather, it must involve all staff, as anything short of a total school commitment is likely to prove inadequate to the task of provid-

ing services and information to meet the varying needs of individual students. When one consults the following goals of guidance, it is clear that the active support of personnel, both within and without the school, is necessary for their attainment:

> (a) helping the student to view himself as a worthwhile person; (b) assisting the student to experience success in his own eyes; (c) assisting the school in providing *meaningful* experiences for *all* students; (d) helping the student to consider, understand, and either accept or reject the values of a work-oriented society; (e) assisting the student to develop an understanding and appreciation of his own talents and interests; (f) helping the student to make appropriate choices from the widest possible range of alternatives available; (g) helping the student to formulate plans for implementing decisions which he has made; and (h) helping the student to accept personal responsibility for such decisions (Bottoms 1969, p. 13).

Counselors Need More of the Training of Vocational Educators and Vocational Educators Need More of the Training of Counselors. Counselors often lack first-hand knowledge of the world of work yet possess guidance skills, whereas vocational educators who are well-informed of the realities of work often lack the skills required in the guidance process.

There Is a Need to Develop and Adopt Job Placement and Follow-Up Models in our Schools. So as to maximize the use of placement and follow-up resources, it is suggested that a cooperative job placement strategy be initiated in which teachers and guidance specialists share the responsibility for providing an organized and systematic job placement program. The job placement function would consist of four distinct phases in which *first,* individuals are assisted in assessing their interests and abilities; *second,* individuals are assisted in acquiring knowledge about occupations; *third,* a job is located, and entrance secured; and *fourth,* follow-through counseling is made available for individuals once placed on the job to assist them in retaining the job and in establishing plans for moving up the career ladder.

Summary

This chapter attempts to show the important role which guidance and counseling personnel can play in a school's program. Guidance is discussed in terms of self-concept, personality and careers, trait factors, and social system approaches. Career development theories, in terms of the periods of fantasy, tentativeness, and realism, are elaborated on. The guidance and counseling roles are discussed, and strengths and shortcomings reviewed. Suggestions are made as to how all teachers can help in the guidance function, and hints as to the value of placement and follow-up are given. Throughout, it is implied that guidance and counseling personnel are not being utilized as much as they should be, nor in the capacity in which they are most capable.

QUESTIONS AND ACTIVITIES

1. Discuss the theory of guidance and counseling and relate it to your own career development.

2. Visit a school's guidance department and determine the approach used by the personnel that make it up.

3. According to Holland's six types, how would you identify the group of students you teach?

4. What group guidance activity would you judge to be the most successful? Which two would you be willing to take part in?

5. Discuss the advantages and disadvantages of the Florida "occupational specialist."

SOURCE MATERIALS

1. Bottoms, Gene, and Matheny, Kenneth B. "Occupational Guidance, Counseling and Job Placement for Junior High and Secondary School Youth." Paper, Mimeograph. March, 1969.

2. Budke, Wesley E. *Review and Synthesis of Information On Occupational Exploratiion.* Columbus, Ohio: ERIC Clearinghouse, The Ohio State University, June, 1971.

3. Campbell, Robert E. *Vocational Guidance for Secondary Education.* Columbus, Ohio: The Center for Vocational and Technical Education, The Ohio State University, December 1968, p. ix.

4. Coe, Burr D., and Zanzalari, Henry J. *After Ten Years: A Ten Year Follow-up of Middlesex County Vocational and Technical High School Graduates.* New Brunswick, N.J.: Middlesex County Vocational and Technical High Schools, 1964.

5. Connecticut State Department of Education. *Graduate Follow-Up: Statistical Data on Connecticut Students Completing Vocational Programs in 1969.* Hartford, Conn.: Division of Vocational Education, 1970.

6. Ginzberg, E.; Ginzberg, S. W.; Axelrod, S.; Herma, J. L. *Occupational Choice: An Approach To a General Theory.* New York: Columbia University Press, 1951.

7.   Herr, Edwin L. *Review and Synthesis of Foundations for Career Education.* Columbus, Ohio: The Center for Vocational and Technical Education, The Ohio State University, March 1972, p. 58.

8.   Holland, John L. "Explorations of a Theory of Vocational Choice: VI. A Longitudinal Study Using a Sample of Typical College Students." *Journal of Applied Psychology Monograph Supplement* (1968): 52.

9.   ————. *The Psychology of Vocational Choice.* Waltham, Massachusetts: Blaisdell Publishing Co., 1966.

10. Kaufman, J. Jacob; Schaefer, Carl J.; Lewis, Morgan V.; Stevens, David W.; and House, Elaine W. *The Role of the Secondary Schools in the Preparation of Youth for Employment.* A comprehensive study of the vocational, academic, and general curricula. University Park, Pa.: Institute for Research on Human Resources, The Pennsylvania State University, 1967.

11. McKay, Jr., Kenneth. "Relationship of Trade and Industrial Educators to the State Legislative Process." *Contemporary Concepts in Trade and Industrial Education.* Washington, D.C.: American Vocational Association, 1971.

12. Moullette, John. "Career Education: Opportunity and Challenge for Vocational Education." Paper presented to California Directors of Vocational Education, Hollywood, California, May 18, 1973, p. 3.

13. Schaefer, Carl J., and Kaufman, Jacob J. *New Directions for Vocational Education.* Lexington, Massachusetts: Heath Lexington Books, 1971.

14. Strong, Merle E. *An Assessment of Wisconsin's Vocational and Technical Education Program.* Conducted for the Wisconsin Advisory Council on Vocational Education by the Cooperative Educational Research and Services Department of Educational Administration, the University of Wisconsin, Madison, 1970, pp. 21–22.

15. Super, D. E. "A Theory of Vocational Development." *American Psychologist* 8(1953): 185–190.

16. Super, D. E.; Starishevsky, R.; Matlin, N.; Jordaan, J. P. *Career Development: Self-Concept Theory.* New York: College Entrance Examination Board Research, Monograph No. 4, 1963.

17. Taylor, Robert E. "Perspectives on Career Education." Paper presented at the meeting of the Oregon Association of School Administrators, Corvallis, Oregon, March 30, 1972, p. 10.

18. U.S. Office of Education. *Follow-Up Study of 1963 Graduates: Trade and Industrial Programs in Public Vocational and Technical Schools.* Washington, D.C.: Division of Vocational and Technical Education, 1964.

Chapter 9 STAFF RECRUITMENT AND DEVELOPMENT

Trade, industrial, and technical education can not be any better than the personnel who staff its programs. If one accepts this proposition as self evident, the concern for staff recruitment and development takes on increasing emphasis. This chapter will provide some idea of the dimensions of staff recruitment and developments, spell out some areas needing attention, and suggest some solutions. In no way will it *provide* solutions; for solutions will only be realized when the personnel who make up trade, industrial, and technical education reach the decision to take seriously the problems of staff recruitment and development.

The United States Office of Education (1970) estimates that there are some 81,000 teachers employed in the trade, industrial, and technical education endeavor. This amounts to 43 percent of the total number of vocational teachers employed. The vast majority of these teachers are employed under some type of certification or credentialing process. This means most have met basic criteria set forth by a certification division of a state department of education. Such criteria usually includes the following:

high school graduation
high moral character
documented occupational experience (not necessarily demonstrated)
some teacher education (not necessarily a college degree)

154

Typically, those engaged in trade, industrial, and technical education can be described as follows (House 1970).

Age: 36–45

Teaching experience: 5 years

Occupational experience: 21 years

Marital status: Married

Family background: Second generation Americans and small families (two siblings or less)

Decision to become a teacher: Thought about it from one to three years; wife or friend had greatest influence

Position procurement: Through another vocational teacher; three or more applications made

Intergenerational mobility: The occupational status of first job was very similar to that of father's job. Upward mobility in job status as compared to father's job was significant

Education: More formal education than father

The House study (1970) summarizes the characteristics of the trade, industrial, and technical teacher as follows:

The skilled worker who aspires to become a teacher, whether his aspirations are translated into reality or not, appears to have certain characteristics which may not be shared with the totality of skilled workers.

Trade and industrial teachers, and those who hope to teach their skill to others, come from small families, in which they are most likely to be the youngest brother, only brother, or the only child. Once married, they tend to produce small families.

The occupational shift into teaching was made or considered when the subjects were in their late thirties or early forties. By that time, they had amassed a considerable amount of trade experience. (It must be emphasized that trade experience does not necessarily connote trade competency.) The decision to teach, which was reached a year or more prior to actual teaching or participation in the pre-service program, was often influenced by another person. This "other person" was most likely a friend, although the wife and former professor (or teacher) were also mentioned.

Those presently teaching had secured their jobs with little effort. Over half had been contacted by the school or heard about the opening through another vocational teacher.

All of the subjects had, in the first job, inherited their father's occupational status. In the course of their work cycle, all groups had been occupationally mobile in respect to their fathers.

The work cycle of all groups exhibited both intergenerational and intragenerational mobility. It may be said that teaching attracts those skilled workers who already have been occupationally mobile and, presumably, successful. Their work cycles—from first, to next to last, to last job—are characterized by a steady rise in occupational status.

The occupational classification of "teacher" represented a significant gain in socioeconomic status for the trade and industrial instructor. It was not until he became a teacher that his occupational status was greater than that of his wife or oldest brother. In contrast, the pre-service dropout had already attained, in his last job in a trade or industry, a status level which exceeded that of his wife or oldest brother.

After the first job, the importance of the father as a reference person appeared to diminish. Later in the work cycle, the wife, the oldest brother, and friends (who were not included in the present study) may be considered key reference persons.

As these skilled workers proceeded through their work cycles, they also acquired more education.

Staff Recruitment

The recruitment of staff for trade, industrial, and technical education is a continuing problem. Not only is it one of assuring adequate numbers to man the expanding shops and classrooms, but, more important, it is a problem of assuring competent functional staffing. It is a fact that even when new schools need to be completely staffed, there seems to be no problem of securing adequate applicants to fill the positions. That is to say, there are enough tradesmen and journeymen types who meet minimum qualifications and who want to be teachers. At times there are applicants who in many respects are overqualified (in terms of their paper credentials), with engineering and advanced degrees. The smart administrator is cautious of seemingly overqualified potential teachers in the recruitment process. The label *caveat emptor* ("let the buyer beware") has not been properly heeded, and in the haste of new staffing or re-staffing, many an incompetent individual has found his way into a critical teaching position.

Recruitment should normally start from a sense of long-range planning, and teachers should be viewed as the key to the success of the entire program. Given good teachers, the program will succeed; given poor teachers, it will fail. Such a precept demands coming to grips with answers to the following kinds of questions:

- What level of occupational competency is needed, and can the individual demonstrate competency at this level?
- Has the individual, through past experience, shown drive and ambition or is he looking at teaching as a "soft" and easy job?

- What does he have in his background that suggests he will be humanistic toward youth and display empathy for them?

- What kind of an intelligence does he possess? Is he well read (broader than just his speciality) and does he communicate well with others?

- Does he have further ambitions for other challenges in the education profession, such as extracurricular activities, department head, administration, and the like? Or is he content only to meet the challenge in the classroom?

- Who is recommending him? Is it someone close to teaching (such as a teacher trainer) or is it someone who does not know education?

- How does he plan on using his summers? Would he be willing to work during the summer as an educator or does he want this time for vacationing, his own employment, etc.?

- Why does he want to teach? And why should he be selected over anyone else for the particular position? Chances are if he cannot convincingly argue that he is the best qualified, he is not the individual to fill the job.

These are but some of the questions that need to be answered in one's search for the best possible teaching staff.

Sources of staff recruitment are generally located within the occupational or trade areas themselves. That is to say, teachers are identified by their subject or content areas and are usually found directly associated with some facet of these areas. For example, sources of information are union or trade associations, joint apprenticeship committee recommendations, industrial training directors, fellow teacher referrals, recommendations by teacher-training institutions, and the like. Less common is the use of direct advertising in the "Help Wanted" ads or the involvement of a placement service such as the state employment service.

The recruitment and initial selection of personnel cannot be treated casually. It is the first and most important step in the development of staff. Techniques commonly used to select trade, industrial, and technical teachers include:

- A review of credentials, including references, resume, occupational experience records, occupational competency examination scores, etc.*

---

*The National Occupational Competency Examination Project, funded by the U.S. Office of Education, will soon band some 44 states into a consortium for occupational competency testing of prospective teachers. Information about this effort may be secured from the National Occupation Competency Testing Institute, Educational Testing Service, Princeton, New Jersey.

- A personal interview, frequently by several individuals or even the entire membership of an advisory committee. The interview technique should include an evaluation of the personal appearance, speech habits, and overall bearing of the interviewee.

- A check on references. If a phone call is made, notes as to the results should be kept, and made a part of the employment application file.

- Tryout. It is not uncommon to use substitute teaching or part-time teaching as a testing ground for selecting full-time teachers. If this is done, some type of observational record should be maintained so it will be available when the need arises to select additional staff from the list of part-time people.

In the final analysis, there seems to be no "fool proof" way of selecting the best person for a particular position, even when all of the techniques mentioned are followed. The profession as a whole must be ever mindful of the need for competent individuals, and the process is one of continual quest for such individuals. This means that the involvement of teachers, teacher educators, and administrators is necessary to recruit the best possible talent into the profession.

Professional Development

Teachers are in need of a systematic, planned program of continued professional development. The New Jersey Educational Association (*NJEA Review* 1971) had the following to say about personnel development and teacher evaluation.

> Most current evaluation of teacher performance is job oriented. Career development has been sadly lacking. . . .
>
> Behavioral psychology tells us that people respond better to challenge than to threat, better to praise than to criticism. The surest way to increase the effectiveness of any professional is to surround him with productive peers, expose him to new ideas, and stimulate him into constructive analysis of his own performance.
>
> Many professionals in all fields operate capably in their jobs at less than their maximal level of production or efficiency. Accordingly, industry spends considerable amounts to upgrade the performance of professional-technical and middle management personnel. Schools make little comparable effort to upgrade the efficiency of their professional personnel—the teachers.

It is unfortunately true that in the vocational education profession it is by chance that teachers keep up-to-date with occupational technology.

Within their particular trade or occupational areas, teachers' expertise is not often esteemed by their tradesmen counterparts. It is also true that college preparatory courses in teacher education are not what they should be, and many teacher educators themselves are out-dated in their subject expertise. The need to produce capable teachers through professional development, and to keep teachers up-to-date by means of inservice vocational teacher education programs, has certainly not diminished over the years.

ADMINISTRATORS

The problem of the professional development of administrators is even more acute. Too infrequently, the most advanced techniques of modern business management practices are injected into administrative programs; and even less frequently, administrative personnel in education make an effort to update themselves in the latest managerial techniques. It rarely occurs that once the peculiar yet effective characteristics of a particular administrator are identified, he or she has the opportunity to apply these attributes to a number of situations and locations in which they are needed. When an exceptionally talented administrator builds a building, for example, his talents and know-how are seldom used to build more than one building. When an administrator is particularly sensitive to curricula needs in one school, the interpersonal relations that are needed with the staff to implement that curriculum are not used in a subsequent situation.

Actual requirements for administrative personnel, both in terms of numbers and competencies required, are difficult to determine. Data available from *The Education Professions* (U.S. Office of Education 1970) indicate the need for a three-fold increase in the number of state and local administrative vocational education personnel. However, recent experience, stemming in part from the severe austerity of state budgets, indicates that the projected need may be far in excess of those new administrators who will actually be employed. The emphasis most surely will be on upgrading present personnel.

ANCILLARY SERVICES

Ancillary services involve a whole new area of personnel development. The notion of the paraprofessional joining the education profession is only now becoming popular. As with administrative personnel, projected requirements are questionable. What is sure, though, is that an ancillary team effort, especially at the local level, will be needed to provide improved instruction. Application of the concept of career education will increase the need for ancillary personnel, especially guidance specialists.

THE DELIVERY SYSTEM

The delivery system for personnel development must be closely tied with both the quality and quantity dimensions of the profession. At this point in time, it may be that the quality dimension outweighs the production of sheer numbers of personnel. As Dale Parnell, Superintendent of Public Instruction for Oregon, put it:

> The past thirty years have seen great emphasis on quantity. It has been all educational managers could do to secure enough teachers, enough buildings, and enough buses. With the enrollment bulge on the flat side, it is safe to say the next ten to twenty years will be spent on dealing with quality in education (Parnell 1971).

As self-evident as Parnell's statement is, in today's teacher employment market little argument can be raised against the need for a delivery system that once and for all guarantees an ample supply of personnel in terms of both quantity and quality.

COMPONENTS OF A PERSONNEL DEVELOPMENT SYSTEM

The components of a personnel development system, whether a statewide or local endeavor, include seven distinct yet related categories: (1) mission and goal specification; (2) needs assessment; (3) priority determination and resource allocation; (4) program design and operation; (5) student/employee recruitment; (6) evaluation; and (7) roles, relationships, and responsibilities determination. Figure 9-1 illustrates these components.

Mission and Goals.   As described by Coster (1969), the mission and goals of a personnel development system must be of considerable breadth. In a forthright manner, he states the mission to be:

> . . . to enhance the educational, social and economic welfare of the state through the preparation and upgrading of personnel who are employed or to be employed in the vocational and technical systems of the state.

He describes the goals as being:

1. To provide an adequate supply of qualified personnel to staff the expanding programs in the vocational educational system of the state.

2. To upgrade the professional competencies of personnel now employed in the system.

3. To develop and implement procedures for a continuing input from the state system of vocational education into the professional development program.

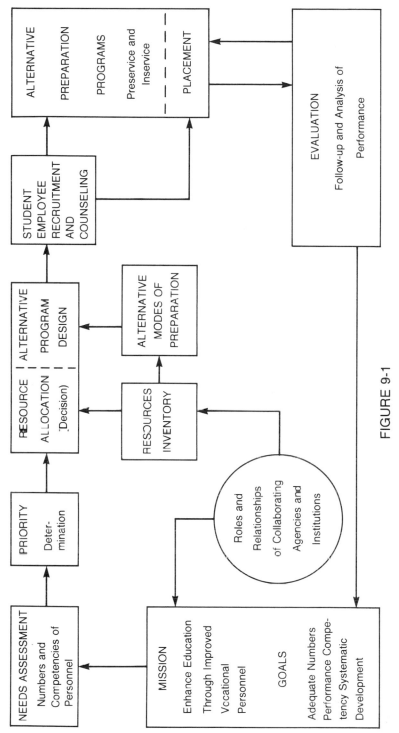

FIGURE 9-1

COMPONENTS AND FLOW OF A COMPREHENSIVE PLAN FOR
PERSONNEL DEVELOPMENT

Once such a mission is found acceptable by those who value personnel development, it then becomes necessary to proceed to the next and by far more complicated component—needs assessment.

Needs Assessment.   Determination of needs, at least in the past, has involved doing something about a situation when confronted by that situation; or, put another way, meeting a crisis when it arises. Such procedures have ignored the fact that personnel development takes time. Too little thought has gone into the process of selecting needed personnel for emerging staffing on a long-range and functional basis. The problem becomes even more complex if the definition of personnel development by performance-based criteria or staff differentiation is accepted as desirable. What is to be the need for the professional, technical, skilled, semiskilled, and unskilled in the profession? How many of each are required and how are they going to be employed at any given time to meet a given situation?

The determination of needs in terms of function applies not only to new personnel but to those already engaged in the system as well. Retraining, then, must be considered in needs assessment. Figure 9-2 delineates the need for instructional (functional) staffing of the total "career education" concept which prescribes the need for both pre- and inservice personnel assessments. Questions that must be raised are: (1) How many personnel are needed for staffing by levels, content, and student-learning styles? (2) Where are these personnel being produced and how (both in quantity and quality) are they being produced? (3) How can present personnel be retrained to fit these new functions?

The same question must be asked about other personnel, such as:

    state directors and supervisors
    assistant state directors
    local directors and supervisors
    state area supervisors
    state guidance specialists
    state research specialists
    state youth specialists
    state teacher trainers
    state itinerant teachers
    institutional teacher trainers
    local and state curriculum specialists
    local guidance specialists
    administrative assistants
    local research specialists
    teaching aides
    clerical aides
    media technicians

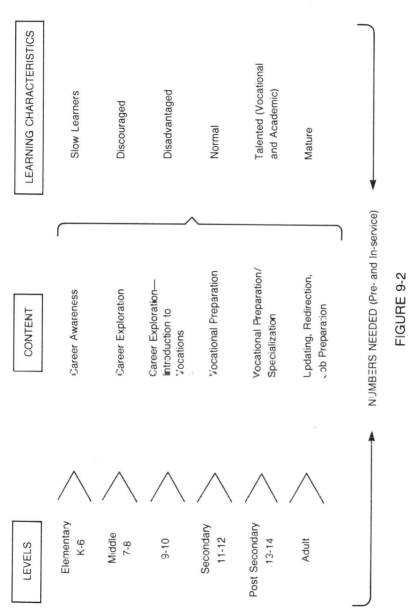

FIGURE 9-2

Instructional (Functional) Staffing Pattern

Priority Determination and Resource Allocation.   Determining priorities obviously depends upon a combination of needs and available resources. The latter has been used as a crutch for far too long in the education enterprise. The *a priori* practice of turning out teachers, all of whom would be assured a position, is past. An overabundance in some teaching and staffing areas and an undersupply in others may be a reality for the future. Where to place priorities then becomes the question. If, as Shoemaker (1971) has stated, management by objectives is the answer, then setting priorities becomes somewhat easier. At the 1971 seminar for state directors of vocational education in Las Vegas, Nevada, Shoemaker explained that the Ohio "management by objectives" plan included (1) identifying the problems (goals); (2) establishing quantified objectives; (3) identifying resources; (4) planning programs; (5) establishing costs; (6) making selections which would make the greatest contribution to goals.

In conclusion, Shoemaker stated:

> Only one thing is sure in vocational education, and that is change. I recognize that not all change is within the control of the state directors of vocational education, the state staff, local staff, or even educational leadership as a whole. Change can be brought about by changes in state budgets, federal budgets, local voting attitude and practices, and parental and student attitudes. Such possibilities for change, however, do not absolve us of our responsibilities to plan boldly, to plan wisely, to invest carefully, and to sell back the services which we believe are important to the solution of social and economic problems facing our nation.

The key here is knowing that the attainment of goals is accomplished through quantified objectives. For example, a quantified objective might be stated as the following:

> To provide by 1975, a career exploration program for 299,170 or 75% of the 378,895 students at the 9th and 10th grade level of 14 and 15 years of age is precise in terms of effort and cost to reach the objective. The setting of priorities can then be seen in the *reality* of the situation by the state vocational decision makers, state boards of education, and state legislatures who are providing the funding necessary in order to achieve the desired goals (Shoemaker 1971).

Program Design and Operation.   All too often the provision for personnel preparation programs has not adequately considered alternative program design. A plan for personnel development in vocational education must take into consideration various alternative modes of preparing the individuals which the plan has identified as priority needs. Resources available for implementation of the plan must be taken into consideration, alternative programs designed, and the preparation of individuals carried out. If at all possible, a system should provide a variety of channels whereby an individual can move into the role which he desires and which institutions and agencies require. The alternative preparation programs must include both pre-service and inservice elements and take into consideration continual upgrading of professional staff, and, in some instances, retraining for those who are in positions and have competencies no longer required.

Student/Employee Recruitment.   How to recruit and select new employees was covered in the first part of this chapter. The recruitment of present employees into a personnel development program is quite another matter. Why should an employee (teacher, administrator, teacher aide, etc.) subject himself to a program of personnel development? The answer to this question is, of course, to become better able to do his job—to be kept up-to-date and to become renewed in a true professional sense.

However, frequently the constraints of time, money, and almost sheer exhaustion prevent those in the education profession from availing themselves of professional development opportunities, even when they are presented. It is these constraints that must be overcome if any real progress is to be made in the quest to keep staff up-dated and renewed. Recruitment into professional development programs, institutes, inservice classes and the like may take such enticements as sabbatical leaves, professional days, visitation days, personal days, and released time in order to assure proper staff development. Some plan must be adopted so that staff members as part of the educational enterprise, receive the renewal and up-dating needed to stay viable. Possibly, as the profession moves toward a two, twelve month operational base, staff development will become a legitimate, ongoing consideration of the profession.

Evaluation.   Structured and formal evaluation of the entire recruitment plan must take place during its operation, but, most importantly, assessment of the end *product* must be conducted. Assuming that the selection is based upon competency required to adequately perform in the role designated, then an assessment plan must also take into consideration the analysis of performance. This will necessitate follow-up of former students and evaluations in terms of their actual performances on the job—both as self-assessed and as assessed by their employers. The importance of product assessment by performance standards cannot be too strongly stressed. Current work by the Bureau of Educational Professional Development through The Center for Vocational and Technical Education at The Ohio State University to develop a model for the evaluation of professional development programs promises to provide helpful procedures and mechanisms for accomplishing such assessment.

A LOCUS FOR PROFESSIONAL DEVELOPMENT

Industry must play a key role in the continuing educational process. The nature of industrial involvement is described in a study performed by the Department of Vocational-Technical Education of Rutgers University (U.S. Office of Education 1964). The study envisioned twelve regional centers, each of which contained a physical complex specifically designed to facilitate a continuing dialogue between industry and occupational teacher education. In this center, pre-service and inservice teachers, drawn from the entire spectrum of occupational education, would be exposed to the most recent developments and concepts within their field by means of a series of specially structured programs.

The technology resource center, as conceived and presented, would embody three elements.

The Technology Function.   The technology building contains a series of laboratories, each of which is empty of permanent equipment but contains highly versatile utilities. The laboratories differ one from the other in that each is able to accommodate a clearly identifiable spectrum of equipment and processes. The laboratories surround a central core that contains the most modern multi-media presentation facilities and audio-visual recording equipment.

Workshops of varying lengths would be set up to demonstrate a given process or piece of equipment to pre-service or inservice occupational teachers in whose occupational specialty the information would be of interest. These demonstrations would be conducted by industrial personnel on equipment loaned by industry for that purpose. The occupational educators would have the opportunity to gain actual hands-on experience, and, in addition, would have available to them the latest in visual or video-tape recording euqipment. Thus, they would be able to document their experience for subsequent curriculum development or enrichment. This same facility would provide the resources for the development of multi-media specialists. A permanent staff of such individuals would be responsible for recording the demonstrations and placing them in the library of the curriculum laboratory.

The Resource Function.   The resource building is a facility for the utilization of the products of the adjacent technology building and translates them into curriculum materials. The curriculum laboratory embodies two main functions: (1) the developmental laboratory, complete with its reference library, single concept films, motion pictures, still photographs, and video-tape recordings; completely equipped duplicating facilities for the production of text materials, manuals, and other training aids, developed for the entire range of occupational courses; and (2) an evaluation component staffed by specialists, to test out materials and training aides produced by the developmental laboratory.

The Computer Center.   A major computer is housed in the lower level of the resource building. Its primary purpose is to provide computer assisted instruction programs to all occupational education institutions in the area by means of isolated student terminals. We are witnessing the beginnings of a revolution in the tutorial process: for the first time, machines can be programmed to interact with humans to enhance the learning process. It is essential that master teachers of the future be able to cope with and master such advanced techniques. In addition, the computer can be used to provide electronic data processing services to the same institutions which use it for instructional purposes, thus reducing administrative and overhead expenses. The computer facility itself would also be used for the training of operations personnel for the major computers found in business and industry.

The principal philosophy of the technology resource center is to directly involve business and industry with occupational educational teacher regeneration. Facilities of this nature must be established in order to demonstrate to the economic sector the enormity of their own interest in the occupational educational process, and to render visible the efforts of occupational education in attempting to meet its responsibilities.

Summary

In summary, trade, industrial and technical education cannot be any better than the personnel who staff its programs. A deep concern for the quality and development of staff is the key to the success of any quality program. The process starts with the recruitment of talent to teach and to administer; provides a viable program of professional development (sometimes called continuing education); and molds personnel at all levels into a working team. The delivery system to provide such a program involves seven important components: (1) setting mission and goals; (2) establishing needs; (3) determining priorities and resource allocation; (4) designing the program's operation; (5) recruiting the student and employees; (6) evaluating the problem; and (7) determining roles, relationships, and responsibilities. The locus or setting for professional development embraces the notion of close school-industrial cooperation carried on in a physical facility called a technology resource center. Ideally, this facility would have the capability to provide technological and pedagogical updating of teachers and administrators alike.

QUESTIONS AND ACTIVITIES

1. Describe the staff of the school system in which you are employed in terms of mean age, educational attainment, and ability to teach.

2. Discuss the status of personnel development in your school system.

3. Make a list of the activities you personally feel necessary for your continuing education.

4. Make a survey of five teaching colleges to determine their personnel development needs.

5. Organize a five-year program of personnel development for your school staff.

SOURCE MATERIALS

1. Coster, John K. *The Development of a Vocational-Technical Education Personnel Development Program in a State.* North Carolina: Center for Occupational Education, 1969.

2. House, Elaine W. "Selected Factors Relating to The Work Cycle of Vocational Skill Subjects Teachers." Unpublished doctoral dissertation. Graduate School of Education, Rutgers University, 1970.

3. "NJEA Speaks out on . . . Teacher evaluation." *NJEA Review* Vol. 44, No. 5, pp. 15–18, 1971.

4. Parnell, Dale. *Confusion on the Bridge.* Paper presented at the Fourth Annual National Leadership Development Seminar for State Directors of Vocational Education, Las Vegas, 1971.

5. Schaefer, Carl J., and Ward, Darrell L. *A Model for a Comprehensive Personnel Development System in Vocational Education.* Columbus, Ohio: The Center for Vocational and Technical Education, The Ohio State University, 1972.

6. Shoemaker, Byrl R. *Management by Objectives and Personnel Development for Vocational Education.* Paper presented at the Fourth Annual National Leadership Development Seminar for State Directors of Vocational Education, Las Vegas, 1971.

7. U.S. Office of Education. "The Development of a Technology-Resource Center." Washington, D.C.: Office of Education Contract Number OE-5-85-043, 1964. Available on microfiche through ERIC.

8. U.S. Office of Education. *The Education Professions:* An Annual Report on the People Who Serve our Schools and Colleges. Washington, D.C.: Superintendent of Documents. OE—58032-70, 1970.

9. U.S. Office of Education. *Summary Data, Vocational Education, Fiscal year 1970.* Washington, D.C.: Division of Vocational and Technical Education, 1971.

Chapter 10 PROFESSIONAL ORGANIZATIONS

As a professional in trade, industrial, and technical education you will want to participate in organizations which will be supportive of your duties and which will contribute to your professional growth. There will always be a dilemma in your mind as to the choice of professional organizations to join. How many can you afford? Do you have the time to participate? What will be the most beneficial?

As a professional educator, another series of questions you should ask relates to how you can best contribute to your profession. Membership in professional organizations provides opportunities not only to acquire new knowledge and competence but also to contribute to the total of education. This chapter will answer some of the questions raised and will assist you in making decisions about your professional involvement.

American Vocational Association

When one thinks of trade, industrial, and technical education he immediately thinks of the American Vocational Association. This organization, headquartered in Washington, D.C., is the professional organization representing all vocational educators. Its membership is composed of over 50,000 vocational educators from all of its fields.

The AVA is a federation of state and territorial vocational associations and is a private, nonprofit, professional education organization devoted exclusively to the promotion and development of vocational, technical, and practical arts education and the professionalism of its members. It was founded in 1925, is an independent organization not affiliated with the federal government or any other professional association. AVA does, however, work closely with representatives of many professional and trade associations. The association also works very closely with agencies of the federal government, the Congress, and other key policy- and decision-makers.

The following Articles of Incorporation describe the particular objectives for which AVA was formed:

1. To establish and maintain active national leadership in all types of vocational and practical arts education, including industrial arts and guidance services.

2. To render service to state and local communities in promoting and stabilizing vocational education.

3. To provide a national open forum for the study and discussion of all questions involved in vocational education.

4. To unify all the vocational education interests of the nation through representative membership.

5. To cooperate with other nations in the further development of vocational education, and to welcome international memberships.

6. To encourage the further development and improvement of all programs of education related to vocational and practical arts education, including industrial arts and guidance services.

7. To emphasize and encourage the promotion, improvement and expansion of programs of vocational part-time and vocational adult education.*

The AVA is a federation of state vocational associations. Educators gain membership through the state vocational associations. The overriding structure of the AVA is its divisions. You will note that there is both a Trade and Industrial Division and a Technical Education Division. Departments have been a more recent innovation in the structure and are designed with the purpose of increasing communication and professional activities among persons with like interests across the Divisions. Designing an organization to effectively accommodate its over 50,000 members is no small task.

Each of the Divisions within the AVA encompasses a number of associations. For example, in the Trade and Industrial Education Division will be found such organizations as the National Association of State Supervisors

*Incorporated under the Laws of the State of Indiana, Dec. 5, 1929.

of Trade and Industrial Education and the National Trade and Industrial Teachers Association. The fact that should be emphasized is that it has been the attempt of the leadership of AVA to accommodate a wide range of special interest groups in such a way that any vocational or practical arts educator could relate to the organization.

Some of the membership services of the AVA include:

Professional Journal.   The *American Vocational Journal,* published monthly, September through May, keeps members informed about new developments and issues and provides vital information concerning vocational, technical, practical arts, and career education. The *Journal* also provides a forum for membership expression through letters to the editor, lists of new equipment and teaching aids, and reader information services.

Publications.   The AVA publishes numerous booklets and pamphlets containing information not available elsewhere. AVA Headquarters maintains a library and information services which can be called upon to help members.

Member-gram.   The AVA communicates with its membership through a quarterly newsletter which provides up-to-date information on matters of interest to membership. The Member-gram is the "awareness" communique which tells you what's going on across the nation.

Program Development.   The AVA staff is dedicated to providing members with ongoing career and leadership development programs. There will be an ever-increasing number of national and regional conferences to help promote professional growth.

Annual Convention.   An annual convention provides AVA members and representatives from all areas of education with a national forum for an exchange of ideas. Thus, progress is furthered and fostered in all aspects of the development of human resources for the world of work. This annual convention gives AVA members and guests an opportunity to discuss educational programs and needs with manufacturers, publishers, and business representatives. Visitors also get a chance to inspect new and innovative equipment, teaching aids, and supplies which are available for use in carrying out educational programs. Usually over 8,000 vocational educators attend this annual affair.

Insurance Programs.   AVA makes available a variety of voluntary insurance programs which benefit its members. In a brochure of the AVA, Lowell A. Burkett, Executive Director, has this to say to the prospective member:

We are indeed pleased that you are considering membership in the American Vocational Association. The AVA is the only national organization that has a professional concern for vocational, technical and practical arts education as its primary goal. As education moves to embrace the concept of career education for all people of all ages in every community, those in the forefront of this movement will be those who join and participate in AVA activities. We are happy that you are making that professional commitment and know that you will profit from it.

AVA is proud of its past record in bringing to members of Congress and other policymakers the accomplishments of vocational, technical and practical arts education as well as the needs for future development. As the scope of our program broadens and as it becomes more complex, those who are engaged in that program must exert their professional influence in shaping its future.

The AVA needs you and you need AVA. A truly professional person asks not what the profession can do for him but what he can do for the profession. This is the hallmark for the future of our profession.

We believe that the professional organization has a unique role to play at the federal, state, and local levels and, therefore, we encourage membership at all these levels. We urge you to join the AVA through your local chapter and your state association.

We look forward to working with you in the years ahead and welcome you into AVA. (American Vocational Association 1972).

The National Association of Industrial and Technical Teacher Educators (NAITTE) is somewhat unique in structure in the AVA in that it is affiliated with three AVA divisions; the Industrial Arts Division, Trade and Industrial Division, and the Technical Education Division. Its purposes as set forth in its constitution and by-laws are as follows:

This Association shall earnestly endeavor:

1. To bring about closer cooperation among those engaged in preparing and improving teachers and other workers in health occupations, industrial arts, technical education, and trade and industrial education;

2. To stimulate and to take appropriate action concerning practices and proposals in industrial and technical teacher education and in other educational phases related thereto;

3. To increase the contribution of the group to the extension and perfection of all phases of industrial arts and vocational and technical education;

4. To foster research and recording of experiences in line with professional interests;

5. To promote other common desires of the group (NAITTE 1972, p. 1).

The AVA through the years has been an effective voice for the profession. It has provided the structure whereby persons in the profession could have dialogue and represent a unified position on federal legislation and policy. It has had a very positive effect on federal legislation throughout the years. In fact, without such an organization it is doubtful that we would have had a continuity of increasingly important federal legislation in vocational and technical education.

Shown on the bottom of the organizational chart of AVA are national organizations associated with AVA; specifically, the National Council of Local Administrators of Vocational, Technical Education and Practical Arts and the National Association of State Directors of Vocational Education. The State Directors organization has been a significant and influential group in the AVA. Attention is also called to the local administrators group which has continued to grow in number, strength, and influence. Although not specifically shown on the AVA organizational chart, it should be mentioned that there is a Trade and Industrial Education Womens' Section; a National Association of State Supervisors of Trade and Industrial Education; and a National Association of Trade and Industrial Instructors. Each of these groups caters to the professional needs of its members and each holds formal meetings at the annual AVA convention.

The National Association of Trade and Industrial Instructors (NATII), with a potential membership of approximately 60,000, has been late in coming to the fore. The gathering of some twenty-five professional vocational educators in Boston during the 1970 AVA Convention brought about the culmination of about three years of previous behind-the-scenes work of other vocational educators. The state of Iowa was the first to organize a state Association of Trade and Industrial Instructors. Its efforts and membership first started the National Association of Trade and Industrial Instructors (NATII). Since Boston, NATII has grown to about fifteen-hundred members representing thirty-two states. Two states, North Carolina and Oklahoma, have joined in a large bloc. Other states are gathering to act in a similar fashion.

A complete set of officers is elected for each year, and currently regional vice-presidents are appointed to represent NATII throughout the country. To facilitate the communications previously mentioned, an associate vice-president is named to represent each state. This has a two-fold effect—(1) leadership is obtained for future NATII officers, and (2) a much closer contact is made with each state to the national organizations. The expressed purposes of NATII are:

1. To have representation on the AVA Board.

2. To have a voice in legislation.

3. To have specific teacher voice in philosophical developments.

4. To plan conferences for instructors.

5. To publish a newsletter for instructors.

6. To review T & I publications, various textbooks, and materials.

7. To exchange teacher experiences and ideas (NATII *News* 1971).

American Technical Education Association

This association's beginning is traced to the American Association of Technical High Schools and Institutes, organized in Detroit in 1928. The Association started with the plan of holding meetings with the Department of Secondary School Principals of the National Education Association. Since most of the members in the early days were from the northern states east of the Mississippi, it was not feasible to go to all of the National Education Association convention cities. Hence, two meetings were held in Brooklyn Technical High School, and one in cooperation with the New York State Vocational and Practical Arts Association at their annual convention in Syracuse, New York. Furthermore, the personnel of NEA showed very little interest in technical education. Therefore, at the meeting held at the Brooklyn Technical High School on December 5, 1944, it was decided to seek affiliation with The American Vocational Association. At the 1949 conference held in Atlantic City, the name of the Association was changed to the American Technical Education Association.

The affiliation with the AVA was continued until 1969. At this time AVA decided to have a Division of Technical Education under the leadership of an AVA vice president. According to AVA by-laws, it was no longer possible for the organization to be affiliated with AVA.

New by-laws became effective July 1, 1972. Provision was made for nine regional representatives—one in Canada, and eight in the United States. Provision was also made for an advisory council in each of the regions, with a council member representing each state in the region. One of the effective activities of the regional representatives and regional councils has been the planning and conduct of ATEA conferences in their respective regions.

Membership includes institutional as well as individual members. The purposes of the association are listed as follows:

- To promote technical education for interested and qualified youth and adults.

- To recommend standards for technical education.

- To provide an opportunity for an exchange of ideas among persons in the Technical Education field (ATEA 1972).

The American Industrial Arts Association

This association is affiliated with the National Education Association (NEA). Its purposes are stated in its constitution as follows:

- To define, stimulate, coordinate, and strive for the ideal form of industrial arts education as a vital aspect of education for all students on all levels: elementary, secondary, and adult, national and international.

- To promote the improvement of the quality of instruction in industrial arts education by assisting educators, students, and all others concerned to keep instructional content, methods, and facilities current with the rapid changes in industry and technology.

Emerging National Organization

It is anticipated that in the near future a new organization entitled The National Association for the Advancement of Trade and Industrial Manpower will emerge. This will be an umbrella-type organization, probably affiliated with the American Vocational Association, and will include the following groups: National Council of Local Administrators of Vocational, Technical Education and Practical Arts; National Association of Trade and Industrial Instructors; National Association of Industrial and Technical Teacher Educators; National Association of State Supervisors of Trade and Industrial Education; Vocational Industrial Clubs of America; Trade and Industrial Womens' Section; and the National Occupational Competency Testing Consortium. If this organization is ever formed, it will assemble under one organization the largest group of trade, industrial, and technical educators ever. Their unification in purpose as well as their concerted action will be a force with which to be contended.

State Organizations

Preceding discussions have related to national organizations. Many of these have state counterparts. The organization with which you should be most closely allied is your state vocational association. The exact nature of the membership of such associations varies from state to state; however, the most common pattern includes membership from each of the vocational education occupational areas with divisions within the organization for trade, industrial, and technical education. The professional benefits of membership and active participation are potentially very great. The effectiveness of the organization depends, however, on how active and committed are its members.

State associations usually conduct an annual meeting and often have regional activities. Most provide a magazine or newsletter. The organization is usually the focal point for providing information and views on legislation or other governmental policy affecting programs or funding.

Summary

This chapter has stressed the desirability of trade, industrial, and technical educators becoming actively involved in professional associations representing their field. This is important in terms of what the individual may gain from membership and participation, but, perhaps even more important, in terms of the contribution that he can make to an important segment of the educational program.

This chapter has not discussed the desirability of membership in the occupation or the occupational group for which training is provided. It should be stressed that these occupational or industrial relationships are also important.

QUESTIONS AND ACTIVITIES

1. Secure materials on your state's vocational association.

2. Evaluate the effectiveness of your state association in terms of:
   Annual meeting
   Legislative activity
   Communication vehicle with profession

3. Secure a copy of the Annual Proceedings of the American Vocational Association. Discuss the report's implication for your particular field.

SOURCE MATERIALS

1. American Industrial Arts Association. *Constitution, Article II, Section 1 and 2.* Washington, D.C.

2. American Technical Education Association. *By-Laws, Article II, Sections A, B, and C.* Delmar, New York: 1972.

3. American Vocational Association. *The American Vocational Association* (brochure). Washington, D.C., (1972).

4. National Association of Trade and Industrial Instructors. *News.* Michigan City, Indiana: 1971.

5. The National Association of Industrial and Technical Teacher Educators. *Constitution and By-Laws,* Kearney, Nebraska: 1972.

RESOURCE AGENCIES

American Industrial Arts Association, 1201 Sixteenth Street, N.W., Washington, D.C.: 20036.

American Technical Education Association, Inc., Box 31, Delmar, New York, 12054.

American Vocational Association, Inc., 1510 H Street, N.W., Washington, D.C. 20005.

National Association of Industrial and Technical Teacher Educators, Kearney State College, Kearney, Nebraska, 68847.

National Council of Local Administrators, % American Vocational Association, 1510 H Street, N.W., Washington, D.C. 20005.

Chapter 11 VICA: TRADE, INDUSTRIAL, AND TECHNICAL EDUCATION'S YOUTH CLUB

Probably one of the most exciting things that has happened recently within both secondary and postsecondary level trade, industrial, and technical programs has been the formation of the Vocational Industrial Clubs of America. Every teacher, supervisor, and administrator of trade, industrial, and technical education must acquaint himself with this high potential development. For this reason, the present chapter has been included in this book—to introduce the reader to VICA.

The purposes of the Vocational Industrial Clubs of America are as follows (VICA *Leadership Handbook 1970,* p. 62):

- To unite in a common bond all students enrolled in trade, industrial, technical, and health education.

- To develop leadership abilities through participation in educational, vocational, civic, recreational, and social activities.

- To foster a deep respect for the DIGNITY OF WORK.

- To assist students in establishing realistic vocational goals.

- To help students attain a purposeful life.

Credit for much of this chapter goes to Larry W. Johnson, Executive Director, and Virginia J. Croft, Director of Public Information of the National VICA Office, 105 N. Virginia Avenue, Falls Church, Virginia 22046.

- To create enthusiasm for learning.

- To promote high standards in trade ethics, workmanship, scholarship, and safety.

- To develop the ability of students to plan together, organize, and carry out worthy activities and projects through use of the democratic process.

- To foster a wholesome understanding of the functions of labor and management organizations and a recognition of their mutual interdependence.

- To create among students, faculty members, patrons of the school, and persons in business and labor a sincere interest in and esteem for trade, industrial, technical, and health education.

- To develop patriotism through a knowledge of our Nation's heritage and the practice of DEMOCRACY.

As a result of this purpose, VICA has grown phenomenally. Since its constitutional convention, held in Nashville, Tennessee, in May, 1965, the organization's membership has grown to over 148,000 and continues to grow at a rate of about 17,000 new members per year. The youth club idea was not new to trade, industrial, and technical educators, as they observed that other vocational students—in agriculture, business, homemaking, and distribution—had long enjoyed the leadership, citizenship, and character-building benefits of youth clubs.*

Trade, industrial, and technical educators have been long aware that their students need more manipulative skills to make their way in the world of work. The VICA movement supplies a vehicle by which many organized cocurricular activities that encourage student motivation, respect for individual capabilities, an understanding of the role of the working community, and an awareness of citizenship roles can be carried on.

Historical Development

In the 1930s, a national organization called the Future Craftsmen of America grew out of a recognition of the needs of students to be prepared for entrance into industrial occupations. This organization failed in its second year of operation, but individual states kept the idea alive with organizations of their own. Prior to the organization of VICA, at least twenty states were involved in some type of trade, industrial, and technical youth club activity on local and state levels. Many states had

---

*The other vocational youth organizations are known as: Future Farmers of America (FFA), Future Business Leaders of America (FBLA), Future Homemakers of America (FHA) and Distributive Education Clubs of America (DECA).

developed sophisticated programs, and even some regional level programs were in existence.

The turning point for translating the need and idea into a usable program of normal scope was reached in 1960. The setting was the American Vocational Association Convention in December,1960, when a committee was set up to study the possibility of a national vocational youth organization and to make recommendations. With the interest and assistance of many educators, the U.S. Office of Education, and national labor and management leadership, the momentum increased and the groundwork was laid for VICA—a national organization for trade, technical, industrial, and health students. Its official beginning was May, 1965, when the First Annual Trade and Industrial Youth Conference in Nashville, Tennessee, was covered. Two hundred persons participated, fourteen states were represented by student delegations, and twenty-four states had adult participants or observers. Twenty-six state trade and industrial club associations with 30,000 members joined the national VICA organization during its first year. Its growth since then is proof of the need for a national program to promote trade, industrial, and technical education.

THE PLEDGE AND CREED OF VICA

With a membership soon to nearly include a quarter of a million, those in trade, industrial, and technical education cannot help but feel proud of the rhetoric exemplified by the pledge and creed of these youth (VICA *Leadership Handbook* 1970).

THE PLEDGE

UPON MY HONOR, I Pledge

- To prepare myself by diligent study and ardent practice to become a worker whose services will be recognized as honorable by my employer and fellow workers.

- To base my expectations of reward upon the solid foundation of service.

- To honor and respect my vocation in such a way as to bring repute to myself.

- And further, to spare no effort in upholding the ideals of the Vocational Industrial Clubs of America.

The Creed, in a like manner, sets forth the seriousness of the philosophy behind VICA.

THE CREED

I Believe in the Dignity of Work

I hold that mankind has advanced to his present culture through the intelligent use of his hands and mind. I shall maintain a feeling of humbleness for the knowledge and skills that I receive from craftsmen, and I shall conduct myself with dignity in the work I do.

I Believe in the American Way of Life

I know our culture of today is the result of freedom of action and opportunities won by our American forefathers, and I will uphold their ideals.

I Believe in Education

I shall endeavor to make the best use of knowledge, skills, and experience that I learn in school in order that I may become a better workman in my chosen occupation and a better citizen in my community. To this end I will continue my learning both in and out of school.

I Believe in Fair Play

I shall through honesty and fair play respect the rights of my fellowman. I shall always conduct myself in the manner of the best craftsmen in my occupation, and treat those with whom I work as I would like to be treated.

I Believe Satisfaction is Achieved by Good Work

I feel that compensation and personal satisfaction received for my work and services will be in proportion to my creative and productive ability.

I Believe in High Moral and Spiritual Standards

I shall endeavor to conduct myself in such a manner as to set an example for my fellowman by living a wholesome life and by fulfilling my responsibilities as a citizen of my community.

In accepting the challenge of the pledge and creed, the youth of VICA have expanded their educational program well beyond the confines of the school walls and well beyond the years of formal education. As stated in the VICA *Leadership Handbook* (1970):

> For your generation, many say there are no frontiers to conquer, no challenges to meet. We see large numbers of youth who say our country has lost its purpose and that the American people are drifting without direction. The Vocational Industrial Clubs of America does not accept this; we see clearly new challenges as important as the frontiers that existed for our forefathers. This generation has greater opportunities than those of any previous. The frontiers that challenge you are those of ignorance, poverty, space and, most important, to assure that our democratic process is preserved.
>
> Each generation must seek the answers to its own problems. How well each generation solves its problems is reflected by its youth. As steel is tempered and made strong by heat, each new generation must be tempered by challenge. You must determine for yourself what you can contribute. To do so, you should be fully aware of the contributions of past young Americans. Too many of our young people feel left out precisely because of their youth. But VICA believes that the future is in the hands of the young, because it is early in life that you are most creative and flexible.

THE EMBLEM

Proudly displayed on the blazer of the VICA member will be found the VICA emblem. (See figure 11-1.)

The VICA emblem colors—red, white, blue, and gold—have the following significance:

THE SYMBOLISM OF THE VICA EMBLEM

The Shield Represents Patriotism

The shield denotes belief in democracy, liberty, and the American way of life.

The Torch Represents Knowledge

The flaming torch reflects the light of knowledge which dispels the darkness of ignorance. In the light of the torch progress will be made toward the vocational goals of the individual.

The Orbital Circles Represent Technology

The circles present the challenge of modern technology, and the training needed to accept and master the challenge of new technical frontiers and the need for continuous education.

The Gear Represents the Industrial Society

The gear, symbolic of the industrial society, denotes the interdependence and cooperation of the individual working together with labor and management for the betterment of mankind.

The Hands Represent Youth

The Hands portray a search for knowledge and the desire to acquire a skill. In the process to attain knowledge and skill the individual will develop a respect for the dignity of work and become a productive and responsible citizen.

FIGURE 11-1

OFFICIAL VICA EMBLEM

The National Structure

Although the local club is central in terms of activities, the national organization offers cohesion and provides the guidance and identification that lend the program strength. Essential to an understanding of VICA is a knowledge of the structure of the program at all levels.

The Vocational Industrial Clubs of America, Incorporated, a nonprofit educational organization, sponsors VICA, the national youth organization. The corporation is composed of the head state supervisors of trade and industrial education from each state having a VICA Association. In each state, the head state supervisor is the official state director or advisor to his association. A Board of Directors composed of members of VICA, Inc., the U.S. Office of Education, and the American Vocational Association, serves as the adult governing body. Ten national VICA officers are elected annually by the student members of each division—the high school and the postsecondary—to serve as the National Executive Council. They are President, Vice-President, Secretary, Treasurer, Parliamentarian, and five Regional Vice-Presidents. (See figure 11-2.)

A National Advisory Council composed of members from education, labor, and business provides counsel, advice, and assistance to the Board of Directors. An Executive Director, appointed by the Board, serves as the administrative officer of the national organization at its headquarters in Falls Church, Virginia.

VICA itself is an organization of state and territorial associations, each operating under approval of the Board of Directors in accordance with and by legal authority derived from a charter granted by VICA, Inc. Charters are issued to eligible states or territories upon submission of a formal application which meets the national requirements.

THE STATE STRUCTURE

The State Association is administered by the State Department of Education as a function of the Division of Vocational Education. The head state supervisor of trade and industrial education is responsible for VICA within each state. The chief advisor for VICA in each state is the state supervisor of trade and industrial education (or his designated representative), and he is the administrative officer of the state association. The designated state VICA director is usually a member of state industrial education supervisory staff. The state structure can take on several forms. Figure 11-3 shows the state structure when secondary and postsecondary programs fall under the responsibility of the head State Supervisor. Figure 11-4 shows the structure when different state staff members head trade, industrial, and technical, and health education programs.

The Local Club Structure: VICA functions as an organization of local clubs affiliated with the national organization through a state association. A Vocational Industrial Club is a group of students in a single school who work cooperatively to develop leadership abilities through participation in worthwhile educational, vocational, civic, recreational, and social activities. Assisting in the organizing and functioning of a club is an adult club advisor. Usually, he is a vocational teacher and is the administrative officer of the club in that school.

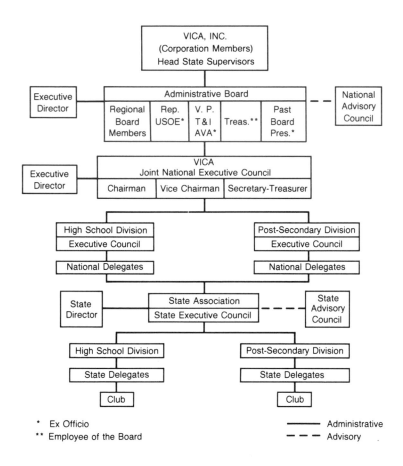

FIGURE 11-2

VOCATIONAL INDUSTRIAL CLUBS OF AMERICA NATIONAL STRUCTURE

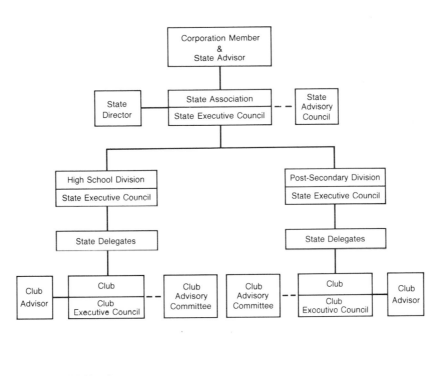

FIGURE 11-3

VOCATIONAL INDUSTRIAL CLUBS OF AMERICA SUGGESTED STATE
STRUCTURE A

Generally, local clubs have one of two organizational structures—the
single-section or multi-section. The single-section is the most common and
is found in schools with only one vocational industrial training course. In
a single-section club, all the students are pursuing the same training under
a single instructor (who is the club advisor). The students elect their officers,
who comprise the club executive council and plan and conduct various
activities in a single body.

The multi-section club (see figures 11-5 and 11-6) is formed in schools
where several vocational courses are offered, such as in large comprehensive
high schools, area vocational schools, or community colleges. In this situa-

tion, a club consists of several sections organized by subject as described above. Each section has its own officers and activities, and the instructor serves as section advisor. Each section elects delegates to the club executive council which coordinates the section activities and plans overall club activities. The club advisor is elected from the section advisors or is appointed by the school principal. Often guidance counselors serve as club advisors in schools with multi-section clubs. Students in large clubs prefer the multi-section structure because it offers a togetherness not possible otherwise. With membership in the hundreds, a single-structure club is not practical because opportunities for participation are greatly reduced. The national organization is essential to the VICA program because it can offer guidance

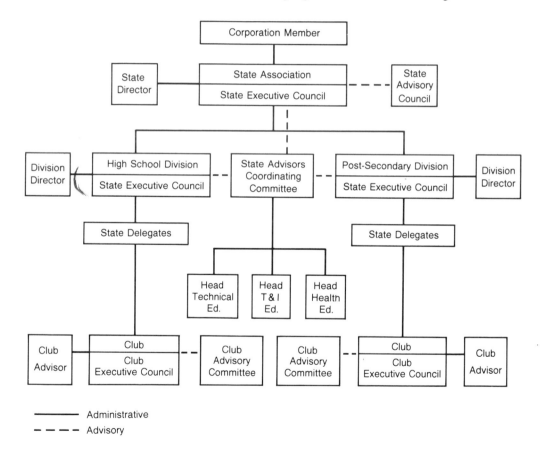

FIGURE 11-4

VOCATIONAL INDUSTRIAL CLUBS OF AMERICA SUGGESTED STATE
STRUCTURE B

and services that could not otherwise be made available. National VICA
offers an organizational hand in getting local club programs moving and it
helps them to continue. It is active in developing programs which offer
guidance and assistance to state departments of education and to local high
schools in the establishment of clubs. It provides information and materials,
conducts workshops and conferences, and offers consulting services on club
organization and youth development.

YOUTH DEVELOPMENT ACTIVITIES

The Youth Development Foundation solicits the financial support of
labor and management so that the National VICA can sponsor major youth
development activities. These include: leadership development conferences,
national competitive activities, leadership awards and leadership development publications and materials.

Leadership conferences have a particularly significant role in the VICA
program. Among the major national conferences held yearly are two national officers' leadership conferences, a state directors' workshop, and the
national leadership conference to which all state associations may send

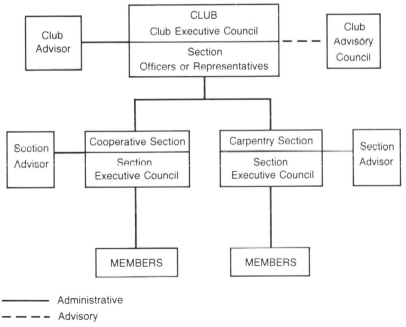

FIGURE 11-5

VOCATIONAL INDUSTRIAL CLUBS OF AMERICA—SUGGESTED LOCAL
CLUB STRUCTURE FOR CLUBS HAVING TWO OR MORE SECTIONS

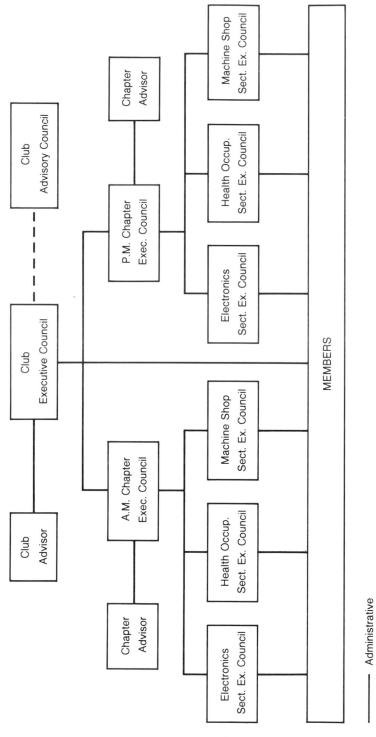

FIGURE 11-6

VOCATIONAL INDUSTRIAL CLUBS OF AMERICA—SUGGESTED LOCAL VICA CLUB STRUCTURE

——— Administrative

– – – Advisory

delegates. In addition, the VICA Youth Development Foundation sponsors the American Industrial-Technical Education Conference (AITEC), whose members are representatives of business, industry, labor, government, and education. All are supporters of the VICA program and attend the conference for progress reports and discussions on vocational trade, industrial, technical, and health education as well as on the problems of VICA. The national student conferences are essential for instilling spirit and a sense of identity among members from all over the nation. They provide the opportunity for students to take part in conducting the business of the organization.

Competitive activities have been included in the VICA Youth Development Program to motivate and develop an enthusiasm for learning. These activities provide practical and valuable experience for students entering trade, industrial, and technical, and health careers and, at the same time, they offer personal enrichment by providing opportunities to achieve a sense of accomplishment and recognition. VICA's contests are of two types: leadership development and occupational expertise. The leadership development contests involve public speaking, club business procedure, safety, ceremonies demonstration, job interview, and overall outstanding club. A student's poise and skill in handling a variety of situations such as those that arise in public speaking, parliamentary procedure demonstration, and job interview situations are proof of his or her ability to cope with various social and business situations. Occupational contests (U.S. Skill Olympics) are held in the areas of building trades, health occupations, automotive technology, electrical/electronics industry, and personal services. In the competitive activities programs, the interests of the student, the school, and the industrial community seem to mesh. Contests encourage industry and the school program to come together in a common cause.

Across the nation, labor and management have shown their commitment to the competitive activities program through their involvement at local, state, and national levels. Input ranges from advice on the planning of contests to financial support, and the provision of supplies, equipment, and qualified judges. Industry's involvement is also helping to publicize the VICA program and industrial-technical and health education. The competitive activities program is one way of giving prestige and recognition to outstanding students and has had great value in raising the status of trade, industrial/technical, and health education in this country.

National VICA also has a program through which every student can strive for and win recognition at various levels of achievement. The Vocational Initiative and Club Achievement Program is designed to motivate students and give recognition in the areas of both club participation and skill development. Emphasis is on developing the well-rounded individual, and every member can participate on an individual basis. In the area of personal development, a student is given goals and levels of achievement for development in citizenship, character, and leadership through club work. In the area of individual skill development, he is recognized for performance in his area of training. The student is encouraged to participate in both aspects of the program although he may choose to participate in only one. Top awards are the American VICA Degree and the International Industrial Degree.

A key aspect of the Youth Development Program is the provision to provide communications and materials between clubs and between National VICA and individual members and advisors. Publications and supplies necessary to the club program are provided through National VICA. Publications include the *Leadership Handbook,* which is a complete guide to club activities and programs such as the Vocational Initiative and Club Achievement program; a *Competitive Activities Guide;* booklets on public relations and the National Program of Work; and a variety of other materials helpful to club members and advisors. VICA also publishes the *VICA Professional News,* which gives items of information valuable to the professional member, and the *VICA Leader,* a newsletter for the club officer. Perhaps foremost among the public information materials is the *VICA* magazine, published four times yearly. Through articles about club activities and club members, VICA broadens the student's perspective and gives him a sense of identity with others of similar interests.

In addition to its publications services, National VICA administers a supply service which gives members an opportunity to purchase official VICA items and club paraphernalia. Supply service items carry the distinguishing VICA emblem. The red VICA blazer and sweater, the official windbreaker, and shop uniforms, and many other distinctively VICA items give members a sense of identity with other trade, industrial, and technical and health students and with the goals and purposes of VICA. They help the member develop feelings of pride and self-confidence in his and her own abilities and roles. Positive recognition through identification with a national organization of high purpose is something to be proud of.

All of these aspects of the total VICA program—leadership conferences, competitive activities, leadership development publications, and the achievement program—are concrete ways through which VICA can serve the student.

ACCEPTANCE IS THE KEY TO GROWTH

VICA will continue to grow dramatically if active attitudes to support its growth are taken by trade, industrial, and technical, and health educators on the local, state, and national level.

Among educators, it is important that the activities of VICA be recognized as *a part* of the total trade, industrial, technical, and health education program. The American Vocational Association has endorsed the VICA program as part of the responsibility of the teachers, thus indicating that teaching goes well beyond mere skill development and includes the development of traits of citizenship and leadership.

Meeting in May, 1967, in St. Paul, Minnesota, a national conference of state trade and industrial supervisors expressed support for the VICA program. These educators recognized that in order to spur the growth of VICA, action had to be taken by federal, state, and local leadership. They felt the United States Office of Education had to accept the premise that youth organizations complement vocational instruction. This became a reality when in the spring of 1970, the late Dr. James E. Allen, Jr., United States Commissioner of Education, directed a memorandum on vocational youth clubs to chief state school officers and executive officers of state boards for vocational education. The memo stated USOE's position in regard to youth organizations including the intention to provide advisory assistance through federal employees designated to serve in this capacity. The memo made clear that federal-state grant funds for vocational education could be used by the states to give leadership and support to youth organizations and activities "directly related to established vocational education instructional programs, under provisions of approved state plans for vocational education."

"The purpose of the Office of Education in encouraging youth organizations," the memorandum said, ". . . is to improve the quality and relevance of instruction, develop youth leadership and provide wholesome experiences for youth not otherwise available within the schools."

Dr. Allen's successor, Dr. Sidney P. Marland, Jr., has reiterated support of vocational youth clubs and said that the USOE welcomes their cooperation, support, and suggestions in strengthening programs of vocational and technical education. Support has come from other than governmental quarters as well. In keeping with their involvement and commitment to VICA, various industry groups representing both labor and management have issued public statements of support over the last several years. Statements of support for the goals of VICA have come from such organizations as the American Federation of Labor-Congress of Industrial Organizations; National Association of Manufacturers; California AFL-CIO; Washington State Labor Council; Chamber of Commerce of the United States; Associated General Contractors of America; Structural Clay Products Institute; National Association of Home Builders; National Tool, Die and Precision Machining Association; National Plastering Industries Joint Apprenticeship Trust Fund; Construction Industry Collective Bargaining Commission; and the National Joint Carpentry Apprenticeship and Training Committee.

National support for all vocational youth organizations has only recently come from the National Advisory Council on Vocational Education. In a letter from Lawrence Davenport to the Honorable Elliot Richardson, former Secretary, Department of Health, Education and Welfare, the Council recently stated its position as follows:

> The National Advisory Council on Vocational Education is pleased to submit as its Seventh Report recommendations for expanding the visibility and support of Vocational Student Organizations.
>
> For many years, Vocational Student Organizations have typified the cooperation between education and the private sector which is being so urgently sought today. These student organizations have supplied their members with the incentives and guidance which we recognize now as essential to bringing relevance to education, and which we accept as an integral part of the emerging career education concept.
>
> We believe that Vocational Student Organizations are a neglected resource which can make great contributions toward expanding the options available to our Nation's student body.
>
> This report attempts to bring their story to the public, and solicit nationwide support for their efforts.
>
> The Council is deeply appreciative of the cooperation of all the student organizations, along with their advocates both in and out of the education field, in assisting us with gathering the background for this report. We are indebted to Council Member Martha Bachman, who is also Chairman of the Delaware State Advisory Council on Vocational Education, for her excellent guidance in preparing the report.

The Seventh Report of the Council (1970) entitled *Vocational Student Organizations* had this to say about youth organizations.

> One splendid, yet neglected, mechanism for industry involvement is already in place: *our national vocational student organizations.* They have existed among us for 45 years. They reach 1.5 million more young people every year—year after year. Industry invests an estimated three million dollars a year to help pay their modest costs, but these contributions are even more important as a measure of the esteem American industry holds for this vital organization. But much more important, thousands of business, industry, labor, and community representatives participate in the daily activities of these organizations. The value of the time they contribute is inestimable, but infinitely more valuable are the solid links between industry and our young people that are being built. These vocational youth organizations, whose membership is voluntary, are quietly doing more to close the relevance gap than any other movement on the educational scene.

It is this kind of support that will place vocational youth organizations on an educational level commensurate with their true value. Such a contribution cannot be overlooked in the full development of trade, industrial, and technical education.

In the long run, the strength of VICA will lie in the acceptance of the philosophy behind it: that youth development should be an integral part of the trade, industrial, and technical and health education program. The VICA concept must be relayed to the trade, industrial, and technical instructor through teacher training programs. This requires an acceptance of club activities as part of every program. To this end, teacher training programs must prepare the future instructor to recognize the centrality of youth development activities; that it is an inseparable part of the total learning experience.

Summary

This chapter points to one of the most significant accomplishments of trade, industrial, and technical education made during our generation of vocational educators; the establishment of the Vocational Industrial Clubs of America. Through the over 125,000 members of VICA a much felt program of youth leadership development has been achieved.

The purpose, historical development, pledge, creed, and emblem attest to the spirit and commitment of the organization. To be a VICA member represents an opportunity well beyond that which is offered through most regular school programs. Sponsorship of VICA, either as an extracurricular activity or as part of the regular school schedule, requires skills not always possessed by teachers. Study and effort through teacher training programs is suggested as being highly beneficial to assure a strong VICA youth movement.

QUESTIONS AND ACTIVITIES

1. Name the five official youth organizations associated with vocational education.

2. Survey your school to determine whether or not there is interest in organizing a local chapter of VICA.

3. How would you structure a local chapter of VICA in your school? By sections (multi-clubs) or by a single club?

4. What kinds of activities are sponsored by the Vocational Industrial Clubs of America?

SOURCE MATERIALS

1. National Advisory Council on Vocational Education. *Seventh Report: Vocational Student Organizations.* Washington, D.C., November, 1972.

2. Vocational Industrial Clubs of America. *Leadership Handbook.* Falls Church, Virginia: 1970.

Chapter 12 PROGRAM EVALUATION AND ACCREDITATION

The rhetoric of determining the effectiveness of educational programs is diverse and elusive. One cannot really evaluate trade, industrial, and technical programs at the present because the base line from which to make judgments is so hazy and vague that justification for almost any effort can be substantiated. This chapter will suggest some ways to achieve precision with regard to evaluation and educational variables.

Measurement and Evaluation

It is appropriate to begin by reminding the reader that "measurement" and "evaluation" are not synonymous:

> Measurement is the process of identifying phenomena by means of assigned dimensional symbols in order to characterize the status of a phenomena as precisely as possible. . . . Evaluation is determining the value of this status by comparing it with some appropriate standard (Bradfield and Moredock 1957).

A classic example of evaluation is to gauge typing ability by *measuring* the number of words per minute the person can produce. The phenomenon being measured is, of course, typing, the status of which is characterized by

195

the number of words per minute. Thus, speed and accuracy (since errors will reduce the score) are precisely measured. Evaluation takes place when a manual is consulted that gives the level of ability attained for a certain score. The evaluation is based on a standard or norm set by repeated testing of many so-called typists. Depending on a given score, the typist may be *evaluated* as excellent, good, fair, poor, or unsatisfactory. Although examples in the trade, industrial, and technical field are not as easy to provide, they exist if one uses a little imagination. For example, the Plymouth Trouble Shooting Contest uses a number of malfunctions to *evaluate* the automotive ability as *measured* by their correction in number of minutes. Cosmetology and practical nursing, both licensed occupations, *evaluate* their product by using a paper and pencil test as the *measure* of competency.

Bradfield and Moredock (1957, p. 191) remind us that the distinction between evaluation and measurement will not be always clearly discerned.

> . . . the unclear distinction between measurement and evaluation is the case where custom and long usage have fixed an association between certain measurement symbols and particular standards of quality. For instance, certain IQ brackets through long association have come to represent certain values of intelligence: 20–50 imbecile, 50–70 moron, 100 normal, 140 and up, genius.

This automatic association of measurement with immediate evaluation does not, however, assure set standards for measurement symbols. That is to say, standards of evaluation "give way" from time to time (usually based on new research and findings) even though the measurement instruments remain the same. In the process of evaluating phenomena in education as well as in most areas of the behavioral sciences, the weakness lies in procuring the measurement.

MEASUREMENT

Measurement involves three imperative criteria: validity, reliability, and efficiency. Briefly stated, validity is the capability of the procedure to measure what it purports to measure. Among other things, the validity of a measuring device involves a clear definition of what is to be measured. For example, the measurement of typing speed involves the number of words accurately typed per minute. Any other measure of typing speed could be said to be invalid.

Reliability is concerned with the consistency of the measurement from one time to another. Reliable measures yield comparable scores upon repeated test administration. Determination of reliability rests with the measuring device's ability to produce the same results time after time.

Efficiency of a measuring procedure involves matters of expense, time, and energy—three factors that have been considered a luxury for the education profession to consider (a notion which in reality has contributed to its weakness). The ideal efficient measuring procedure is the one which provides the needed measurement techniques with a minimum of time, expense, and energy when compared with other possible measuring procedures.

EVALUATION

Standards are used as the basis for making judgments or evaluations. A standard represents a scale and is subject to change as its appropriateness changes. The standards of dress, dance, and hair-dos serve as classic examples of change of standards. Frequently a "purpose" is a standard; for example the purpose of retraining programs might be to provide individuals with immediate employment. Evaluation of such a purpose could thus be based on the measurement signs of days, weeks, or months it takes to have all the graduates of the program become employed. The evaluative standard (scale) could be set with one to three days necessary to find employment being *excellent,* four to seven, *good;* eight to twelve days, *fair;* thirteen to fifteen days, *poor;* and fifteen days and over, *unsatisfactory.* During times of severe unemployment the evaluation scale could be changed upward from the ideal just cited. Evaluations, therefore, can be changed, depending on circumstances.

Criteria for determining evaluative standards are at least five-fold.

1. Evaluative standards should be expressed in qualitative terms and not vaguely implied. The standards should be concerned with the question of quality.

2. Variations of quality should be well defined. Clear boundaries that may exist between different quality levels, such as apprentice, journeyman, master mechanic, serve as an example.

3. Evaluative standards should be reasonably stable. Standards subject to rapid changes should be avoided.

4. Evaluative standards should be expressed in terms that lend themselves to good procedures of measurement. That is to say, evaluative standards and measuring procedures are highly interdependent, and properly stated standards produce good measuring devices.

5. Evaluative standards should reflect societal acceptability. They should emphasize the culture and value structure of time. The dignity of work, creativity, innovation and such should receive high ratings; whereas, laziness, lack of initiative, and complacency should receive low standards.

Measurement and evaluation constitute a two-fold action. The elimination of either step jeopardizes the other. The first part is to precisely appraise the phenomenon and the second is to compare it with an appropriate standard. The remainder of this chapter will deal with these two parts and their application to the *internal* and *external* evaluation of trade, industrial, and technical education programs.

INTERNAL EVALUATION: EDUCATIONAL VARIABLES AS A BASIS FOR EVALUATION

It is quite clear that our nation, largely due to technological and scientific development, has reached the stage of a truly mass society, as contrasted to the communal society of some decades ago. The local option—closely knit, self-sufficient, neighborhood and family life atmosphere—is rapidly giving way to complex social forces and interrelationships which act on individuals and have an increasing effect. The unrest caused by unequal opportunities and the suppression of certain racial and ethnic groups breaks out without regard to geographic location. The blight of the slums and the poverty-stricken grows into open exposure as society moves as a mass.

As a result of population growth and technological advances, the mass society is confronted with critical economic problems. A transportation strike in New York City has a measurable effect on the lives of the shoppers in Tulsa, Oklahoma, and the temperature in the South affects the citrus consumption in the North. Moreover, the educational level attained by a youth in New Jersey affects his ability to change occupations several times throughout his life span, not to mention his ability to be mobile in a geographic sense. Changes in labor structure, the rise and fall of occupational areas, and various levels of unemployment have their impact on educational training programs. Times of full employment suggest broadening educational offerings in contrast to the specificity of a low employment picture. Such forces and their effect on the necessities of life must be reflected in educational training programs.

Against this backdrop it seems appropriate to restate some underlying beliefs held by most educators involved in trade, industrial, and technical education:

- Society benefits when each individual has the opportunity to develop his abilities to make a maximum contribution.

- One of the most important contributions which any individual can make to society is that of economic independence, whether on the farm, in the store, in the factory, or in the home.

- The education of the individual, to be properly balanced, must include training for efficient self-support.

- Changes in agriculture, industry, distribution, and service occupations must be recognized in adapting vocational education to the changing demands of our dynamic society.

Quality trade, industrial, and technical programs can be discussed from several perspectives. The approach taken here is to suggest the possibility of incorporating what will be referred to as *internal* and *external* evaluation. In this sense, internal evaluation would give concern to the educational variables definable in terms of the program *in-put*. Those components that make possible a successful program of trade, industrial, and technical education are recognized through past experience and are evident within any good program. They can be looked upon as the *in-put*. They consist of such variables as: distinguishing characteristics, philosophy and objectives, matching objectives to need, achievement of objectives, organization and management, occupational advisory committees, program research and evaluation, the teaching-learning process, curriculum, learning resources, supplies and equipment, and instructional space and facilities (American Vocational Association 1971).

Input variables of this type, judged within the context of a specific program, serve as a basis for making evaluations for purposes of self-improvement and accreditation. An attempt is usually made to have expert evaluators structure their responses to be consistent with the aims and objectives of the program under study. Statements or guiding principles as supplied by the American Vocational Association's National Study for Accreditation of Vocational/Technical Education are used as a guide to make observations.

By use of such a judgmental procedure and structured instrument, certain appraisals can be made. However, all such instruments appear to conform to the same weakness of subjectivity and bias of the evaluators. Appraisals are based on the response ratings of the evaluators, who are usually experts from the field but are subject to their own biases. Responses are placed on a scale to indicate their strength of agreement or disagreement. The responses across items reflect a raw score or a mean score for an overall assessment. In this manner, an indication of the worth (evaluation) of the program is made. The biases of the evaluators must be accepted as part of such a procedure and can only be reduced by having several evaluators or a team, all equally competent, respond using the same instrument. Probably the most noted of these measures have been developed by the American Vocational Association (1971), the National Study for Secondary School Evaluation, and the States of New York (1962) and Ohio (1964).

EDUCATIONAL VARIABLES

The educational variables most appropriately considered may be defined as follows.

Organization.   This variable implies a structure, arrangement, and administrative plan for carrying forth the training program. It concerns itself with questions of operation, funding, and management. In its broadest sense, it involves a plan so designed as to meet a diversity of situations within the stated purposes of the program. Administrative staff and their functions are usually considered part of this variable.

Nature of the Offerings.   This variable deals with the specific aims and objectives of the offering. It justifies them in terms of the general plan and shows how they were arrived at, that is, analysis, specifications, advice, and so forth. In many respects the nature of the offering is the most important of all educational variables. How aims and objectives are arrived at can vary a great deal, but once stated, they must remain as a bench mark until changed on a justifiable basis. The lack of specificity of aims and objectives can negate their measurement.

Physical Facilities.   The variable of physical facilities is a function of both appropriateness and adequacy. The setting, architectural design, physical structure, heating, lighting, ventilation, and so forth can be appraised in terms of the nature of the offering and the purpose for which they are used. The vintage of structures attest to some extent to the value attached to certain programs. The status of the apprenticeship program in Cleveland, Ohio, for example, increased many fold with the completion of the new Max S. Hayes School which provides such training.

Direction of Learning.   There are four variables to be considered here: instructional staff, instructional activities, instructional materials, and methods of evaluation. Each is explained as follows:

Instructional staff: The concern here is with the qualifications, experience, and personal traits of those who carry on the instruction. Differences in formal preparation, certification, and up-to-dateness constitute considerable variability both in terms of purpose (meeting objectives) and capability.

Instructional Activities: The appropriateness of pedagogical techniques, correlation of course content, and the carrying out of the instructional processes are variables under this heading. This category depicts the role of the teacher(s) in terms of performance and manipulation to maximize learning.

Instructional Materials: The tools and devices for instruction are important variables to consider. Audio-visual aids such as models, mock ups, films, slides, and exploded views are essential to good instruction. Their availability and extent of use serves the purposes of motivation for learning and clarification of instruction. Text books, trade journals, industrial pamphlets, occupational monographs, and other such materials can be appraised as to their availability and use in the classroom.

Methods of Evaluation: This concerns the extent to which appropriate measures, such as tests, records, reports, and instructor interviews represent evaluative variables. Evaluation has to be thought of as continuing throughout instruction. The objectivity of the technique is an important consideration. Student "feedback" through the use of posted progress charts is evidence of a good evaluative procedure.

No doubt other educational variables could be cited and other categorical classifications made. The American Vocational Association's Pilot Test Edition, *Instruments and Procedures for the Evaluation of Vocational/Technical Education Institutions and Programs* (1971) is one such example. However, the limitations of the process and the constraints of the judgmental procedure for the purpose of internal evaluation of training programs should be recognized.

The procedure becomes increasingly complex when specificity of purpose (nature of the offering) is not clear and precise, and when the aims and objectives do not lend themselves to given dimensions. For example, *aims and objectives* which are stated in high sounding, unmeasurable, undimensional terms as "the understanding of," "a knowledge of," "desirable citizenship," or "saleable skills," are not appropriate. One cannot argue the worthiness of such terms, but their appraisal, and thus their capability to be measured, become most difficult.

More appropriately stated, *aims and objectives,* at least for purposes of evaluation, are phrased in terms such as "the ability to identify," "to interpret," "the ability to apply," "to comprehend," and so forth. Cast in such a context, a basis for using the judgmental procedure takes on new and more precise meaning.

Kaufman and Schaefer (1967) used this procedural method to investigate the effectiveness of secondary school vocational and technical education programs. Among some of the problems they encountered were the lack of clear and well-defined objectives of the programs under study and vast differences in interpretation of the purposes of vocational programs at the local level of implementation. At least from the standpoint of evaluation, it appeared to these two researchers that the locally stated purpose of vocational education was so vague that the local school administrator simply did not know where his program was headed. Moreover, the needs of students were so diverse that a singularly designed occupational program made the internal evaluation, in terms of the criteria mentioned, almost impossible to judge. That is to say, for various levels of occupational training (programs for students with special needs, for example) the organizational pattern must differ as to the physical facilities, instructional activities, teacher characteristics, materials involved, and so forth. In assuming this difference does not exist, one returns to the one room-one teacher schoolhouse concept, which has been proven ineffective in terms of quality education when the needs of all youth are considered. The obvious plea is for more specificity in defining objectives and in the structure necessary to meet them.

Internal evaluation has played and will continue to play an important role in improving instructional programs. The processes, if used as a "self evaluation" technique, can be of benefit both to the individual staff member and to the program as a whole. However, it mainly finds its value as a tool for proclaiming accreditation or certification of programs. Examples can be cited of accreditation for almost any level and type of educational program. Correspondence schools have their own accrediting body, colleges are accreditated, programs within colleges request the respectability of accreditation, teacher education programs (both undergraduate and graduate) are evaluated for purposes of accreditation, and associated degree programs receive the attention of accrediting bodies.* This "good housekeeping" seal or stamp of approval is a coveted honor. Depending on the expertness of the individuals involved, the instrumentation used, frequency of administration, and the type of feedback given, accreditation can be perceived as a valuable method of not only improving the effectiveness of programs, but also as a valid method of evaluation. Much more could be said for the application of this procedure in upgrading secondary-vocational training, apprenticeships, MDTA, job corps, and other such training programs.

The worth of this procedure is self evident. Its use in a highly sophisticated manner for accreditation purposes would undoubtedly have a measurable effect on the quality of programs oriented toward the world of work, no matter at what level of education the technique is used.

EXTERNAL EVALUATION: BEHAVIORAL VARIABLES AS A BASIS FOR EVALUATION

Testing to determine what individuals gain from training is another way of evaluating a program's effectiveness. Did they indeed learn manipulative skills and knowledge? Has their attitude toward work changed? Are they employable? How well do they perform? Answers to these questions can be

---

*Among these accrediting bodies are the North Central Association of Colleges and Secondary Schools (and five other similar associations for this purpose); National Council for Accreditation of Teacher Education; Engineer's Council for Professional Development; Council for Medical Education; American Bar Association; and the National Architectural Board.

measured in quite a different manner than the use of the previous procedures. To ignore measurement of the "end product" of the training program is to ignore a source of more precise measurement than the internal variables previously presented. Here the term *external* evaluation is being used to distinguish between the two kinds of evaluations in the types of procedures used and the kinds of data to be collected. Tuckman (1966) is of the following opinion:

> The judgmental approach is a necessary but not sufficient approach to evaluation. It must be supported and strengthened through the use of data gathered from the students themselves, indicating the extent to which they have realized the objectives of the program. This realization must be determined not only by the judgments of the students, but by their actual performance and behavior.

Gagne (1965, p. 5) has a similar opinion, and he states his case by defining learning as, ". . . a change in human disposition or capability, which can be retained, and which is not simply ascribable to the process of growth." Such change, he relates, exhibits itself as a change in behavior, and "may be, and often is, an increased capability for some type of performance. It may also be an altered disposition of the sort called 'attitude', or 'interest', or 'value'. "

The work of Bloom et al. (1956) stands as a bench mark in presenting a general classification of educational goals stated as basic dimensions of student achievement. The Bloom taxonomy is based on educational objectives so stated as to make it possible to measure their attainment by means of measuring the behavioral changes in individuals.

Besides the taxonomy or classification advocated by Bloom, the measurement of student behaviors represents the intended outcomes of the educational (training) process and is of prime concern to the topic under discussion. What is attempted in the external evaluation process is to determine as precisely as possible the intended behavior of students, such as the ways in which they act, think, or feel as the result of participating in trade, industrial, and technical programs.

The taxonomy approach attempts to imply a hierarchical order of the different classes of objectives, ranging from the simple to the complex. For example, to assist in such clarification, the Dewey decimal classification system for libraries was adopted. Subsequently, six major classifications were arrived at in order of their importance: (Bloom 1956, p. 18).

1.00 Knowledge

2.00 Comprehension

3.00 Application

4.00 Analysis

5.00 Synthesis

6.00 Evaluation

Such a classification scheme has particular relevance when one realizes that the classification and evaluation of educational objectives must be considered as part of the total process of curriculum and training program development. In developing curriculum, consideration must be given to:

1. The educational (training) purpose or objectives;
2. The learning experiences that need to be provided to bring about attainment of these objectives;
3. How those learning experiences can be interrelated to reinforce each other;
4. How the experiences can be evaluated by use of testing and other means of measurement.

Step one in constructing curriculum objectives must be defined and clearly identified if time and energy are not to be wasted. Moreover, objectives (goals) must be feasible in terms of time available, facilities, and equipment (conditions), and the aptitudes of the students.

What this suggests is the use of Bloom's taxonomy as a tool of program establishment on the one hand and as a means of evaluating (testing) on the other. Assuming program objectives (goals) have been so identified, it then becomes possible to develop testing procedures, especially achievement tests, as a valid measure of evidence that the students are attaining each of the objectives of the program.

In this vein, it is appropriate for one to look more closely at the behavioral variables being discussed and classified by the Bloom taxonomy.

1.00 Knowledge—Knowledge concerns itself with the recall of methods and processes, patterns, and structures or settings. The mind is depicted as a file to empty its store of information upon request. Knowledge is further broken down into:

1.10 Knowledge of Specifics

1.11 Knowledge of Terminology

1.12 Knowledge of Specific Facts

1.20 Knowledge of Ways and Means of Dealing with Specifics

1.21 Knowledge of Conventions

1.22 Knowledge of Trends and Sequences

1.23 Knowledge of Classifications and Categories

1.24 Knowledge of Criteria

1.25 Knowledge of Methodology

1.30 Knowledge of the Universals and Abstractions in a Field

1.31 Knowledge of Principles and Generalizations

1.32 Knowledge of Theories and Structures

2.00 Comprehension—This represents the lowest level of understanding. It involves understanding of what is being communicated without necessarily relating it to other material or seeing its full implications. Comprehension is further broken down into:

2.00 Translation

2.20 Interpretation

2.30 Extrapolation

3.00 Application—Application concerns itself with abstractions and concrete situations that utilize technical principles, ideas, and theories.

4.00 Analysis—Analysis is intended to clarify the communications and to organize and serve as a basis for arrangement. Analysis is further broken down into:

4.10 Analysis of Elements

4.20 Analysis of Relationships

4.30 Analysis of Organizational Principles

5.00 Synthesis—This involves the fitting together of the parts to form a whole. It concerns itself with providing structure and clarity. Synthesis is broken down into:

5.10 Production of a Unique Communication, i.e., the getting of ideas, feelings, etc. across to others; the ability to make an extemporaneous speech, etc.

5.20 Production of a Plan, or Proposed Set of Operations: i.e., the ability to set down step-by-step procedure, the design, etc.

5.30 Derivation of a Set of Abstract Relations: i.e., ability to formulate appropriate hypotheses based on analysis of factors involved.

6.00 Evaluation—This concerns the use of a standard of appraisal. Based on quantitative and qualitative data, decisions are made about the value of the materials and methods used for a given purpose. Evaluation is further broken down into:

6.10 Judgments in Terms of Internal Evidence: i.e., the ability to apply criteria (based on internal standards such as consistency) to the judgment of work.

6.20 Judgments in Terms of External Criteria: i.e., evaluation based on criteria derived from a consideration of the *ends* to be served and the appropriateness of specific means for achieving these ends.

What is being suggested here is the use of Bloom's educational objective classification as a tool not only for curriculum development, but as a means of constructing tests to ascertain attainment of the curriculum. More specifically, such tests might well be constructed to accompany secondary school vocational, apprenticeship, and retraining programs as local, state, and even national indicators of program success. The standardization of achievement tests has long been a belief of New York State in the form of State Regents examinations; College Board Examinations are used for establishing acceptability for college entrance, and certain local, state, and even national examinations are required for licensure purposes.

Measurement of the effectiveness of programs in this manner would enable the establishment of a basis for comparison and subsequent meaningful evaluative (normative data) insights. Obviously the problem becomes more complex when the manipulative or motor-skill area is seriously considered. Tests of manipulative skills have been developed, but, without a doubt, much more needs to be done if we are to move into a high degree of evaluation on this basis. The development of tests as evaluative instruments has long been a topic of discussion and study. Among those contributing to the refinement of testing both as a process and procedure of evaluation are Lindquist (1951), Dressel (1950), and Taylor (1949).

At the present time a group of states are working on the development of examinations to measure the occupational competency of prospective teachers for certification and/or college credit. The effort is known as *The National Occupational Competency Testing Institute* and is located at the Educational Testing Service, Princeton, New Jersey. Examinations are planned and administered twice a year through regional coordinators of the Institute.

Needless to say, in order to assess total program offerings by any testing procedure, a major breakthrough would be necessary on many levels, such as apprenticeship, retraining, job corps, secondary vocational, and the like. The present status of the art is both lacking in appropriateness and in amount of real effort shown, the most obvious being the lack of manipulative skills tests.

INTERNAL AND EXTERNAL EVALUATION

As already indicated in this chapter, *internal evaluation* is identified in terms of educational variables within the ongoing program. *External evaluation* is defined as those testable aspects founded in behavioral changes of the student(s). Their relationship exists in terms of the quality of the instructional program and the validity of measurement. Certainly, one without the other could lead to questions as to the relative merit of a program or curriculum. That is to say, the internal evaluation needs to be cross-validated with the actual attainment of the students. Testing to determine student progress must be compared with the in-put evaluation so as to assure an efficient and economical means of arriving at that attainment.

When combined in this manner, an evaluation of the educational and behavioral variables can be said to be based on valid measurement. This is precisely the point that is missing in the evaluation of most training programs. To be able to say that trade, industrial, and technical education program is good by all indications of good pedagogy is far less accurate than to say that a program is good because of the instructional processes (pedagogy) and attested to by the end product (students) being turned out.

Probably an outstanding example, which at least approaches the relationship that is being discussed, can be cited in the State of Ohio relative to its trade and industrial high school offerings. The Ohio State Department of Education (1972) has developed and utilized a series of achievement examinations for measuring student attainment in the areas of auto mechanics, auto body, carpentry, electronics, machine trades, welding, sheet metal, and printing. These examinations are administered to each graduating class, on a voluntary basis, for the purpose of indicating the strengths and weakness of the instructional areas. In addition, individual student profiles are plotted to show each graduate how he ranked when compared with his fellow class students and fellow state students. The Ohio State Department of Education (1964) also possesses evaluative criteria for assessing high school trade and industrial education programs by means of an internal evaluation. In this instance, it is not hard to envision the use of both of these procedures to attest to the quality of Ohio's high school trade and industrial education programs. By combining the two measures, a high degree of validity of measurement can be claimed and eventually appropriate standards of evaluation can be developed.

Undoubtedly, one of the deterents in this combined process is the tremendous amount of time and cost involved in developing both measures to the high degree of sophistication necessary. The problem is certainly of great magnitude if significant results of assessment are to be made.

SOCIOECONOMIC VARIABLES AND THEIR MEASUREMENT

For too long we have ignored the evaluation of educational programs in terms of how investment in training contributes to the processes of social and economic growth. As Nicholas DeWitt (1966) puts it:

> Human resource development is the social process of the production, distribution, and utilization of the knowledge, the skills, and the capabilities of all of the people in a society. If a society is unable to develop its human resources, it can not develop much else, be it technology, political, or social institutions, material or culture welfare, or its economy.

There have been but spotty endeavors to evaluate trade, industrial, and technical terms of economic variables; and even fewer attempts have been made to measure the value of programs designed for the world of work in relation to social variables. The methodology used by educators, when indeed such attempts have been made, has been that of follow-up studies. Both the paucity of such studies and their lack of breadth probably attest to the inadequacy of educators themselves to pursue an evaluation on this basis. The panel of consultants in the report, *Education for a Changing World of Work* (U.S. Department of Health, Education and Welfare 1963) readily admitted this deficiency. Other attempts can be cited in the form of the *North Atlantic Region Follow-up Studies of Graduates of Trade and Industrial Programs in Public Vocational-Technical High Schools* (U.S. Office of Education 1950–1966), and, on the local level, *After Ten Years* (Coe 1964), completed by the Middlesex County Vocational and Technical High Schools, New Jersey.*

If accurate social and economic evaluations of training programs are to be made, and certainly they should be made, it seems appropriate that they be carried out with the vigor and precision that the disciplines of sociology and economics can lend to the problem. That is to say, the work of Ginzberg (1964), Kaufman (1972), and others must begin to truly focus on the value of education to the wealth of the nation. Such work must be directed to the problem of relating trade, industrial, and technical programs to social and economic variables.**

The very image of work has changed over the years as technology has changed the world of work. Prior to the Industrial Revolution, for example, the function of work was the production of goods. The primary instruments of production were human and animal strength. Work, in other words, was measured to a large extent in human effort; and man's status was measured in terms of the amount of work he could produce.

Today muscle power is more and more displaced by automated machinery, and vast surpluses of production are conceivable.

As Venn (1964, pp. 10–11) puts it:

> This situation leads to the problem at hand . . . any hard work that a machine can do (and that includes virtually all such work) is better done by a machine; "hard" these days means mostly boring and repetitive, whether in the factory or the office. But the instinct for workmanship, the need to feel needed, the will to achieve, are deeply felt in every human

---

*This study followed up the class of 1953 ten years after graduation in order to determine the occupational, educational, marital, and armed service experiences of these graduates during the time period June 1953 to June 1963.

**Among the most noteworthy economic variables are: mobility, structural unemployment, level of employment, occupational demands, and employment opportunities. The social variables include: equality of opportunities, maintaining a balanced curriculum, status of occupations, flexibility of choice, national goals, and the like.

heart. . . . In place of work we have substituted the job. A man's occupation in American society is now his single most significant status-conferring role. Whether it be high or low, a job of status allows the individual to form some stable conception of himself and his position in the community.

The social and psychological effects of joblessness are painfully apparent in America today. They can be seen in the faces of those citizens standing in line for relief checks; none of them may be starving, and there may be work around the home that could keep them busy, but without a job they are lost.

Without an occupation or job, Brookover and Nosow (1963, p. 26) remind us, "the individual has few other statuses which are capable of offering him a respected position in the community." The sociologist, being well aware of this situation, cannot leave the consequences for such ultimate frustrations entirely in the hands of educators.

The relationship between education and economic development is generally agreed upon by economists, but the technical problems of measuring the economic returns on a particular investment remain great. Attempts have been made to relate earnings and educational attainment and to compare them with the earning power of those with less education. Needless to say, such an approach is confounded by the technical difficulty, among other things, of measuring the cost of providing educational programs. In the public sector, and especially at the secondary education level, the parcelling out of costs for buildings, instruction, etc., is a difficult task. Nevertheless, such an approach has merit, and, if adequately arrived at, represents a meaningful indicator to even the skeptic. There are indications that the World War II G.I. Bill of Rights (which was measured in this manner) proved the worth of the investment. Refinement of this method of assessing the relationship between trade, industrial, and technical education and economic development must capture the assistance of the economists. Their role in this endeavor has been too long underemphasized. Educators will not be surprised to be informed, as Gordon (1965) points out in her study, *Retraining and Labor Market Adjustment in Western Europe,* that:

> . . . retraining was regarded in several countries as a permanent instrument of labor market adjustment policy, rather than as merely a means of facilitating the transition from a wartime to a peacetime economy (p. 26).
> . . . the usefulness of retraining programs as a means of combating shortages of workers with particular types of skills or training under tight labor market conditions has come to be increasingly recognized . . . (p. 57).

The dialogue in this vein must be continuous and vocal and must be heard by those who have the responsibility for organizing and carrying forth programs designed for the world of work. It may be some time before the entire evaluative picture (educational, behavioral, and socioeconomic) can be brought into clear perspective, but the ultimate objective should not be for anything less.

Recommendations

If, but to clinch the points made in this chapter, recommendations relative to the picture (educational and behavioral) can be made, they can be stated succinctly as follows:

1. Evaluation of trade, industrial, and technical programs should culminate in a form of accreditation on a regional or national basis. They should receive the prestige of being found acceptable to produce the end product they purport to produce. They should be subject to review and investigation far beyond local and even state standards. And if these standards are not in accord, a dialogue should be established to reason out why there are differences.

2. Evaluation of trade, industrial, and technical programs should be based on a combination of the internal and external evaluation procedures. Neither the former nor the latter in their own right are enough. The combined instrumentation of the two procedures is needed to acclaim the merit of a program and to attest to its accreditation.

3. Evaluation of trade, industrial, and technical programs should, in addition, seek the prestige of the end product (graduates) being awarded certification equivalent in prestige and authenticity to licensuring practices now found in a large number of occupations. The license, thus, reflects attainment and up-to-dateness of ability to perform in an acceptable manner.

It would be hoped that such recommendations, regardless of their difficulty to implement, would bring about substantial changes in the effectiveness of trade, industrial, and technical programs. There is evidence that one need but look at the respectability and acceptance of the present day practical nurse to observe what can be accomplished if a profession sets its mind to assuring attainment of program effectiveness.

Summary

This chapter has discussed the educational and behavioral variables that must be considered in evaluating educational (training) programs. The need for their measurement in a precise and accurate manner was emphasized. The internal evaluation procedure and its lack of objectivity brought about by the biases of evaluators was examined in relationship to the input variables of the nature of the offerings, organizations, physical facilities, and direction of learning.

The testing procedure to measure behavioral change of the students in training programs was pursued. The Bloom taxonomy of measuring behavioral change and its contribution to making valid tests was reviewed. The combining of the two procedures into an accreditation type structure, utilizing both internal and external evaluation was recommended as a plausible, if not a much-needed entity, to assure the effectiveness of programs oriented toward the world of work.

A plea for the measurement of the socioeconomic variables of education by the sociologist and economist in order to round out the evaluation was made.

QUESTIONS AND ACTIVITIES

1. How is your trade, industrial, and technical program evaluated? What types of measures do you use?

2. What methods do you use to determine internal evaluation? External evaluation?

3. Check your examination (mid-term or final) against Bloom's taxonomy to see if it conforms to the classification system.

4. Why do you think the Bloom classification dealing with application is the most difficult to assess?

5. In your estimation, should the educator be concerned with the socioeconomic goals of a trade, industrial, and technical program?

6. Discuss the three recommendations in terms of their desirability and/or appropriateness.

SOURCE MATERIALS

1. American Vocational Association. *Instruments and Procedures for the Evaluation of Vocational/Technical Education Institutions and Programs. Pilot Test Edition 12–71.* Washington, D.C.: 1971.

2. Bloom, Benjamin S., ed. *Taxonomy of Educational Objectives, Handbook I, Cognitive Domain.* New York: David McKay Company, 1956.

3. Bradfield, James M., and Moredock, Steward H. *Measurement and Evaluation in Education.* New York: The Macmillan Company, 1957.

4. Brookover, Wilbur B., and Nosow, Sigmund. "A Sociological Analysis of Vocational Education in the United States." *Education for a Changing World of Work: Report of the Panel of Consultants on Vocational Education, Appendix III.* Washington, D.C.: U.S. Government Printing Office, 1963, p. 26.

5. Coe, Burr D., and Zanzalari, Henry J. *After Ten Years: A Follow-up Study of Middlesex County Vocational and Technical High School Graduates, Class of June 1953.* New Brunswick, N.J.: Middlesex County Vocational and Technical High Schools, 1964.

6. De Witt, Nicholas. "Investment in Education and Economic Development," *Phi Delta Kappan* 47, (December 1965).

7. Dressel, Paul L. "Evaluation Procedures for General Education Objectives." *Educational Record,* April 1950, pp. 97–122.

8. Gagne, Robert M. *Conditions of Learning.* New York: Holt, Rinehart and Winston, 1965.

9. Ginzberg, Eli, ed. *Technology and Social Change.* New York: Columbia University, 1964.

10. Gordon, Margaret S. *Retraining and Labor Market Adjustment in Western Europe.* Washington, D.C.: Manpower Administration. U.S. Government Printing Office, 1965.

11. Kaufman, J. J.; Cohn, Elchana; Hu, Tch-Wei. *The Cost of Vocational and Nonvocational Programs: A Study of Michigan Secondary Schools.* University Park, Pa.: Institute for Research on Human Resources, The Pennsylvania State University, 1972.

12. Kaufman, J. J. et al. *The Role of the Secondary Schools in the Preparation of Youth for Employment.* University Park, Pa.: The Pennsylvania State University, 1967.

13. Lindquist, E. F., ed. *Educational Measurement.* Washington, D.C.: American Council on Education, 1951.

14. Ohio State Department of Education. *Achievement Test Program.* Columbus, Ohio: Trade and Industrial Education Services, 1972.

15. Ohio State Department of Education, Division of Vocational Education, Trade and Industrial Education Service. *Trade and Industrial Education Program Analysis Questionnaire,* Columbus, Ohio, 1964.

16. Taylor, Ralph W. "Achievement Testing and Curriculum Construction." *Trends in Student Personnel Work.* E. G. Williamson (ed.). Minneapolis, Minn.: University of Minnesota Press, 1949, pp. 391–407.

17. The University of the State of New York. *A Guide for the Review of a Program in Trade and Technical Education.* Albany, N.Y.: The State Department of Education, Cooperative Review Service, 1962.

18. Tuckman, Bruce, W. "The Development and Testing of an Evaluation Model for Vocational Pilot Programs." Rutgers–The State University. An unpublished proposal for 4-C funds under The Vocational Educational Act 1963, 1966.

19. U.S. Department of Health, Education and Welfare. *Education for a Changing World of Work.* Report of the Panel of Consultants on Vocational Education. Washington, D.C.: Superintendent of Documents, 1963.

20. U.S. Office of Education. *North Atlantic Region Follow-Up Studies of Graduates from Trade and Industrial Education Programs,* (by year). Washington, D.C.: Division of Vocational Education, 1950–1966.

21. Venn, Grant. *Man, Education, and Work.* Washington, D.C.: American Council on Education. 1964.

Chapter 13 MAJOR ISSUES IN TRADE, INDUSTRIAL, AND TECHNICAL EDUCATION

To say there are not problems in the trade, industrial, and technical field would be untrue. The present day scene has contributed to its share of confusion of the issues as at no other time in the history of the field. It has been the intent of this entire text to clarify some of the "fuzzy thinking" that has confounded the area of trade, industrial, and technical education. Moreover, it is the purpose in this chapter to reemphasize some of the issues and to raise others which need attention and solution through research and study. Although not in order of priority, these issues are as follows:

What is the present day philosophical basis of trade, industrial, and technical education?   At this time of "career education," the mission of trade, industrial, and technical education is confused. Its role at the secondary and postsecondary levels of the educational enterprise is not clearly delineated; and its contribution as a delivery system is questionable. Moreover, the place of trade, industrial, and technical education in the total concept of "career education" appears confounded in terms of the curriculum to be offered, the requisites of the teacher, and the type of physical facility required to support the learning process. The general notion of job clusters and the apparent demise of industrial arts, especially at the high school level, further confound the issues.

What is the philosophy behind the teaching of specific trades and occupations as part of public school education? Is the philosophical base the same as it was a half century ago? Should such training be "put off" until the postsecondary years? Is the labor market really willing to accept youth—especially those under twenty-one years of age—or should they be retained longer in school? What are the motivations of youth toward career choices, and how strong and valid are occupational choices at different age levels? These are but some of the legitimate questions of a philosophical nature that need study and research.

What should constitute the curriculum of trade, industrial, and technical education?   The problems of curriculum construction and its implementation and revision continue to plague trade, industrial, and technical education. What constitutes a good curriculum and how it can be delivered are questions which need answers. In the past, occupational analysis techniques have been relied upon as the means to elicit curriculum content. Are these techniques still appropriate today?

The lengths of trade, industrial, and technical programs differ dramatically—from two to four years. Scheduling practices vary in terms of the delivery of the content. Sometimes related instruction is taught within the shop or laboratory, by the shop or lab teacher. Other plans call for separate teachers.* Staff utilization is related to the scheduling and curriculum delivery. The correlation or relationship of science, mathematics, and drawing with the performance aspects of the occupation implies a need for proper staff utilization and scheduling. Scheduling is frequently looked upon as a process to maximize the use of teachers and facilities, and not as a means of meeting the needs of students. The whole process of scheduling can become rigid and nonflexible—a device to assure teacher expediency, and not student-centered; administratively convenient, and not educationally sound. The excuse that, "It is difficult to schedule this building" is heard far too often.

All of this adds up to the need for the study and generation of "hard data" on the advantages and disadvantages of varied plans of curriculum building, scheduling practices, and staffing patterns.

How can staffs, curricula, and physical facilities be maximized as a delivery system?   At the present time the full potential of trade, industrial, and technical education is not being utilized. Staffing is employed on a ten-month basis, only to leave dormant for a period of time the existing curricula and physical facility. Meanwhile, manpower training centers, job

---

*Frequently referred to as Type A and B programs. Type A uses additional periods outside the shop time to teach related mathematics, science, and drawing. Type B teaches these related subjects within the shop time.

corps, and the like have sprung up to duplicate (in many respects) the already existing offerings of trade, industrial, and technical education. Questions arise such as: Can we afford dual programs when there are limited dollars available? How can existing staff be maximized in the effort? What about the physical facility and its use in terms of "down time" and duplication costs? Can teachers relate equally well to youth and adult students? What should be the role of trade, industrial, and technical education as a delivery system?

Answers to these and similar questions are needed to substantiate the full potential of trade, industrial, and technical education as a viable delivery system for the producing of skilled manpower. The duplication of small entities or pieces of education without overall coordination has lead to much confusion. What appears to be needed is a "locus" for the continuing education throughout life which serves the needs of youth and adults. And certainly a paramount need lies in the area of occupational preparation, up-dating and retraining. In this, trade, industrial, and technical education has an important role to play—but one which has not been fully accepted either in philosophy or implementation.

Why has not trade, industrial, and technical education addressed itself more to the occupational needs of females and minority groups?
The ranks of skilled employment and job opportunities are conspicuously void in terms of minority populations. Blacks, especially, do not find their way into the skilled and technical-level jobs. At a time when the manpower needs of the nation are pleading for greater and greater skills and technical knowledge, it appears that minority groups are not being prepared in great enough numbers for such roles. Why more such individuals are not being enrolled in trade, industrial, and technical education programs is a problem needing study.

Somewhat the same question could be asked about the lack of females. It appears that there are "typical" curricula—and only such curricula—for females in trade, industrial, and technical areas. Are opportunities being made available for girls to enroll in the curricula they desire and where they have the motivation and ability to achieve? Why are there not more girls in various drafting curricula, for example?

Questions of exclusiveness need to be raised as to how open are trade, industrial, and technical education programs. Moreover, answers need to be found for problems encountered in placement and follow-up of minority and female graduates of programs.

What degree of occupational versus pedagogical competency should be expected of trade, industrial, and technical teachers?   Does the concept that a teacher must first and foremost be a master of his subject matter still hold today? Occupational competency of trade, industrial, and technical teachers has long been acclaimed to be the most important ingredient of a teacher. Certification in many states has been written to help attest to such competency. Too frequently, however, mere number of years of experience has not proven to be a foolproof criterion. College and university degree programs are now beginning to recognize the worth of accumulated experience and knowledge as a legitimate currency for the granting of college credit, especially, if it is substantiated through examination.

Should trade, industrial, and technical teachers receive credit toward degrees if they can substantiate occupational competency through examination? How such tests will be developed and administered becomes a question. Moreover, what about the ability to teach as well as possess knowledge of the subject being taught. How can the sincerity and empathy for teaching be assessed? After all, the heart of the education profession is the teacher: his personality, ability to relate to the particular student population with whom he is entrusted, his skill in organizing and delivering the learning, and his dedication to the "end product" being produced. Therefore, the teacher of trade, industrial, and technical education is a most important element to the program's success. Study of the teacher, including his competencies, personality, human relations, modes of operation, and the like is important.

How can professional development be maintained?   Occupational knowledge and teaching skills rapidly become outdated if not periodically refreshed. What can be done to provide the continuing education of educators—the self-renewal of those in the trade, industrial, and technical fields?

From time to time, skills need sharpening, knowledge needs up-dating, and self-confidence needs restoring. Up to this point in the history of trade, industrial, and technical education there has not been a planned and generally accepted program of "self-renewal" for its personnel. Hit-and-miss summer work activities for teachers leaves much to be desired in achieving this goal.

Questions of staff occupational obsolescence and lack of professionalism originate from nonexistent personnel development programs. Questions of added cost and cost benefit of formalized workshops, professional days, institutes, seminars and the like need to be studied. Moreover, the whole problem of accreditation of programs and the up-to-dateness of the teacher within the accreditation needs to be explored.

How can the U.S. Office of Education report the differences between trade, industrial, and technical education and career education clusters?   The acuteness of such problems as previously discussed is further emphasized when one looks at the U.S. Office of Education's annual reporting scheme. What constitutes bona fide trade, industrial, and technical education programs and staffing in such reports is hard to distinguish. Moreover, as the career education cluster concept becomes operationalized, the distinguishing characteristics of the reporting system could become even more clouded. What is needed is a system that closely ties together those trade, industrial, and technical education programs with the definitions found in the *Dictionary of Occupational Titles*. In this way, employers and consumers will have a sense of what graduates of the specific trade, industrial, and technical education programs were trained to accomplish. The career education graduates would thus be identified as occupational-cluster types who would either go on to further training or be eligible for employment in a more broad sense.

A classification scheme of this type would eventually show a larger and larger number at the high school level enrolled in the career education cluster endeavor (as compared with the more specific trade, industrial, and technical education programs). Possibly, when this becomes a reality it will mean that those enrolled in trade, industrial, and technical education programs will be more highly motivated and vocationally talented. For the first time, teacher competency, physical facilities, and curricula could be maximized to benefit the high skill classification required by the specific occupation. Hopefully, the future classification and reporting system of the U.S. Office of Education will recognize the need to be sensitive to such a problem.

How can the effectiveness of trade, industrial, and technical education programs be measured and evaluated?   The present day emphasis in education in general is on accountability. This imposes measures of effectiveness and benefit upon the system being used to deliver graduates from trade, industrial, and technical education programs. What does it cost per graduate? How good is the product? What happens to the graduate ten or more years after graduation? These are questions needing answers if trade, industrial, and technical education is to prove its worth.

It has always been admitted that curricula of trade, industrial, and technical education are expensive to implement and to operate. But something costing a great deal may, in the long run, be quite reasonable—if the "pay-off" is substantially great; that is to say, if it can be shown that the effect is such that to not make the initial investment would result in even greater cost at some subsequent time in terms of societal needs. Thus, initial costs, although high, may actually be quite cheap. Studies to date have failed to prove that trade, industrial, and technical education at the secondary and postsecondary levels result in the best investment.

The techniques thus far developed for measuring effectiveness leave much to be desired. Internal evaluative techniques of the accreditation nature, such as evaluative criteria, are not conclusive, and the external technique of student follow-up has its limitations. In fact, few follow-up studies of a span of several years (ten to twenty) are ever conducted. There has to be a better and more accurate way to ascertain the value of the various curricula of trade, industrial, and technical education for those who invest their time and energy in pursuing them.

Problem solving at its best is a costly and time-consuming endeavor. This is probably the reason why so little information of a "hard data" type is available in most states relating to the issues just described. The one ray of hope appears to emanate from the state research coordinating units—if they are astute to recognize the real issues at hand. Facts and relatively hard data must be accumulated to support the various propositions which trade, industrial, and technical education has accepted as valid. Without such evidence the field can only move forward on conjecture.

Summary

In summary, the issues facing trade, industrial, and technical education are many and are as prevalent today as they were in the past. Solutions to such problems as changes in philosophy, curriculum, delivery systems, staffing, outreach to females and minority groups, teaching competencies, in-service preparation, and the reporting system need to be found. It is one thing to identify the problem, but another to bring to bear a body of knowledge which helps in its solution. This latter element (hard factual data) has eluded those in trade, industrial, and technical education far too long. It is time something is done about it, and the state research coordinating units appear to be a good place to start.

QUESTIONS AND ACTIVITIES

1. Make a list, according to priority, of five major issues you see facing trade, industrial, and technical education. How does this list differ from that given in this text?

2. Research has been said to be lacking in trade, industrial, and technical education. State what appears to be the trouble with the present research effort.

3. Debate the issue of twelve months versus ten months of school. Choose either side and support your position with "hard data" wherever possible.

4. If provided financial resources to implement a personnel development system, how would you use the monies?

5. Describe what is meant by "accountability" and give an example of "being accountable" in your local school system.

SOURCE MATERIALS

1. U.S. Office of Education. *National Planning and Development Committees in Trade and Industrial Education.* Washington, D.C.: Division of Vocational and Technical Education, 1968.

2. _____. *Vocational Education: The Bridge Between Man and His Work.* Washington, D.C.: Superintendent of Documents, 1968.

3. _____. *Trade and Industrial Education for the 1960's.* Washington, D.C.: Division of Vocational Education, 1959.

APPENDIX A

Introduction

The statements which follow represent discussions which were held over a three-year period by a joint committee appointed by the Industrial Arts and Trade and Industrial Education Divisions of the American Vocational Association. The Statements have been approved by both Divisions for the purpose of providing educators, students, and the lay public with a better understanding of the two programs. The members of the joint committee reaffirmed the belief that their deliberations, as reflected in this report, produced positive, constructive suggestions for mutually strengthening industrial arts education and trade, industrial, and technical education.

Committee Members

Representing Industrial Arts Education	Representing Trade and Industrial Education
Pat H. Atteberry, co-chairman	Burr D. Coe, co-chairman
Ralph Bohn	C. Thomas Olivo
Leonard W. Glismann	William B. Steinberg
Frederick D. Kagy	Clyde E. Stiner
John H. Koenig	Eurus V. Stoltz
William R. Mason	James W. Wilson
Marshall L. Schmitt, ex officio	Merle E. Strong, ex officio

Definitions

Industrial Education is a generic term which broadly defines that part of the total educational program which includes instruction in industrial arts education and trade and industrial/technical education.

Trade and Industrial/Technical Education is a program of vocational education and training for gainful employment in trades, service, and industrial/technical occupations, as described below.

Industrial Arts is a program of education relating to the broad study of selected industries, as described below.

Industrial Arts Education   Trade and Industrial/Technical Education

Curriculum

Content is derived from a broad study of selected industries; including the use of tools, materials, and processes.

The content is determined by an analysis of the various job titles in an occupational field for which training is being given, such as machine industries occupations.

Provides for the development of conceptualized skills and understandings.

The curriculum is developed, reviewed, and updated with the assistance of management/labor representatives from industry.

Provides opportunity to apply basic principles of the man-made world as a designer, planner, and user.

The content is continuously changing and is updated to reflect technological changes in each occupational field.

Programs are kept current with technological advances and changes in educational media.

Instructional materials include recent industrial publications and modern industrial devices and techniques as an integral part of the instructional programs.

Includes instructional programs

The curriculum provides

which are:

—Designed to acquaint students with the general functions and procedures of industry, including guidance for the broad spectrum of industrial occupations.

—Designed to provide a study of the interrelationships of industrial activities leading to the production and manufacture of industrial products.

—Designed to provide an opportunity for a student to concentrate in a broad subject field such as electricity/electronics, drafting, graphic arts, automotive and power materials and processes.

—Designed to foster creative abilities and interests in the use of the tools and materials of industry.

in-depth learning experience and techniques which duplicate those found in industrial/technical employment.

The time schedule, and level and amount of instruction must be adequate to develop necessary skills and related technical understanding essential for successful entry into and progress in a trade, service, industrial or technical occupation.

Pre-employment programs are provided immediately preceding employment in order to be most effective.

Programs are designed to meet the full spectrum of needs, from the single-purpose operatives to the highly skilled trade and industrial/technical craftsman.

Pre employment education and training is usually provided from grades 9 through 14.

Programs provide open-ended curriculum to permit vertical articulation from secondary to post-secondary levels.

Programs are provided around-the-clock and throughout the year. Such programs include pre-apprentice and apprentice training, retraining, occupational extension, and foremanship, supervisory and management development training.

Types of Schools

Industrial arts programs are offered in elementary schools, junior high and senior high schools, colleges, and universities.

Instructional programs in trade and industrial/technical education are offered at secondary and post-secondary levels. These are provided in a broad range of institutions, including: industrial plants, departments in comprehensive high schools, vocational schools, departments in junior and community colleges, and in programs of less than baccalaureate level in some four-year institutions.

Teachers

A baccalaureate degree program with an approved major in industrial arts education is required for initial entry into the profession with the curriculum taught and 100% approved by industrial arts teacher educators.

Must have completed a program of professional preparation, including a supervised internship or student teaching experience.

Work experience is desirable as a basis for a broad understanding of industry and the world of work.

The prerequisite occupational proficiency is developed under actual wage earning situations in a trade, service, industrial, or technical occupation.

High school graduation or the equivalent is required as the minimal education for acceptance into trade and industrial/technical teacher education.

Potential teachers recruited from industry must possess personal, physical, and moral qualities essential for the development of a successful teacher.

Quality vocational industrial/technical teacher education programs are required. Such programs are planned, directed, and supervised by qualified vocational industrial teacher educators.

Instructional Facilities

Must meet standards set by regional accreditation associations and individual state requirements.

Must include the tools, equipment, materials, and space necessary to implement the proposed curriculum.

The plans for instructional shops, laboratories, and related instructional classroom facilities are based upon occupational analyses and recommendations of vocational industrial advisory committees. The nature of the instructional plant and the variety of equipment are comparable, where practical, to those found in industry.

Instructional supplies and materials are comparable to those found in industry and are available in sufficient quantity to develop adequate marketable skills.

Students

All students K through 12, post-secondary, college, and adults, regardless of their occupational goals, could benefit from experiences offered in industrial arts.

Programs are planned for a large variety of student objectives such as:
—Pre-collegiate programs providing industrial information preparatory to professional study
—General education programs providing a broad understanding and consumer experience in industrial subjects
—Elementary programs providing occupational and industrial guidance and introductory experiences in industrial arts

For youth and adults whose goal is entry into, retraining for, or upgrading in trade, industrial/technical occupations.

Students are selected in terms of potential employability.

The minimum entry age into the program is determined by the employability age at the completion of the education and training program.

Students receive: A high school diploma endorsed in an occupational field upon completion of secondary programs; a certificate or associate degree with

—Special programs for students who have mental and physical handicaps, but who are still capable of profiting from special courses planned for their abilities.

occupational endorsement for post-secondary programs; and a certificate of occupational competency for ungraded programs.

Persons with special occupational needs are served in vocational programs.

Guidance and Counseling

Industrial arts educators provide the student with basic experiences which help him make his occupational, educational, or professional choice.

Organized programs of vocational guidance provide for recruiting, testing, and selecting students.

Vocational counseling services are provided for in-school and out-of-school youth and adults as an integral part of preparatory, retraining, or upgrading programs in trade and industrial/technical education.

Job placement and trainee follow-up are an integral part of the program.

APPENDIX B

Industrial Service Occupations
Education Programs

Trades, industrial, and related service occupations are administered through a branch of vocational education which is concerned with preparing persons for initial employment or for upgrading or retraining workers in a wide range of trades, industrial, and related service occupations. Such occupations are on the skilled, semiskilled, and operative levels and are concerned with designing, producing, processing, assembling, testing, maintaining, servicing, or repairing any product or commodity. Instruction is provided in (1) basic manipulative skills and the accompanying trade theory, safety and occupational hygiene, industrial and labor relations, and related occupational information in mathematics, blueprint reading, sketching and drafting, and science required to perform successfully in the occupation; and (2) through a combination of shop or laboratory experiences simulating those found in industry and classroom learning. Included is instruction for apprentices in apprenticeable occupations and for journeymen already engaged in a trade or industrial occupation. Also included is training for certain semiprofessional occupations considered to be trade and industrial in nature, for foremanship, management (middle-level and supervisory positions), and public service occupations.

17.01 *Air Conditioning Industries*—Classroom and shop learning experiences which enable the student to become proficient in the installation, repair, and maintenance of commercial and domestic air conditioning systems. Included is learning in the theory and application of basic principles of conditioning of air: cooling, heating, filtering, and controlling humidity; the operating characteristics of various units and parts; blueprint reading; the use of technical

Adapted from *Vocational Education and Occupations.* Washington, D.C.: U.S. Department of Health, Education and Welfare, 1969.

reference manuals; the diagnosis of malfunctions; the overhaul, repair, and adjustment of units and parts such as pumps, compressors, valves, springs, and connections; and repair of electric and pneumatic control systems.

17.0101   *Cooling*—Learning experiences specifically concerned with the installation, operation, testing, and trouble shooting of various types of air cooling equipment and of the controls needed for operation.

17.0102   *Heating*—Learning experiences specifically concerned with the installation, operation, testing, and trouble shooting of various types of heating equipment and of the controls needed for operation.

17.0103   *Ventilating (Filtering and Humidification)*—Learning experiences specifically concerned with the installation, operation, testing, and trouble shooting of various air quality control equipment such as humidifiers, filters, fans, and related equipment.

17.0199   *Other Air Conditioning*—Include here other specialized subject matter and learning experiences emphasized in air conditioning, refrigeration, and heating which are not listed or classifiable above. (Specify.)

17.02   *Appliance Repairing Services*—Classroom and shop learning experiences concerned with the theory of electrical circuitry; simple gearing, linkages, lubrication in the operation; and maintenance, and repair of components including relays, time switches, pumps, and agitators used in appliances such as washers, dryers, vacuum cleaners, toasters, water heaters, and stoves. Related training is provided in the use of familiar tools, test equipment, and service manuals and in making cash estimates for repairs.

17.03   *Automotive Industries*—Classroom and shop learning experiences which include training in all phases of automotive maintenance repair work on all types of automotive vehicles. Includes training in the use of technical manuals and a variety of hand and power tools. Instruction and practice are provided in diagnosis of malfunctions, disassembly of units, parts inspection, and repair or replacement of parts, and includes engine overhaul and repair, ignition systems, carburetion, brakes, transmissions, front end alignment, and installation of a variety of accessories such as radios, heaters, mirrors, and windshield wipers.

17.0301   *Body and Fender*—Specialized learning experiences concerned with all phases of the repair of damaged bodies and fenders including metal straightening by hammering; smoothing areas by filing, grinding, or sanding; concealment of imperfections; painting; and replacement of body components, including trim.

17.0302　*Mechanics*—Learning experiences concerned with the components of the vehicle, including engine, power transmission, steering, brakes, and electrical systems. Included is training in the use of diagnostic and testing equipment and tools in the repair process.

17.0303　*Specialization*—Learning experiences which involve more detailed training in the adjustment and repair of the automobile, including the radiator, transmission, carburetor, brake system, and other units to provide greater proficiency in the servicing of selected components.

17.0303　*Other Automotive Industries*—Include here other organized subject matter content and learning experiences emphasized in automotive industries which are not listed or classifiable above. (Specify.)

17.04　*Aviation Industries Occupations*—Classroom and practical experiences which include instruction relating to aircraft maintenance, aircraft operation, and ground support.

17.0401　*Aircraft Maintenance*—Classroom and shop learning experiences concerned with the inspection, repair, servicing, and overhauling of all airplane parts, including engines, propellers, instruments, airframes, fuel and oil tanks, control cables, and hydraulic units. Involves learning the use of technical manuals and various kinds of testing equipment.

17.0402　*Aircraft Operations*—Classroom and practical experiences concerned with the in-flight operation of commercial planes, including piloting, navigating, and passenger services (e.g., flight engineer, pilot, and stewardess training).

17.0403　*Ground Operations*—Classroom and practical experiences concerned with the ground-support of commercial planes, including passenger service, aircraft pre-flight service, and flight control (e.g., baggage handler, ticket agent, and traffic controller training).

17.05　*Blueprint Reading*—Classroom and practical experiences concerned with visualizing, preparing, developing, and interpreting blueprints. Included are the study of principles of sketching and drawing objects or structures; understanding and utilizing symbols, plans, sections, and details for communicating through blueprints; interpreting blueprints and their related specifications, and then translating them into actuality.

17.06   *Business Machine Maintenance Services*—Classroom and shop learning experiences concerned with maintaining and repairing a variety of office machines such as typewriters, dictation machines, calculators, and data processing equipment used for correspondence, recording and processing data, duplicating, and mailing. Instruction includes diagnostic techniques; understanding of mechanical principles such as those involved in gears, cams, levers, and eccentrics; nomenclatures; use and care of special hand and power tools; soldering; mechanical drawing; principles of electricity and electronics; use of testing devices; business procedures and customer relations.

17.07   *Commercial Art Occupations*—Organized specialized learning experiences which include theory and laboratory and shop work as they relate to the design and execution of layouts and making illustrations for advertising, display, and instructional manuals. Instruction includes advertising theory and preparation of copy, lettering, poster design, fashion illustration, silk screen, air brush and touch-up, inks and color dynamics, package and product design, drawings for line and halftone reproduction, and other display devices and exhibits. Instruction leads to preparation for various types of employment such as fashion illustrator, technical illustrator, interior decorator, and advertising artist.

17.08   *Commercial Fishery Occupations*—Organized specialized learning experiences which include theory and laboratory and shop work as they relate to seamanship, navigation, and communications; utilization of rigging and other equipment; maintenance and repair of boats; techniques for finding fish; shipboard preservation and refrigeration; processing catches afloat and on shore; and operation and maintenance of all fishing gear and power plants. Instruction leads to preparation for various types of employment such as fisherman, processor, weigher, and equipment and special gear maintenance man.

17.09   *Commercial Photography Occupations*—Organized specialized learning experiences which include theory and laboratory and studio work as each relates to all phases of camera uses and photographic processing. Instruction includes composition and color dynamics, contact printing, and enlarging; developing film; air brush and retouching, coloring, and copying; utilization of cameras, meters, and other photographic equipment; portrait, commercial, and industrial photography, including such processes as microfilming and preparing copy for other printing and graphic arts processing.

Instruction also emphasizes development of skills and knowledge essential for employment in planning, developing, and producing in such areas as audiovisual materials and telecasting, and for employment as a commercial photographer, air brush man, camera man (offset printing), audiovisual projectionist, and camera man (broadcasting).

17.10   *Construction and Maintenance Trades*—Classroom and shop learning experiences concerned with the erection, installation, maintenance or repair of buildings, highways, airports, missile sites, and earth and other structures using assorted materials such as metal, wood, stone, brick, glass, concrete, or composition substances. Instruction is provided in a variety of activities such as cost estimating, cutting, fitting, fastening, and finishing; in the use of a variety of hand and power tools; and in blueprint reading and following technical specifications. Knowledge is provided concerning the physical properties of the materials.

   17.1001   *Carpentry*—Classroom and shop learning experiences involving layout, fabrication, assembly, installation, and repair of structural units. Included is instruction in the care and use of hand or power tools, equipment and materials; common systems of frame and sound construction; and drafting, blueprint reading, applied mathematics, and materials estimating.

   17.1002   *Electricity*—Classroom and shop learning experiences concerned with the layout, assembly, installation, testing, and maintenance of electrical fixtures, apparatus, and wiring used in electrical systems. Instruction is provided in the reading, interpretation, and understanding of residential, commercial, and industrial wiring based on controlling electrical codes.

   17.1003   *Heavy Equipment (Construction)*—Classroom and practical work experience concerned with the operation, maintenance, and repair of heavy-duty equipment such as bulldozers, cranes, graders, tractors, concrete mixers, crawler-mounted shovels, trailer-mounted compressors, and the gasoline or diesel engines powering the equipment.

17.1004   *Masonry*—Specialized classroom and shop experiences concerned with the cutting, chipping, and fixing in position of concrete blocks, brick, and glass blocks using bonding materials and hand tools. Included is training in reading architectural plans, planning, and estimating.

17.1005   *Painting and Decorating*—Specialized classroom and shop learning experiences concerned with the preparation and finishing of exterior and interior surfaces by the application of protective or decorative coating materials such as lacquer, paint, and wallpapers. Includes instruction in scraping, burning, or sanding surfaces; making, mixing, and matching paints and colors; applying coating with brush, roller, or spray-gun, or by cutting, pasting, and hanging wallpaper.

17.1006   *Plastering*—Specialized classroom and shop learning experiences concerned with the application of plaster, stucco, and similar materials to interior and exterior surfaces of structures. Instruction includes the preparation of surfaces and the smoothing and finishing of them.

17.1007   *Plumbing and Pipefitting*—Specialized classroom and shop learning experiences concerned with layout assembly, installing, altering, and repairing piping systems and related fixtures and fittings in structures by the use of pipe-cutting, bending, and threading tools; welding, soldering, and brazing equipment; and other hand and power tools and equipment.

17.1099   *Other Construction and Maintenance Trades*—Include here other subject matter content and learning experiences emphasized in construction and maintenance trades which are not listed or classified above. (Specify.)

17.11   *Custodial Services*—Classroom and shop learning experiences which are concerned with all phases of care and cleaning of buildings, fixtures, and furnishings, including all types of building interiors such as linoleum, plastic, terrazzo, tile, and wood floors; rugs; and plastic, wood panel, paint, and synthetic wall coatings. Skills are taught in the use and care of hand and power tools for such operations as dusting, dust mopping, wet mopping, scrubbing, waxing, and refinishing, and the cleaning of toilet rooms, windows, and walls.

Additional emphases are placed on (1) characteristics of various cleaning agents and protective coatings—including their reactions on surfaces—and procedures for applying them; (2) sanitation and disinfectants; (3) scheduling work, and (4) purchasing custodial supplies.

17.12   *Diesel Industrial Occupations*—Classroom and shop learning experiences which are concerned with all phases of repair work on diesel engines used to power buses, ships, trucks, railroad trains, electric generators, construction machinery, and similar equipment. Instruction and practice is provided in diagnoses of malfunction; disassembly of engines; examination of parts; reconditioning and replacement of parts; and repair and adjustment of fuel injection systems, oil and water pumps, generators, governors, auxiliary and accompanying power units, controls, and transmissions. The uses of technical manuals, a variety of hand and power tools, and testing and diagnostic equipment are also studied.

17.13   *Drafting Industries Occupations*—Organized specialized learning experiences which include theory, use of drafting room and laboratory, and shop work as each relates to the gathering and translating of data or specifications, planning, preparing, and interpreting mechanical, architectural, structural, pneumatic, marine, electrical/electronic, topographical, and other drawings and sketches. Instruction includes experiences with drawing reproduction materials, equipment, and processes; the preparation of reports and data sheets for specifications writing; the development of plan and process charts and drawings; and model development.

Instruction emphasizes the development of skills and knowledge essential for employment in ancillary capacities such as tracers or reproduction equipment operators, and for occupations such as mechanical draftsman, structural draftsman, detailer marine draftsman, tool designer, fixture designer, and punch and die designer.

17.14   *Electrical Industries Occupations*—Organized subject matter and experiences which include theory, laboratory, and shop work as each relates to planning functions, generating and transmitting electricity, installing and maintaining electrical and communications systems, and equipment and components. Instruction emphasizes practical applications of mathematics, the sciences, circuit diagrams, blueprint reading, sketching, and other subjects essential to preparation for employment in the electrical occupations.

17.1401   *Industrial Electrician*—Specialized classroom and practical instruction related to the maintenance and repair of a variety of industrial machinery which is driven by electrical motors or which is electrically controlled.

17.1402   *Lineman*—Specialized classroom and practical experiences concerned with the installation, operation, and maintenance of local, long-distance, and rural lines, including pole- and tower-line erection and construction.

17.1403   *Motor Repairman*—Specialized classroom and practical learning experiences concerned with the assembly, installation, testing, maintenance, and repair of electric motors, generators, transformers, and related equipment.

17.1499   *Other Electrical Occupations*—Include here other subject matter content and learning experiences emphasized in electrical occupations which are not listed or classifiable above. (Specify.)

17.15   *Electronics Industries Occupations*—Organized specialized learning experiences which include theory, laboratory, and shop work as each relates to planning, producing, testing, assembling, and installing and maintaining electronic communications equipment such as radio, radar, and television; industrial electronic equipment including digital computers, new electronic systems, components, and equipment; and control devices. Emphases are placed on solid state devices and components, electron tube characteristics, low frequency amplifiers, LC and RC Oscillators, transistors, and amplitude and frequency modulation.

Instruction is designed to develop knowledge, understandings, and skills essential for employment in communications, industrial electronics, radio/television, and other electronics occupations.

17.1501   *Communications*—Specialized classroom and practical experiences concerned with the assembly, installation, operation, maintenance, and repair of communications equipment and systems of all types, e.g., industrial and entertainment sound systems, data processing, telephone dial systems, two-way radio, central circuits, hearing aids, and high-fidelity sets.

17.1502   *Industry*—Specialized classroom, laboratory, and practical experiences which are concerned with the basic elements of vacuum tubes and circuitry; using and servicing testing equipment and trouble shooting circuits; the study of and experience in repairing photoelectric controls, timers, selector switches, counters, recorders, and transducers; and the study of the characteristics and intricacies of equipment and components used in industry and research centers.

More advanced study includes study, analysis, and repair of magnetic amplifiers, motors, motor controls, electronic heating, saturable reactors, servomechanisms, pulse circuits, computers, and test instruments—including basic principles and servicing procedures. Field trips are frequently emphasized.

17.1503   *Radio/Television*—Specialized theory and practice which are concerned with the construction, maintenance, and repair of radios and television sets. Training also prepares pupils to diagnose troubles and make repairs on other electronic products such as high-fidelity sound equipment, phonographs, and tape recorders.

17.1599   *Other Electronics Occupations*—Include here other subject matter content and learning experiences emphasized in electronics occupations which are not listed or classifiable above. (Specify.)

17.16   *Fabric Maintenance Services*—Classroom and laboratory learning experiences which are concerned with all phases of maintenance service on all types of fabrics. Instruction emphasizes identifying, marking and entering, sorting, assembling, wrapping, and bagging clothing and other fabrics; a wide range of information dealing with drycleaning and spotting agents, detergents, bleaches and dyes; effects of heat on various fabrics; skills involved in the use of hand tools and power equipment such as power presses for flat work, roller presses, washers, extractors, and dryers, and alteration and repair of fabrics.

17.1601   *Dry Cleaning*—Classroom and practical experiences concerned with theory and knowledge in drycleaning plant management and processes. Instruction includes receiving garments, inspecting, dry and wet cleaning, identifying spots and spotting, pressing, dyeing, sorting and wrapping of wearing apparel, household furnishings, and other articles of textile construction or leather. Also emphasized are experiences concerned with various cleaning agents, kinds of fabrics, alteration and repair of fabrics, and uses of hand and power tools and equipment.

17.1602   *Laundering*—Classroom and practical experiences concerned with theory and knowledge in laundering, and plant management and processes. Instruction includes receiving garments, inspecting, washing of fabrics, spotting, ironing and processing, dyeing, bleaching, sorting, and folding and wrapping of wearing apparel and household and other articles of textile construction. Also emphasized are experiences concerned with various cleaning agents (including detergents), type of fabrics, alteration and repair of fabrics, and uses of hand and power tools and equipment.

17.1699   *Other Fabric Maintenance Services*—Include here other subject matter content and experiences emphasized in fabric maintenance services which are not listed or classifiable above. (Specify.)

17.17   *Foremanship, Supervisory, and Management Development*— Planned learning experiences designed to assist the supervisor in effectively utilizing the men, machines, and materials under his supervision by broadening his background and developing his leadership abilities. Included is the study of human behavior; organization and management; oral communication; labor laws; personnel procedures; job analysis; work simplification; employee utilization; and development techniques of writing as applied to preparation of letters, memos, and technical reports, speed reading, and safety and first-aid practices.

17.18   *General Continuation*—Part-time classes for persons under eighteen years of age who have left full-time instruction to enter the labor force, providing instruction designed to increase civic intelligence rather than to develop specific occupational competence.

17.19   *Graphic Arts Industries Occupations*—Organized specialized learning experiences which include theory and laboratory and shop work as they relate to all phases of hot and cold typesetting, layout, composition, presswork, and binding, including flexography, lithography, photoengraving and others related to the printing industry. Emphases are also placed on typographical layouts and design, hand and machine typesetting, camera and plate work, imposition, type casting, offset and platen press makeup and operation, paper cutting, ink and color preparation, binding, and production by silk screen process.

Instruction leads to preparation for various types of employment such as typesetter, compositor, camera man, platemaker, cost analyst, expediter, and production planner.

17.20   *Industrial Atomic Energy Occupations*—Organized specialized learning experiences which include theory and laboratory and shop work as they relate to the construction, operation, and maintenance of reactor plants and industrial "x-ray" equipment and the industrial uses of radioisotopes for production and control operations. Almost every form of mechanical, electrical, electronic, and chemical skills and equipment generally used in industry may be involved.

17.2001 *Installation, Operation, and Maintenance of Reactors*—Organized learning experiences which are concerned with atomic reactor plants and their use. Emphasized in addition to the knowledge and skills required in general construction of reactor plants are the related factors of reactor theory, operating characteristics and limitations, instrumentation, radiation hazards, maintenance, and emergency and safety procedures.

17.2002 *Radiography*—Organized learning experiences which are concerned with the installation, safe operation, interpretation, and maintenance of industrial "x-ray" equipment. Training also includes atomic theory, operating procedures, radiation protection standards and instruments, photographic film, and interpretation of film exposures.

17.2003 *Industrial Uses of Radioisotopes*—Organized learning experiences which are concerned with the industrial use of radioisotopes in production and control operations. Training also includes atomic theory, electrical and electronic theory, operating procedures, specialized instrumentation, radiation protection, process and quality controls, interpretation, and record keeping.

17.2099 *Other Industrial Atomic Energy Occupations*—Include here other subject matter content and experience emphasized in industrial atomic energy occupations which are not listed or classifiable above. (Specify.)

17.21 *Instrument Service Occupations* (Including watchmaking and repair)—Classroom, laboratory, and practical learning experiences concerned with maintaining and repairing meters, instruments, watches and clocks, and other physical measuring devices. Instruction includes experiences in diagnosing malfunctions, disassembling or repairing and/or replacing faulty parts, cleaning, assembling and adjusting, and using special bench and hand tools, meters, and standards.

17.22 *Maritime Industries Occupations*—Related theory and instruction and practice in performing the tasks required of un-licensed personnel serving aboard merchant ships in deck, engine, and steward departments. Firefighting, lifeboat work, and swimming are taught to all students. In the deck department instruction is offered in fiber and wire rope handling and splicing; chipping and painting for maintenance of the ship's hull; maintenance, operation, stowage, and rigging of cargo handling gear and ground tackle; and general duties as a watch stander and lookout. In the engine department, instruction is given in basic machine shop and pipefitting; maintenance, operation, repair, and servicing of main engines and auxiliary steam, refrigeration, water, and electrical systems. In the steward department, emphasis is placed on storekeeping, food preparation and service, cabin upkeep, and provision of other housekeeping conveniences for a ship's crews.

Included within the maritime occupations are various trade classifications such as in (a) deck department (able-bodied seaman, ship's carpenter, deck maintenance man, quartermaster and boatswain); (b) engine department (oiler, fireman-watertender, electrician, deck-engine maintenance man, and junior engineer); (c) steward department (cook, room steward, and chief steward).

17.23   *Metalworking Industries Occupations*—Organized specialized learning experiences which include theory and laboratory and shop work as they relate to the planning, manufacturing, assembling, testing, and repairing of parts, mechanisms, machines, and structures in which materials are cast, formed, shaped, molded, heat treated, cut, twisted, bent, pressed, stamped, fused, marked, or worked upon.

Instruction emphasizes knowledge, skills, and understandings which lead to preparation for various types of skilled and semi-skilled employment, such as sheet metal man, tool maker, foundry man, welder, millwright, production machine tool operator, production molder, metal stamping operator, and metal patternmaker; and helper-type jobs, such as materials handler, and machine clean-up man.

17.2301   *Foundry*—Specialized classroom and shop learning experiences designed to provide a knowledge of the theory and applications of foundry practice in ferrous and non-ferrous foundries. Instruction emphasizes foundry equipment, various sands and refractories, sand and machine molding, foundry chemistry and metallurgy, coremaking, chipping, and grinding.

17.2302   *Machine Shop*—Specialized classroom and shop learning experiences which are concerned with all aspects of shaping metal parts. Instruction involves making computations relating to work dimensions, tooling, feeds, and speeds of machining. Also emphasized is work on the bench, lathes, shapers, milling machines, grinders and drills; the use of precision measuring instruments such as layout tools, micrometers, and gages; methods of machining and heat treatment of various metals; blueprint reading; and the layout of machine parts. Preparation prepares the pupil to operate and repair all machines.

17.2303   *Machine Tools*—Specialized learning experiences to prepare a semiskilled worker to run only one machine, e.g., lathe, grinder, drill press, milling machine, and shaper.

17.2304   *Metal Trades* (combined)—Specialized learning experiences designed to prepare an all-around metal worker capable of fabricating and assembling a variety of products in many industries. Instruction includes layout; sequence of operations; setting up and operating fabricating machines; positioning, aligning, fitting, and welding parts together; and designing and constructing templates and fixtures.

17.2305   *Sheet Metal*—Specialized classroom and shop learning experiences which are concerned with the layout, fabrication, erection, installation, and maintenance of items made of steel, copper, stainless steel, and aluminum, such as ventilating, air conditioning and heating ducts, kitchen equipment, signs, furniture, and skylights. Instruction includes the use of hand tools and machines such as cornice brake, forming rolls, and squaring shears; and drafting and blueprint reading.

17.2306   *Welding*—Specialized classroom and shop learning experiences which are concerned with all types of metal welding, brazing, and flame cutting. Instruction emphasizes properties of metals, blueprint reading, electrical principles, welding symbols, and mechanical drawing.

17.2399   *Other Metalworking Occupations*—Include here other organized subject matter content and learning experiences emphasized in metalworking occupations which are not listed or classifiable above. (Specify.)

17.24   *Metallurgy Industries Occupations*—Classroom and laboratory learning experiences concerned with assisting in examining and testing metal samples under the direction of physical metallurgists for determining the physical properties of metals, e.g., crystalline structure, porosity, homogeneity, and other characteristics. Instruction includes examining metals with x-ray, gamma ray, and magnetic-flux equipment for detecting defects, and the use of pressure devices, hot acid baths, and other apparatus to test hardness, toughness, and other properties of metals. (See also, 16.0114 *Metallurgical Technology* under TECHNICAL EDUCATION)

17.25   *Nucleonic Industries Occupations*—Organized specialized learning experiences which include theory and laboratory and shop work as they relate to the construction, operation, and maintenance of reactor plants and industrial "x-ray" equipment and the industrial uses of radio-isotopes for production and control operations. Almost every form of mechanical, electrical, electronic and chemical skills and equipment generally used in industry may be involved.

17.26   *Personal Services Occupations*—Planned learning experiences concerned with rendering a variety of personal services related to the physical appearance of individuals. These experiences include giving various kinds of beauty treatment, applying makeup to faces of studio and stage performers, attending clients taking baths, administering elementary massage, and fitting wigs.

   17.2601   *Barbering*—Classroom and practical learning experiences which are concerned with hair cutting and styling, shaving, shampooing, and massaging. Emphases are placed on hygiene, skin and scalp diseases, and sterilization of instruments and utensils. Instruction is designed to qualify pupils for licensing examinations.

   17.2602   *Cosmetology*—Classroom and practical learning experiences which are concerned with a variety of beauty treatments, including the care and beautification of the hair, complexion, and hands. Instruction includes training in giving shampoos, rinses, and scalp treatments; hair styling, setting, cutting, dyeing, tinting, and bleaching; permanent waving, facials, and manicuring, and hand and arm massaging. Bacteriology, anatomy, hygiene, sanitation, and salon management (including keeping records), and customer relations are also emphasized. Instruction is designed to qualify pupils for licensing examination.

   17.2699   *Other Personal Services*—Include here other organized subject matter content and learning experiences emphasized in personal services which are not listed or classifiable above. (Specify.)

17.27   *Plastics Industries Occupations*—Classroom and shop learning experiences dealing with plastics and their characteristics, and with bench molding, fitting, internal carving, and finishing plastic and fiberglass materials into products. Instruction includes using hand and power tools.

17.28   *Public Service Occupations*—Planned learning experiences concerned with training for the performance of occupations in local,
state, and federal government agencies. These occupations usually
are concerned with specialized activities limited to local, county,
and state governments, and do not occur elsewhere in the economy.
Typical activities include police and fire protection, emergency and
rescue squad work, safety, sanitation, transportation, and school
bus driving.

17.2801   *Fireman training*—Specialized class and practical learning
experiences which are concerned with the practices and
techniques of firefighting. Instruction treats the organization
of a community fire department; the chemistry of fire; the
use of water and other materials in fighting fires, the various
kinds of firefighting equipment and aids and their uses, such
as extinguishers, pumps, hose, rope, ladders, gas masks, hy-
drants, and standpipe and sprinkler systems; methods of
entry, rescue principles, practices, and equipment; salvage
equipment and work; fire and arson investigation; inspection
techniques; and radiation hazards.

17.2802   *Law Enforcement Training*—Specialized class and practical
learning experiences that are designed to supplement the
training provided by officially designated law enforcement
agencies. Instruction includes acquiring and maintaining the
uniform; patrolling on foot or in an automobile during the
day or night; dealing with misdemeanors, felonies, traffic
violations and accidents; making arrests; and testifying in
court.

17.2899   *Other Public Services*   Include here other organized subject
matter content and learning experiences emphasized in public service occupations which are not listed or classifiable
above. (Specify.)

17.29   *Quantity Food Trades and Service Occupations*—Organized specialized learning experiences which include theory and laboratory and
shop work as they relate to planning, selecting, purchasing, preserving, preparing, and serving quantity food and food products. Included is the study of a variety of foods and their nutritional values,
food processing, quantity cooking, storing equipment, and sanitation in food handling and management.

Instruction emphasizes quantity food service occupations in
commercial food service establishments such as restaurants, cafete-
rias, drive-ins, tea rooms, bakeries, and meat, fish, and poultry

markets; in other retail food shops which are operated independently or are located in enterprises such as hotels, travel terminals, industrial plants, hospitals, or club houses; and in special food services such as those associated with airline catering or with take-out food establishments. Instruction is designed to prepare pupils for occupations such as baker, cook, chef, and meat cutter; or in planning, purchasing, preparing, storing, and preserving foods; or in services such as bus boy, waiter, or waitress.

17.2901   *Baker*—Specialized classroom and practical work experiences associated with the preparation of bread, crackers, cakes, pies, pastries, and other bakery products for retail distribution or for consumption in a commercial food service establishment. Training includes making, freezing, and handling of baked products; decorating; counter display; and packaging of merchandise. Training prepares the pupil as an all-around baker (although he may be employed in the production of any one type of goods, such as pastries).

17.2902   *Cook/Chef*—Specialized classroom and practical work experiences concerned with the preparation and cooking of a variety of foods. Included is study of the use and care of equipment, food standards (such as the selection and preparation of food), and the determination of size of servings; sanitation procedures, including food handling; cooking methods such as broiling and steaming; and the preparation of special dishes such as soups, salads, garnishes, souffles, and meringues. Although the pupil qualifies as an all-around worker, he may, depending on the size of the establishment, specialize in the preparation of specific types of foods, e.g., meats, vegetables, or sauces.

17.2903   *Meat Cutter*—Specialized classroom and practical work experiences concerned with the cutting, trimming, and preparation of carcasses and consumer-size portions for sale by wholesale or retail establishments, or for cooking in a food service establishment. Instruction is provided in the use of certain meat-cutting tools; identification of and techniques used in cutting different cuts of meats; dressing poultry; processing fish; counter display; and refrigeration of meats, poultry, and fish.

17.2904   *Waiter/Waitress*—Specialized classroom and practical work experiences in table preparation, food handling, and serving. Instruction is provided in personal cleanliness and appearance, sanitary handling of food and equipment, setting a table, receiving and seating guests, taking orders and interpreting the menus, carrying the tray and dishes, placing orders in the kitchen, serving procedures, making out checks, accepting money and making change for checks, and proper relations with fellow employees and customers.

17.2999   *Other Quantity Food Occupations*—Include here other organized subject matter content and learning experiences emphasized in quantity food occupations which are not listed or classifiable above. (Specify.)

17.30   *Refrigeration Services*—Classroom and shop learning experiences concerned with commercial chilling and freezing systems, including theory, application, and operation of compressors, expansion and float valves, thermostats, and pressure controls; diagnosing overhauling, and testing methods and procedures; charging and discharging systems with refrigerants; and testing hermetic units, relays, and overload devices.

17.31   *Small Engine Repair Services (Internal Combustion)*—Classroom and shop learning experiences which are concerned with maintaining and repairing a variety of small engines used on portable power equipment, e.g., lawnmowers, outboard motor-boats, chain saws, and roto-tillers. Instruction includes principles of internal combustion engine operation, reading technical manuals, and customer relations.

17.32   *Stationary Energy Sources Occupations*—Organized specialized learning experiences including theory, laboratory, and shop work as each relates to the installation, operation, and maintenance of large power sources for purposes such as generating electricity, pumping, and heating. Major equipment involved may be turbines (steam, gas, or hydro), engines (diesel or gas), atomic reactors, or furnaces.

17.3201   *Electric Power and Generating Plants*—Organized learning experiences which are concerned with the installation, operation, and maintenance of electric power generating stations from which the electricity may be either for sale or industrial use. Instruction, in addition to that required in general construction, also includes theory, operation, and maintenance of gas, oil, or coal furnaces; atomic reactors; boilers; electrical generators; steam, gas, hydro turbines, and diesel engines; special instrumentation, control; and emergency and safety procedures. Occupational preparation may be designed to provide specialization for a specific type of electric power generating plant construction or operation, e.g., steam, hydro, atomic, diesel, or gas turbine.

17.3202   *Pumping Plants*—Organized learning experiences which are concerned with the installation, operation, and maintenance of pumping installations handling liquids, gases, or solids, for remote delivery through pipe lines or for local use. Pumps are commonly driven by electric motors, diesel engines, or gas turbines. Instruction includes theory, operation, and maintenance of pumps, pipe lines, motors, engines, and gas turbines, as well as instrumentation and control.

17.3299   *Other Stationary Energy Sources Occupations*—Include here other organized subject matter content and learning experiences emphasized in stationary energy sources occupations which are not listed or classifiable above. (Specify.)

17.33   *Textile Production and Fabrication Industries*—Classroom and shop learning experiences which are concerned with all aspects of the fabrication of textiles and kindred materials. Instruction emphasizes the fabrication and repair of garments constructed of cotton, wool, synthetic fibers, or fur; apparel accessories, e.g., handbags, belts, shoes, and gloves; white goods such as sheets and pillow cases; and furnishings such as slip covers, drapes, and curtains.

17.3301   *Dressmaking*—Specialized classroom and laboratory learning experiences which are concerned with the construction, alteration, and fitting of women's apparel such as dresses, coats, and suits. Instruction includes sketching; style, line, and color in fashion design; patternmaking; cutting fabric to patterns; draping; machine and hand stitching; altering finished garments, including cleaning and pressing; classification, identification, and selection of fabrics.

17.3302   *Tailoring*—Specialized learning experiences which are concerned with the fabrication and alteration, by hand and machine, of all types of men's, women's, and children's outer garments. Instruction includes taking measurements, preparing patterns, cutting, sewing, and fitting; hand and powered machine sewing; hand and machine pressing; and making repairs and alterations, from start to finish, according to patterns and designer's specifications.

17.3399   *Other Textile Production and Fabrication*—Include here other organized subject matter content and learning experiences emphasized in textile production and fabrication which are not listed or classifiable above. (Specify.)

17.34 *Shoe Manufacturing/Servicing Industries*—Classroom and shop learning experiences which are concerned with the fabrication and repair of all types of footwear, e.g., shoes, boots, moccasins, sandals, slippers. Instruction emphasizes types and care of shoes; kinds and uses of tools and machines; shoe construction; shoe repairing, including replacement of worn parts such as heels and soles, and sewing parts that need mending; orthopedic shoe-making and repair; leather refinishing and dyeing; salesmanship; and simple bookkeeping. Repairing of other leather articles such as handbags, luggage, and belts may be included in instruction.

17.35 *Upholstering*—Classroom and shop learning experiences which are concerned with all aspects of upholstering, including furniture, automobile seats, caskets, and mattresses and bedsprings. Instruction includes history and styles of furniture; installing, repairing, arranging, and securing springs, filler, padding, and covering material; patternmaking; cutting, sewing, and trimming outside coverings; cushion filling; styling and designing; tufting and buttoning; and wood refinishing.

17.36 *Woodworking Industries Occupations*—Classroom and shop learning experiences which are concerned with woodworking occupations other than construction carpentry. Instruction emphasizes laying out and shaping stock; assembling complete wooden articles or sub-assemblies; marking, binding, sawing, carving, and sanding wood products; and repairing wooden articles. Also emphasized are various hand and power tools and their uses.

17.3601 *Millwork and Cabinet Making*—Specialized class and practical work learning experiences which are concerned with mass producing products such as window frames, moldings, trim, and panels; and with making such products as furniture, store fixtures, kitchen cabinets, and office equipment. Instruction includes training in cutting, shaping, and assembling parts by means of hand tools and woodworking machines; refinishing furniture; installation of hardware, e.g., hinges, catches, drawer pulls; planning layouts; blueprint reading; drafting; and kinds of woods.

17.3699 *Other Millwork and Cabinet Making*—Include here other organized subject matter content and learning experiences emphasized in millwork and cabinet making which are not listed or classifiable above. (Specify.)

17.37   *Other Trades, Industry and Service Occupations*—Include here other organized subject matter content and learning experiences emphasized in trades and industrial occupations which are not listed or classifiable in one of the above major categories. (Specify.)

Technical Industrial Education Programs

Technical/Industrial Education is concerned with that body of knowledge organized in a planned sequence of classroom, laboratory, and shop experiences which prepare students for a cluster of job opportunities in a field of industrial technology. It requires a knowledge of mathematics, sciences, drafting, and design associated with the technology; an understanding of the methods, skills, materials, and processes commonly used in the technology; and an extensive knowledge of a field of specialization, complemented by instruction in the basic communication skills and general education. Technical education prepares for the occupational area between the skilled employee and the professional employee (such as the engineer and the scientist) and is on the continuum nearest to the professional employee.

The technical curriculum must be structured so that it prepares the graduate to enter a job and be productive with a minimum of additional training after employment, and provides him with a background which will give him a reasonable amount of experience and additional education and training to advance into positions of increased responsibility, keeping abreast of developments in the technology.

The technician is usually employed in direct support of the professional employee. For example, the engineering (industrial) technician will be capable of performing such duties as designing, developing, testing, modifying of products and processes, production planning, writing reports, preparing estimates, analyzing and diagnosing technical problems that involve independent decisions, and solving a wide range of technical problems by applying his background in the technical specialities—mathematics, science, and communicative skills.

16.01   *Engineering Related Technology*—Engineering related technology is that part of the engineering field which requires the application of scientific and engineering knowledge and methods combined with technical skills in support of engineering activities. Persons prepared in this technology are a part of the engineering manpower team which includes the skilled craftsman, the technician, the engineers, and work as technicians in close support of the engineer.

16.0101   *Aeronautical Technology*—A planned program of classroom and laboratory experiences, including mathematics, the physical sciences, and a combination of aerodynamics, structures, materials, and electronics as applied to the design, testing, and development of aircraft. This program is designed to produce the ability to understand the propulsion, control, and guidance system of the airplane and to collect pertinent engineering data in a research and development activity. This program prepares the graduate to work in direct support of the engineer in the aerospace industry.

16.0103   *Architectural Technology (Building Construction)*—A program of instruction designed to provide the pupil with knowledge and understanding of scientific principles, mathematical concepts, and communicative and technical skills combined with laboratory experiences, including creative design, testing, and model building, which will enable him to be supportive to the architect and the architectural engineer. The subject matter emphasizes design, estimating, inspection, supervision, contracts, and specifications primarily in the field of building construction with attention to the art of form.

16.0104   *Automotive Technology*—A sequence of classroom and laboratory experiences which includes mathematical and scientific principles leading to an understanding of the design, development, and testing of internal combustion engines and related component parts of the motor vehicle including transmissions, electrical systems, and braking systems. This program enables the graduate to perform duties concerned with designing, testing, and development in direct support of the automotive engineer.

16.0105   *Chemical Technology*—A program of instruction designed to provide the pupil with scientific principles, mathematical concepts, and communicative and technical skills combined with appropriate laboratory experiences which will enable him to be supportive to the chemical engineer. The subject matter content emphasizes qualitative, quantitative, and analytical analyses in general and organic chemistry. In the unit operation laboratory he studies material handling, crushing, grinding, and sizing. By pilot plant operation he studies the chemical machinery and methods used in extraction, distillation, evaporation, drying, absorption, and heat transfer. He designs, installs, and operates pilot plants for chemical manufacturing processes.

16.0106   *Civil Technology*—A planned program of classroom and laboratory experiences including the study of mathematics, physical
sciences, surveying, strength of materials, and other specialty
courses leading to preparation for designing, testing, and supervising the construction of highways, railroads, airports, bridges,
harbors, irrigation works, sanitary plants, and structures. The
graduate works in direct support of the civil engineer.

16.0107   *Electrical Technology*—An organization of subject matter and
laboratory experiences designed to provide preparation in specialty courses, physical sciences, mathematics, and general education as applied to the design, development, and testing of
electrical circuits, devices and systems for generation, distribution and utilization of electrical power. These electrical systems
incorporate the knowledge and application of electronic and instrumentation devices.

The program is designed to produce the capacity to perform
in such areas as: model and prototype development and testing;
systems analysis and integration, including design, selection, installation, calibration, and testing; development of corrective and
preventive maintenance techniques; application of engineering
data; and the preparation of reports and test results in support
of the electrical engineer.

16.0108   *Electronics Technology*—Subject matter and laboratory experiences organized to provide preparation in the specialty courses,
physical sciences, mathematics, and general education concerned
with the design, development, and testing of electronic circuits,
devices, and systems. Content incorporates solid state and mi-
crominiaturization devices and representative systems such as:
microwave systems, computers, and controls.

The program is designed to produce the capacity to perform
in such areas as: practical circuit feasibility; prototype development and testing; development of maintenance techniques; systems analysis including design, selection, installation, calibration
and testing; application of engineering data; and preparation of
reports and test results in support of the professional personnel
in the electronics field.

16.0109   *Electro-Mechanical Technology*—A selection and integration of
specialized classroom and laboratory learning experiences in
both the mechanical and electrical fields. Instruction is planned
to provide preparation concerned with design, development, and
testing of electro-mechanical devices and systems such as auto-

matic control systems and servo-mechanisms including vending machines, elevator controls, missile controls, tape control machines, and auxiliary computer equipment. The program of instruction is designed to develop understanding, knowledge, and skills which will provide the capacity to perform effectively in such areas as: feasibility testing of engineering concepts; systems analysis, including design, selection, and testing; application of engineering data; and the preparation of written reports and test results in support of mechanical and electrical engineers.

16.0110 *Environmental Control Technology*—Classroom and laboratory experiences designed to develop in the pupil knowledge and understandings concerned with the basic mathematics and scientific principles dealing with the control of temperature and quality of air, and the design, testing, installation, and development of heating and cooling systems.

16.0111 *Industrial Technology*—A program of instruction designed to develop knowledge and understanding of scientific principles, mathematical concepts, and communicative and technical skills, combined with appropriate laboratory experiences which will prepare the student to be supportive to the industrial engineer in production and planning. The subject matter content emphasizes design and installation of integrated systems of materials, machinery, equipment, and personnel.

16.0112 *Instrumentation Technology*—A sequence of classroom and laboratory experiences supported by mathematics and physical sciences which will provide an understanding in the fields of electricity, electronics, mechanics, pneumatics, and hydraulics as they pertain to the application of the principles of control and recording systems and automated devices. The program is designed to prepare the pupil to design, develop prototypes, and test and evaluate control systems or automated systems and to prepare graphs, written reports, and test results in support of the professional personnel working the field of instrumentation.

16.0113 *Mechanical Technology*—A program of instruction designed to develop knowledge and understandings concerning scientific principles, mathematical concepts, and communicative skills, combined with appropriate laboratory experiences which will prepare a pupil to become supportive to the mechanical engineer.

16.0114 *Metallurgical Technology*—An organization of subject matter and laboratory experiences including specialty courses, physical sciences, mathematics, and general education concerned with the production, research, and/or quality control of metals. The program is designed to prepare pupils for performing in such areas as: Conducting tests on the properties of metals; pilot and production plant design and development; the development, operation, and alteration of test procedures and equipment, operation, and alteration of test procedures and equipment; and the collection and analysis of data and preparation of comprehensive and detailed reports in support of professional personnel in the metallurgical field.

16.0115 *Nuclear Technology*—A combination of subject matter and experiences designed for the study of scientific principles, mathematical concepts, and communicative and technical skills which, when combined with appropriate laboratory situations, prepare the pupil to be supportive to professionals engaged in developing, manufacturing, testing, researching, maintaining, storing, and handling materials in the nuclear science and energy field. The subject matter content emphasizes nuclear physics, radioisotopes, chemistry, electronics, nuclear instrumentation, and safety procedures. Graduates may enter and develop in this field as reactor technicians, radiation safety technicians, and radioactive materials technicians.

16.0116 *Petroleum Technology*—A planned program of classroom and laboratory experiences which include mathematics, chemistry, physics, petrology, sedimentation, and geophysics as applied to the recovery and use of oil and gas. Instruction leads to preparation for: oil field exploration; supervision of rig construction; drilling; oil field services; crude petroleum production; petroleum refining; and work in direct support of the engineers and geologists in the oil industry.

16.0117 *Scientific Data Processing*—A combination of subject matter and experiences including scientific principles and mathematical concepts combined with specialty courses and applied laboratory experiences necessary in preparing pupils to: convert scientific engineering and other technical problem formulations to processable forms by computer; resolve symbolic formulations; prepare logical flow charts and block diagrams; encode resolvent equations for processing by applying knowledge of advanced mathematics, such as differential equations and numerical analysis; and to gain understanding of computer capabilities and limitations.

The program is designed to provide the capacity to perform such functions as: consulting with engineering and other technical personnel to resolve problems of intent, inaccuracy, or feasibility of computer processing; observing the computer during testing or processing runs to analyze and correct programming and coding errors; reviewing results of computer runs for determining necessary modifications and reruns; developing new subroutines or the extension of the application of available programs and the development of scientific machine languages to simplify programming statements and coding of future problems.

16.0199   *Other Related Technology*—Include here other organized subject matter and experiences emphasized in engineering related technology which are not classifiable or listed above, e.g., ceramics engineering technology, marine engineering technology, and mining engineering technology. (Specify.)

16.01   *Other Technical Education, NEC*—Examples of other aspects of technical education which may be classified in selected categories above, as appropriate, (or here, if not appropriate to one of the above categories), are: (Specify.)

16.0105   Chemical Technology

16.0601   Commercial Pilot Training

16.0602   Fire and Safety Technology

16.0604   Marine Technology

16.0605   Police Science Technology

Health Industries Occupations Educational Programs

Education for health industries occupations comprises the body of related subject matter, or the body of related courses, and planned experiences designed to impart knowledge and develop understandings and skills required in the supportive services to the health professions. Instruction is organized to prepare pupils for the occupational objectives concerned with assisting qualified personnel in providing diagnostic, therapeutic, preventive, restorative, and rehabilitative services to people, including understandings and skills essential to care and health services to patients.

Education for health workers is conducted by recognized education agencies with the cooperation of appropriate health institutions and services that can make available the quality and kind of experiences needed by the trainee in developing the competencies required for his occupational goal.

Instructional programs which prepare persons for occupations that render health services directly to patients (people) provide planned clinical instruction and experience in appropriate clinical situations. For those occupations that render health services which do not involve direct services to patients, planned instruction and experience in laboratories and/or appropriate work situations are provided as an integral part of the instructional program.

Included under this heading are items of information which describe selected aspects of education for health occupations. In the ensuing definitions the term "subject matter" includes theoretical course content that may be given either in a school or in a clinical setting, and the term "experiences" includes the applied course content which is provided in a clinical setting.

07.01   *Dental Services*—Included in this category are occupations concerned with services supportive to the dental profession.

07.0101   *Dental Assistant*—A combination of subject matter and experiences designed to prepare a person to assist the dentist at the chairside in the dental operatory, to perform reception and clerical functions, and to carry out selected dental laboratory work.

07.0102   *Dental Hygienist (Associated Degree)**—A combination of subject matter and experiences designed to prepare a person to provide services to patients, such as performing complete oral prophylaxis, applying medication, and providing dental health education services, both for chairside patients and in community health programs under the supervision of the dentist.

07.0103   *Dental Laboratory Technician*—A combination of subject matter and experiences designed to prepare a person to execute the work in producing restorative appliances required for the oral health of the patient as authorized by the dentist.

07.02   *Medical Services*—Included in this category are occupations concerned with services supportive to the medical professional.

07.0201   *Cytology Technician (Cytotechnologist)*—A combination of subject matter and experiences designed to prepare a person to stain and screen smeared slides for determination of abnormalities of exfoliated cells that may assist in the diagnosis of cancer. This work is performed under the supervision of a physician.

07.0202   *Histology Technician*—A combination of subject matter and experiences to enable a person to prepare, section, and stain tissues

---

*Registration, licensure, and certification: a statement concerning registration, licensure, and certification as applied to items identified by an asterisk (*) in this subject area is to be developed.

for microscopic study, usually by a pathologist or other clinical scientist.

07.0203   *Medical Laboratory Assistant*—A combination of subject matter and experiences organized to prepare a person to work under the supervision of medical technologists, clinical pathologists, or physicians to perform routine clinical laboratory procedures.

07.0301   *Nurse, Associate Degree**—A combination of general and nursing education and clinical experiences designed to prepare the person to work with the nurse supervisor, the physician, and other members of the health team in providing nursing care.

07.0302   *Practical (Vocational) Nurse**—A combination of subject matter and supervised clinical experiences designed to prepare a person to give direct nursing care under the supervision of a nurse or physician.

07.0303   *Nurse's Aide*—A combination of subject matter and experiences which prepares a person to perform simple tasks involved in the personal care of individuals receiving nursing services. These tasks are performed under the supervision of a nurse.

07.0908   *Hospital Food Services Supervisor*—A combination of subject matter and experiences designed to qualify a person for preparing and serving meals in a hospital or other health institution under the supervision of the dictitian.

07.0903   *Inhalation Therapy Technician*—Preparation includes a combination of subject matter and experiences designed to prepare a person to perform procedures and operate and maintain equipment used in supporting respiratory functions, including the administration of oxygen and other sustaining gases, as directed by a physician.

07.0501   *Medical X-ray Technician (Radiologic Technologist)*—A combination of subject matter and experiences designed to prepare a person for the safe use of X-ray equipment in both laboratory and clinical settings under the supervision of a radiologist or other physician.

07.0601   *Optician*—A combination of subject matter and experiences designed to train a person to prepare, assemble, and fit corrective lenses as prescribed by a physician or optometrist.

07.0305   *Surgical Technician (Operating Room Technician)*—A combination of subject matter and experiences designed to prepare a

*Registration, licensure and certification: a statement concerning registration, licensure, and certification as applied to items identified by an asterisk (*) in this subject area is to be developed

person to serve as a general technical assistant on the surgical team in the operating suite.

07.0401   *Occupational Therapy Assistant*—A combination of subject matter and experiences designed to prepare a person to assist the occupational therapist in implementing the plan of therapy for a patient as prescribed by a physician.

07.0402   *Physical Therapy Assistant*—A combination of subject matter and experiences designed to prepare a person to assist the physical therapist in implementing the plan of therapy for a patient as prescribed by a physician.

APPENDIX C

Project E.V.E.N.T., John F. Kennedy Memorial High School, Iselin, New Jersey

Graduate Questionnaire

In order to determine the value of the vocational offerings at John F. Kennedy Memorial High School, the Guidance Department has undertaken Project E.V.E.N.T. (Evaluation of Vocational Education Now and Tomorrow). Your frank and complete answers on this questionnaire will be used not only to evaluate what presently exists, but also to make recommendations for changes and innovations which will better meet the needs of all of those involved. Thank you for your cooperation.

1. Name: _____

2. Employer: _____ Address: _____

3. In which vocational program were you enrolled?

   A. __ Office Work Experience   F. __ Vocational Drawing
   B. __ Data Processing   G. __ Introduction to Vocations
   C. __ Office Practice   H. __ Distributive Education
   D. __ Clerical Practice   I. __ Power Mechanics
   E. __ Basic Electricity   J. __ Fundamentals of Nursing

4. Why did you enroll in this program? (Check one)

   A. __ Preparation for job   D. __ Suggested by teacher or counselor
   B. __ Easy five credits   E. __ Earn salary while attending school
   C. __ Parents desired program

5. Describe briefly what you are doing on your present job.

6. How well did the vocational training which you received in high school prepare you for your job?
   Very helpful _____   Some help _____   No help _____

7. Are you now taking additional training? Yes _____ No _____
   If yes, where?

8. Would you advise other students to take the same type of course in high school? Yes _____ No _____

9. How would you rate the course in terms of:

	Good	Fair	Poor
A. Instruction	____	____	____
B. Skills learned	____	____	____
C. Equipment available	____	____	____

10. Does the type of work you are doing give:

    Much satisfaction _____   Some satisfaction _____   No satisfaction _____

11. Would you select the same vocation again? Yes _____ No _____

12. Please comment on your reactions to the course:

    A. Strong points _____
       _____

    B. Weak points _____
       _____

    C. Additional suggestions:

INDEX

INDEX